NEW WRITING SCOTLAND 5

Edited by
CARL MACDOUGALL
and
EDWIN MORGAN

Managing Editor
HAMISH WHYTE

Association for Scottish Literary Studies

Published by the
Association for Scottish Literary Studies
c/o The Department of English, University of Aberdeen
Aberdeen AB9 2UB

First published 1987

© Association for Scottish Literary Studies

ISBN 0 948877 02 2

The Association for Scottish Literary Studies acknowledges
with gratitude subsidy from the Scottish Arts Council
in the publication of this volume

New writing
Scotland 5

X6

980846

Printed by AUP Aberdeen

CONTENTS

INTRODUCTION

In recent years there has been a remarkable growth in writers' groups across the country which, together with the interest in writing generally, has once again been reflected in the large number of submissions to *New Writing Scotland*. We received almost three thousand manuscripts from over five hundred individuals. And once more we have a larger anthology which publishes more acceptances than our predecessors.

This enormous response is further evidence that *New Writing Scotland* has become established as the country's leading outlet for new work, a fact which was recently underlined by news that the writer of a collection of stories being published this year, was approached by the publisher who first saw his work on these pages.

Yet we must make what is becoming an annual plea for more outlets for writers in this country. The more outlets there are and the more varied their approach, then the more opportunities we have for advancement and experimentation.

In fact, the shortage of other regular outlets has begun to affect us. For though we are now publishing more and we believe better work, we have been forced to return work from contributors who have regularly appeared in *New Writing Scotland* simply because we do not have the space and we believe we must offer an equal opportunity to other new writers.

It is impossible to do this job and not be aware of those who have done it before us and we are pleased to acknowledge and recognise the fine work done by James Aitchison and Alexander Scott. Their efforts and care established *New Writing Scotland* and we hope to extend and develop from the fine base they gave us to work from.

This year we are fortunate in being able to publish new work by some of Scotland's most distinguished writers alongside work by those who appear in print for the first time. The stories this year are perhaps longer than we have published in the past, but they are all diverse, fluent and imaginative pieces where imagination is used as a process of discovery as well as invention and where personal experience is the starting point for fiction, rather than the subject of it.

And despite the melancholy forecasts we are glad to welcome some interesting new work in Scots, particularly in prose where the language and style have more than simple curiosity value, but, as with any good story, the reader finds it difficult to imagine the story told in any other way or in any other language.

And in poetry we are happy to find Scots once again being used as a springboard for new talent, proving itself to be a sturdy survivor as well as a vehicle which is more than capable of carrying new ideas and images. There is a welcome confidence about this year's poetry as well as a diversity of style and content.

Again, because of the large number of submissions, we felt it was only right to use a number of single poems which we hope will serve as an introduction to writers whose work is already known or will become better known.

Carl MacDougall

Glasgow: May 1987

Edwin Morgan

NEW WRITING SCOTLAND 6

Submissions are invited for the sixth annual volume of *New Writing Scotland*, to be published in 1988, from writers resident in Scotland or Scots by birth or upbringing. Poetry, drama, short fiction or other creative prose may be submitted but not full-length plays or novels, though self-contained extracts are acceptable. They must be neither previously published nor accepted for publication and may be in any of the languages of Scotland.

Submissions should be typed, if possible, on one side of the paper only and the sheets secured at the top-left corner. Each individual work should be clearly marked with the author's name and address.

Submissions should be accompanied by two stamped addressed envelopes (one for a receipt, the other for return of MSS) and sent, by 30 January 1988, to:

Hamish Whyte, Managing Editor *NWS*
c/o Rare Books and Manuscripts Dept
The Mitchell Library
North Street
Glasgow G3 7DN

Fred Urquhart

ROBERT/HILDA

I

After she died Robert Greenlees took to dressing up in his wife's clothes. It started when he had driven himself to go through Hilda's belongings to see what he could give away to her friends or to a jumble sale. He knew his daughter-in-law wouldn't even consider them. Alison had been scarcely civil when he'd asked her if she'd sort them out for him. 'Not at the moment, Father,' she had said. 'I'm very busy just now. Later on, maybe, if I can be of any help I'll give you what advice I can.'

He would never ask her again. So, one evening, he pulled out a drawer in Hilda's mahogany chest and took out a few folded garments: a blouse, three night-dresses, some silk scarves, a couple of cardigans. Hilda had been a great knitter; she'd been a dab hand at cardigans for herself and pullovers for him and Donny. She had sold them, too, to many of his customers in the Lothian and Borders villages within a radius of thirty to forty miles around Curlerscuik. Sold them at a profit: Hilda in her way had been as good a businessman as her husband. Robert rifled through the drawers and counted the cardigans, but he stopped when he got to seventeen. It was a wonder how Hilda had managed to wear them all turn about, but of course she'd liked a change. And she'd been fond of bright colours: orange, scarlet, emerald green, magenta, cherry, as well as more sedate heliotrope, powder blue, shell pink and the occasional striped ones, and she'd tried to outdo the fairisle knitting folk of Shetland with elaborate designs. He didn't fancy seeing them on any of Hilda's friends, and they were miles too good to send to a jumble.

Hilda had been a big woman. Not as big as him, but big enough. A pity to keep the cardigans in the drawers when he might be wearing one himself. They'd keep him warm. He could wear one in bed maybe, over his pyjamas. He needed something now he couldn't cuddle up against Hilda. Poor lass, lying in that cold old kirkyard at Otterheath, all on her own, waiting for his box to come and lie on top of hers. Though that, he hoped, would not be for a good while yet. And so he put on a pink and grey cardigan to try it. It fitted better than he'd expected. He kept it on for the rest of the evening. Next night he put on one of the fairisles and stood for a long time admiring himself in the mirror, smoothing the cardigan down over his hips. And then one night he thought he'd try on another kind of garment. And so it wasn't long before he had a great desire to go out to see and be seen. He was desperate to talk to somebody and what's more to talk dressed like this. He was fed up sitting on his own night after night. Of course he went out during the day dressed as he'd always been dressed, for a walk along the back roads in the afternoon when he wasn't likely to meet anybody, and to the village shop sometimes in the morning.

He hated the visit to the shop, for there were always women there who'd almost throttle him with sympathy, talking about Hilda and offering to help; some wanted to do his housework, some went the length of making meals and bringing them to his door just when he'd made a nice simple meal for himself, so that he was forced to eat the neighbour's meal, to show good faith, and often waste his own. Though he'd become cunning enough now and never made a meal that would spoil after a few hours in the fridge or the pantry safe. But what irked him most about these women was the fact that several were widows, and he knew fine they were after him. There was Mrs Nairn who'd been a widow for only two years since poor David got himself killed by the tractor that was the darling of his life, the tractor he'd christened *Peg o' my Heart*. Robert knew Peggy Nairn was after him like a game hunter in Africa with a rifle.

He didn't want to marry again. He didn't need a helping hand from any of these women. He'd been dominated enough all his life by women, and he wanted a change.

Robert was gregarious. When he was a travelling packman and a draper he had been used to meeting people, talking and laughing with them. He loved a good-going clash, sharing other folk's opinions, hopes and experiences. He never read books. He skipped through the newspapers, and he only half-listened to what he still called the wireless. They had been getting on in years when Hilda and he bought a television, and now that she was gone he hardly ever switched on the set, and when he did he often sat with his eyes shut, half-asleep.

In the old days Hilda and he had gone to the cinema once a week, but he had not watched a film on television for a very long time. In his first years in Curlerscuik he got to know everybody in the village: every man, woman and child was his friend. When Donny was young Robert had gone to the pub, *The Stag*, one or two evenings a week and always on Saturday nights. He was well known as 'one of our regulars' until, after several years, he cast out with the landlord and his lady, Dan and Effie Moffat, over the affair of the pissy professor, and Robert never darkened *The Stag*'s door again. Sometimes he regretted it, yet he still felt, though it was many years ago now, that he'd been right to take the stand he did.

The pissy professor was a gentle unassuming little fat man who had retired from one of the great universities and come to live in a fine stone-built late Victorian mansion about half a mile from the village. The professor was an alcoholic, though that was not the description used about him then. The villagers said he was a nice auld gentleman that was fond of his dram. He was so fond of it that every night at six o'clock he came into *The Stag*'s saloon bar, laid a pound note on the counter and asked in a quiet voice that was almost a whisper for 'A double whisky, please.' By closing time he'd had many double whiskies, and he'd also bought many other double whiskies, pints of beer, sherries and gins and tonics for many other inhabitants of Curlerscuik. He was fair game for the avaricious, the mean, the bold and the brash.

After about six months of observing the pissy professor and the locals who hung around, always ready to swallow quickly and thrust out empty glasses at his invitation, and sometimes himself accepting the professor's 'What's yours, Mr Greenlees?' — though he always made sure he returned the compliment immediately — Robert talked forcibly to Mr and Mrs Moffat. He accused them of helping to rook the professor by aiding and abetting the villagers who battened on him for drinks. 'He may be a rich man for all I know,' Robert said. 'He may be well able to afford to fling his money around like he does on a pack of scrounging buggers, but I don't hold with it. I don't approve, and what's more I don't approve of you letting him do it. You encourage him, and you've no right to do it. He's your best customer, but if you go on like this you're going to kill the goose that lays the golden eggs.'

Robert had never gone near *The Stag* again. He'd stamped out of the door with Effie Moffat shouting after him: 'You'll live to regret this, Greenlees, you big fat shite that lets your wife sit on you. You'll come back here crawling one o' thae days.'

He remembered it all as he put on a pair of Hilda's silk stockings and then a skirt of fawn and brown checks that had been one of her favourites. It was a pity he couldn't dander along to *The Stag* and have a whisky and a nice wee gossip with old friends. But he daren't do it. The Moffats had retired a while back, and their daughter and son-in-law, Nell and Jock Jackson, had taken over, but any time Robert had seen either of the Jacksons in the shop or the village street he'd known by their sour looks that the time wasn't ripe yet for returning to his old haunts. It was a great pity, for he'd like fine to get a breath of fresh air. He was desperate to get out of the house for an hour, so to hell with anybody who saw him.

II

'A big change this morning, Mrs Fletcher,' Mrs Nairn shouted across the garden fence to her neighbour. 'It's turned very cauld.'

'Has it?' Mrs Fletcher said. 'I cannie say I've noticed. I'm a bit ahint this mornin' and I've been hurrying to make up.'

'Oh ay, it's much caulder,' Peggy Nairn said. 'It was quite warm last night, but there's a nip in the air the day. It was that warm last night I had to open our front door and stand out on the step for a while to get a breather.'

'Rather you than me, dear,' Mrs Fletcher said. 'I'm no keen on lookin' out at the dark.'

'Ay, but it's wonderful the things you see in the dark,' Mrs Nairn said. 'Fabulous things. I've had my eyes opened many's a time. One thing I've seen lately is that Greenlees has got a fancy woman.'

'Aw no, Mrs Nairn, I don't believe it.'

'It's gospel,' Peggy Nairn said. 'I've seen her with my own eyes. Not once, but at least half a dozen times. It's aye late at night she visits him. After I saw her the first time by accident, I've watched for her. She's very furtive-like. Very furtive. She sneaks past my gate and into his like a sleekit tabby cat. And little wonder. I wouldn't like to swear to it — after all, it was in the dark — but I think she was wearing Hilda's green tweed coat. It's dreadful. Giving away the poor woman's clothes and her not dead six months yet.'

'Are you sure?'

'Of course I'm sure,' Mrs Nairn said. 'I've got good eye-sight, haven't I? Oh yes, she just scuttled past. A right sleekit scuttle. Just like a tabby that's stolen the cream.'

'Fancy that now,' Mrs Fletcher said. 'It just goes to show, doesn't it? If there's anything sleekit it's that Robert Green-lees. I've aye thought he was two-faced. I could never be doing with him. It was her I liked. Hilda was a fine woman and too good for him. Mind you, he's a good enough neigh-bour. He minds his own business. But there's something about him I've never taken to. He's a real salesman. Very smarmy, and full o' gush. He'll gas away like an auld wife until he has your head fair birling.'

'It hasn't taken him long, has it, to forget poor Hilda?' Mrs Nairn said. 'After all the roaring and greeting there was at her funeral. Will you ever forget the fuss he made? He had the cheek to choose yon hymn *O Love that Wilt not let me go* for the service and then he grat like a bairn in the middle of it. I saw him with my own eyes and was fair ashamed of the spectacle he made. I saw the minister looking at him very funny-like. No wonder. A man that is a man would never greet like that. Greenlees should think black burning shame. And now he's got this woman and Hilda hardly cauld in her grave.'

'Ay, she's been soon forgotten, poor lass,' Mrs Fletcher said. 'I'll tell you something that I was going to keep to my-self, but now you've told me about this fancy woman it's high time I aired my views. I made it my business last Sunday to go to Otterheath kirkyard and have a wee keek at her grave. And it was neglected. Shamefully neglected. Only a few withered flowers in a jar full o' stinking water. They'd been there for weeks.'

'Ah well, he'll not get away with it if I have my way,' Peggy Nairn said. 'I'll soon let the whole village know what a monster we've got in our midst.'

'I wonder who she is, Peggy?' Mrs Fletcher said. 'Did you get a good look at her?'

'I tell you it was dark every time. So I saw nothing, though it wasn't for the want of trying. I even went out to my gate to get a better look. I think she must be a stranger. I didn't ken her walk. But one thing I will swear to, and that is that she was wearing one of Hilda's head-scarfs — yon bonnie one with the Chinese figures — forby her green coat. I made no mistake about that.'

Peggy Nairn pursed her lips, tossed her head, growing

squint-eyed with spleen, and added: 'You and me must get to
the bottom of this, Mrs Fletcher, and then it's our duty to let
Donny and his wife ken what a snake in the grass their father
is.'

III

Robert Greenlees was born in the small Midlothian town of
Otterheath. Like his father before him, he was an only child.
His mother was nearly forty when he was born. She had only
one relative, her sister Bertha who was ten years older. Robert
had no other near relatives. Auntie Bertha had been house-
keeper and companion to an old lady who had left her some
money and a cottage in the village of Curlerscuik, five miles
from Otterheath. The money not being enough to keep her in
idleness, Bertha had become the District Nurse, cycling
around the countryside and making herself both a blessing
and a nuisance.

Auntie Bertha was the bane of Robert's life when he was
a child. Every Sunday, unless she had an urgent nursing case,
she cycled to Otterheath and spent the afternoon with the
Greenlees. Bertha was a big domineering woman, always
interfering in other folks' affairs. She never stopped telling
her sister about her brother-in-law's faults and how she wasn't
bringing up Robert in the proper manner. Even when he was
a grown boy, fifteen or sixteen, Auntie Bertha would seize
him by the ear and say: 'Your lugs are dirty and you've got a
tidemark round your neck. If you were mine, my lad, I'd
make you fonder of soap and water and I'd fairly ginger you
up.'

'But he's not yours, Bertha,' his mother would say. 'He's
mine and I'm quite satisfied with him.'

When he was fourteen Robert went to work in the Otterheath paper mill. Before he had time to look around and become pals with one of his workmates he was taken under the
wing of Hilda Wishart, a typist in the office, a dark-haired
determined young woman with plain heavy features. Hilda
had been one of the big girls when Robert was at school and
she had never spoken to him. She made up for this as soon as
she got him into her clutches in the mill. She smothered him
in her engulfing wings, and he never had a chance to seek
other company. They went together to the pictures twice a
week. She was waiting for him every night when the mill
stopped work, and she walked home with him, and they

stood for half an hour, daffing and chaffing, until Robert's
mother called out of the window that it was time he came in
for his high tea.

On Sundays in summer they went for long walks over the
Pentland Hills, always avoiding contact with other young
people hiking in pairs and quartets; they wanted no company but their own. In the winter Robert played cards after
tea with Hilda and her parents, then he stayed to supper,
going home always just before half past ten when his mother
often opened the door before he had time to put his key in
the lock.

Hilda was twenty-two when she decided it was time they
got married. Neither lot of parents objected, though Auntie
Bertha, who thoroughly approved of Hilda, said she didn't
think Robert should settle down quite so quickly: 'He's only
nineteen, and he must ha'e more wild oats to sow yet.'

They could not get a house, so they rented two rooms
from old Mrs Pendreich, a friend of Hilda's mother. Seeing
she had no housework to contend with, Hilda kept on her
job, and every night, as usual, she met Robert at the paper
mill gates, cleeked arms, and they walked home together.
They still went to the pictures twice a week, and on Sundays
they had high tea at the Greenlees' home and then went to
play cards and have supper with the Wisharts.

At twenty-five Robert left the paper mill and became a
travelling packman. This change was caused by the death of
Auntie Bertha. She got knocked off her bike by a runaway
horse dragging an empty coal-lorry, and she died two days
later in the infirmary in Edinburgh. She left her cottage in
Curlerscuik to Robert.

By this time the young Greenlees had moved to other
lodgings; they had got tired of Mrs Pendreich dogging their
footsteps and always asking if Hilda was expecting. They
could not find an empty house at a reasonably cheap rent in
Otterheath, and they were tired of being lodgers in nosey old
women's houses, so Auntie Bertha's death was a great blessing. But the five miles stretch between Curlerscuik and Otterheath was not.

Robert did not fancy cycling back and forrit every day to
the paper mill, and Hilda did not fancy spending her days
cleaning and dusting a four-roomed cottage in a village where
she knew nobody. As luck would have it, there was a sudden
and unexpected solution. Old Jimmy Nairn, the travelling
packman, whose cottage with its adjoining field and roughly-

built stable was next door to Auntie Bertha's, decided to
pack up for good and sell his stock and the goodwill of his
many customers within a forty-mile radius of the Lothians
and Borders. Hilda said it was just the very job that would
suit Robert to perfection; the dust and the din of machinery
in the paper mill were bad for his health. Having endured
them for over ten years, Robert was ready enough to agree
with her, and he liked the idea of a life travelling from place
to place in a pony-and-trap, selling his haberdashery to
women customers in outlying cottages, farms and villages, the
very thing the doctor had ordered. And so they bought
Jimmy Nairn's business and set forth together to make it a
good paying one.

Hilda did her housework in the morning while Robert
was grooming the pony and getting his wares packed into the
trap. Then about eleven o'clock they'd set out at a spanking
pace along the village street waving to any neighbour wifie
who happened to be at her door or had her head stuck out of
a window. They drove a different route every day, for the
main point of the business was a weekly visit to each customer.
On this visit Robert would take his pack or packs into the
house after his customer had greeted him at the door and
she'd exchanged a few words with Hilda, who always sat in
the trap and knitted while her husband was inside. Hilda always said she did not want to interfere with what, after all,
was Robert's own business, but she made an exception whenever it was raining or if the customer invited her in for a cup
of tea.

Whether Hilda came into the house or not, Robert's procedure was always the same. He would chaff the cottar wifie
and then he'd spread out his wares — camisoles, scarves,
knickers, petticoats, men's underwear, shirts, blouses, sheets,
cushion-covers, bedspreads and the like — and the customer
would finger her way through them while she talked about
her family and her neighbours. Then, after she'd made her
choice of the articles she wanted, Robert would get out his
notebook and say: 'Well now, Mrs Nisbet, if we add this to
what you're owing me, it comes to fourteen pounds, nine
and sixpence. Is that all right with you? And what can you
afford to pay me this week? Five bob or ten bob?'

Sometimes she said: 'I think I'll manage a pound this
week, Mr Greenlees. My man had a nice wee win on the
Grand National.' But more often she said: 'I can only afford
to give ye four shillings, Mr Greenlees. I'm awful short at the

moment. But I hope to give ye more next week. In fact, I think I can promise ye ten bob. My youngest laddie starts a new job on Monday, and he's going to give me twenty-five shillings a week for his keep. That pair of pants and the semmit are for him, so I'll see that he pays for them.'

And so the transaction would go down in Robert's note-book, and he and Hilda would depart, waving gaily to Mrs Nisbet or whoever it was, on their way to another customer in the next village or isolated cottage or farmhouse. In this way Robert and Hilda, for he always repeated the gist of the conversation to her as they clopperty-clopped along, got to know the history of all members of the family of each customer.

Robert was a good salesman. He was always good-natured, and the women knew his cheeriness was not just put on for their benefit. He was reasonable, too, about bad debts, and always willing to stretch a point and not press for pay-ment when he knew the women's pleas for more time were genuine. Many a customer got herself into debt just by listen-ing to banter, and most of them were susceptible to his flow of words and often bought things they hadn't thought of or didn't need. 'You could sell sunglasses to a blind man at the North Pole, Mr Greenlees,' said one old woman after he gave her what she called his 'patter' when showing her sheets she had not asked for.

'Ach away with your flattery, Mrs Bruce,' Robert said, laughing. 'These are the best and cheapest sheets you're ever likely to get, so be a devil and lash out. I ken you're not needing new sheets at the moment, but be a devil and buy a couple of pairs to put away. I tell you, woman, in another couple of years you'll have to pay double the price for sheets like these. Look at the quality. That's no cheap cotton. That's as near as dammit to good old Irish linen from Belfast.'

'Ye're an awful man, Mr Greenlees. You'd worm a body's false teeth out of her.' Mrs Bruce tee-heeheed and gave him a dig with a bony elbow. 'I'll buy a pair,' she said, opening her purse. 'They can aye be kept. They'll come in handy for my winding sheet.'

'Ach, you're not likely to need a winding sheet for a long time yet, Mrs Bruce. These sheets are too good for a shroud. If you want a shroud, if you want to put it by for your future like, I've got a nice line in cheap shrouds. Might as well buy one now, Mrs Bruce, when they're going a-begging as wait ten, twenty years when you need it and have to pay ten times the price.'

'Oh, ye're a shameless creature, Mr Greenlees, wheedlin' an auld woman's life blood out of her like that.'

The packman's business prospered. In 1936 it was flourishing so well that Hilda and Robert decided to sell the pony and trap and buy a car. The pony was old and ought to be retired, and the trap was too slow a means of travel. But they were dilatory about making the decisive move, for Robert was fond of the old pony and didn't like to think what might happen after it was sold; he didn't want it to end in a slaughterhouse. And then Hilda became pregnant, so the idea was allowed to lapse.

Hilda had a miscarriage, and after a lot of talk they bought a car in 1938. They were helped in their decision by Jimmy Nairn's son David, who was anxious to buy back the field and the old stable where the pony was housed; David had plans to set up as a smallholder producing necessary foodstuffs if the war with Hitler came. He also agreed to teach Robert to drive. It was an uphill struggle, though. Robert did not have a mechanical mind, and he could not get his feet, eyes and hands to coordinate. In the long run, after Robert had rammed the car into a stone wall and done quite a bit of damage and David had grabbed the wheel from him before he did more, David cried: 'You silly stupid bugger, you'll never be able to drive, so give it up before you kill yourself or somebody else.'

Robert was glad to give up the struggle; he would willingly have bought back the pony and trap. But Hilda was not to be downfaced by David Nairn or anybody else. She asked David to teach her, and in no time she was driving the car as if she'd been driving for years and had, actually, been born in a car.

For the next two years Robert and Hilda ignored the coming and then the outbreak of war. Five days a week they set forth at eleven o'clock every morning, Hilda driving the fawn-coloured Austin, and in no time they had extended their territory and their profit. While Robert was gossiping with his customers, encouraging them to forget the war and their men being in the army, Hilda sat in the car and knitted steadily. This way of Greenlees life was interrupted for a short time in 1940 when Hilda became pregnant again and gave birth to their only child Donald. For a few weeks Robert had to hire another driver, an elderly man who nearly drove him daft by his monologues about the merits and demerits of different Scottish football teams. In a few weeks, however, Hilda

was back in the driving seat and they had a passenger, baby
Donny, in a wicker basket amongst the packs of haberdashery.
After the war trade started to fall off. It was a gradual decline, not very noticeable at first. The war was really respon-
sible. Many families had become more prosperous during it,
owing to women doing well paid work while drawing their
husbands' army allowances. People have always put by
money for a rainy day, but in the years 1939-45 many
families saved more money and spent more than heretofore.
A large number of Robert Greenlees' customers had never
been so well off. At the same time their ideas and ambitions
widened. Many, far enough away from bombing and death,
had a very good time and enjoyed themselves with new
found prosperity. And so they were dissatisfied with the
type and quality of the goods Robert provided. They wanted
to go to Edinburgh to stravaig through the classy shops in
Princes Street, Leith Walk and The Bridges to look at the
greater variety of jumpers, blouses, frocks and knickers and
choose what appealed most to them rather than accept the
kind of things Robert brought in his packs. And because
their newly-affluent sons and daughters were buying cars instead of bicycles many country-women were able to go forth
on a shopping spree whenever they felt like it rather than
having to wait for the packman. Old women who distrusted
cars and never ventured on public transport stayed at home
as they'd always done, but the younger generation was only
too delighted to get into the family car and go to Edinburgh.
    As soon as Hilda noticed the decline in trade — for Hilda,
after all, kept the account books — she said it was time to
make a change. They had made money with the packman
business, had put it in the bank and had invested their
profits. No sense in losing what they had gained, and they
were too young to retire yet. They would get a shop. The
decline had never really dawned on Robert, although he'd
seen that many old customers weren't buying as much as
usual. Some, in fact, were not buying at all; instead, every
week they paid only a few shillings towards what they
owed him, and spent the rest of his visit gossiping. Robert
did not want a shop. 'It would tie us down too much,' he
told Hilda. 'I don't want to spend the rest of my life being
behind a counter either. You'd miss travelling from place to
place, woman. We'd both miss it, and we'd miss the fine fresh
country air. I couldn't thole looking through a window and
watching folk walk by. I'd miss clashing with the likes of Mrs

Nisbet and Mrs Stoddart and auld Jessie Finlayson. And you'd miss all the titbits of gossip I get from them.'

Hilda ignored his arguments. She read advertisements and went to see estate agents. She surveyed several shops in the small towns round about, but none satisfied her. Meantime she nagged away at Robert, trying to make him see reason. But he saw this and decided to give up only when an old customer, Mrs Gibson, a woman nearly fifty and a poor payer, always in arrears, said: 'Well, that's the last of what I owe ye, Mr Greenlees. Paid up to the last shilling. I've always enjoyed your company and many's the good laugh we've had thegither, but I don't think ye need come here again. It would be a waste of my time and yours, for I'll no' be buyin' any more from ye. Yer goods are no' fashionable enough. And my auldest laddie has just bocht a car, so I can gang further afield now and get what I want.'

In less than a week after Mrs Gibson's valediction, Hilda found a shop for sale in Otterheath. It would make a grand draper's, which Otterheath badly needed, and there was a house above it, which would suit them fine and save travelling. She told Robert to bid for it, and after Hilda had haggled about the price, getting it for a few hundreds less than the asking-price, it was theirs. Robert wasn't keen about going back to Otterheath; his parents were dead, and he hardly ever thought about the days of his youth. But Donny was growing, and he needed a better school than the Curlerscuik village one.

The draper's shop did even better than Hilda had prophesied. It was a busy life and not as entertaining as a packman's, but the profits mounted and Donny did well at the Otterheath school. Robert was content. Hilda wanted to sell the Curlerscuik cottage, but for once in his life Robert put down his foot; it had belonged to Auntie Bertha, she'd left it to him, and he was going to hold on to it. Then Hilda said they'd let it at a high rent, but Robert wouldn't have that either. There was no knowing what kind of tenants they'd get and what damage they might do; it was better to leave it as it was and allow it to idle; it wasn't eating up anything, and it was always there for them to bide in at weekends and holidays. Not that there were many free weekends, though they always went to Curlerscuik on Sundays, and there were no holidays. The only kind of holiday they ever got was to have two or three evenings out each week at a restaurant or a pub. Hilda liked eating out; it saved her making an evening meal and it gave them an opportunity to see people other than their shop customers. They went far afield on many evenings, visiting villages where they met old customers: women who, in the packman's time, had never ventured far from home but who now, with prosperity, liked to eat out and see and be seen. It was often around midnight when the Greenlees got home, but no matter how late Hilda always drove with calm deliberation. Hilda often got tipsy, but she never got drunk. She drove the car without fear or favour, and never once did she have an accident.

Like his father before him, Donny got married at nineteen. Like Robert, he'd been taken in tow by a very determined and domineering young woman. Except that Alison was younger than Hilda when she popped the question. Alison was two years younger than Donny. She was a little sharp-faced blonde with a precise polite voice that became shrill when she lost her temper.

Robert had hoped that Donny might be clever enough to go to Edinburgh University; Robert had a great respect for learning though he had no pretence to any himself. Robert still remembered the pissy professor with admiration. He and the professor had had many an interesting talk, and Robert often wondered what happened to the old man after he left Curlerscuik. Donny, however, had no desire to be academic. As soon as he left school at fourteen he got a job in a garage. He soon became so proficient about the mechanism of cars, as well as the selling of them, that he was able to persuade his father to buy him into the business, and he took over the garage when his former boss retired.

When Donny married Alison they could not find a house that Alison considered suitable for a couple of their status, so Hilda and Robert gave them the house above the shop and themselves returned to Curlerscuik. In this way it was as if they'd gone back to their early years as packmen. Hilda drove Robert to Otterheath every day, and this helped to change their view of the draper's and its customers. At last Robert realised that instead of dealing with the friendly cottage wifies of pre-war days he was dealing with small town women who imagined they were sophisticated and, therefore, threw their weight around when choosing garments. He often had to choke down his pride in his goods and his salesmanship. Hilda, on the other hand, was not prepared to be sat on by women she disliked on sight, so she often gave vent to acid-tinged remarks and lost sales. Not that either she or Robert

cared about that. They were counting the days until they retired and handed over the business to Alison, who spent a
few hours every day learning the trade and bossing her father-
in-law.
Their retirement was delayed because Alison had a baby.
No sooner had she produced her son than she became pregnant again. It was another son. As soon as the two little boys
were old enough for Alison to take over the shop, Hilda and
Robert retired. But they had only two years of peace and
happiness together in the Curlerscuik cottage before Hilda
died. She'd had cancer for a long time without ever telling
Robert.
The Greenlees car was taken over by Alison who said:
'You'll have no further use for it now, Father. Donny is
always here to take you wherever you want to go.'
Not that Donny was. Donny was too busy in his garage,
buying and selling second-hand cars and making money, to
have time to take his father for jaunts in the car. Every Saturday night, though, he drove to Curlerscuik and took his
father on a pub crawl while Alison stayed at home and
looked after the children. She kept telling Donny and Robert
how unselfish it was of her to do this after a hard week's
work in the shop. 'Very few wives would let you go out on
your own gallivanting like this,' she said. 'I should get a
medal.' She always succeeded in making Donny feel guilty,
though he knew that as soon as she'd got rid of him she
hustled the children to bed and then sat down and watched
television until he came home about midnight.

IV

One Saturday night when Donny came to take Robert out
for their weekly spree at two or three or more pubs, he found
his father wearing a skirt and blouse, his mother's best green
tweed coat with the mink collar and cuffs, and a green velour
toque that Hilda had kept for best. Robert's lips were well
encarmined with lipstick, and there was powder on his face.
'What in God's name are you doing, Dad?' Donny said.
'Have you gone cuckoo?'
'No, I thought I'd wear this,' Robert said. 'I thought we
might go to *The Stag* tonight. It'll save petrol.'
'I'm not going into *The Stag* with you dressed like that,'
Donny said. 'It's all very well for a laugh in our own house,
but I'm not setting one foot outside the door with you.'

'Why not?'

'Ach, be your age, Dad. What do you think the folks in the village would say if you walked in like that in Mother's clothes? They'd send for the police and the doctor. Anyway, I thought you didn't like *The Stag*. You haven't been in it for years to the best of my knowledge.'

'I'm not keen on it,' Robert said. 'I used to like it before I had yon barney with the Moffats and said I'd never enter it again. But the Moffats have been retired for years, and their son-in-law and daughter hardly know me.'

'They'd know you soon enough if you go in dressed like that. What do you think it is? Hallowe'en? And you're a guiser?'

'I'm not guising, son,' Robert said. 'I'm very serious. However, if you don't want to go to *The Stag*, we'll go somewhere else. Let's get into the car and then we can make up our minds where we're going.'

'I've made up my mind already, Dad. We're not going any place with you dressed like that.'

'We're going to *The Red Lion* at Lasswade,' Robert said. 'Nobody there will ken me. They'll think I'm your mother. Remember to call me "Ma".'

'I'll do no such thing,' Donny said. 'I like a laugh as well as the next one, but I draw the line at capers like this.'

'It's not a caper, son. I don't see anything funny about it. I like wearing your Ma's clothes. They do something to me.'

'They do something to me, too,' Donny said. 'What would my mother say if she saw you? She wouldn't like it.'

'Your mother would've loved it,' Robert said. 'She'd have laughed fit to burst. I can just hear her saying: "What'll you get up to next, you silly auld kipper?" '

'I don't believe it. She'd say you'd turned kinky.'

'Well, maybe I have,' Robert said. 'It's something that happens sometimes to men of my age. I'm androgynous.'

Donny said: 'Androg what?'

'Androgynous.'

'Where did you learn a word like that?' Donny said. 'I thought you never read the papers, Dad?'

'I don't, but I saw this in one that was wrapped round a packet of soap powder I got from the village shop. I had nothing else to do, so I read this article about what happens often to both old men and old women. They begin to look like each other. You must surely have noticed how a lot of old women look like old men.'

'You're pulling my leg, Dad. You're no more androg-whatever-it-is than I am.'

'It's a change of personality in old people,' Robert said. 'I'm not alone in this. Just you wait till you get to my age. Maybe you'll become androgynous too.'

'Not on your nelly,' Donny said. 'Nobody will believe it. Folk'll just laugh and say you've gone off your rocker.'

'Let them laugh,' Robert said.

'That's all very well,' Donny said. 'But they'll think you should be put away. Some bright spark is sure to call the police and have you put in the loony bin.'

'Let them think what they like,' his father said, going to the mirror and prissing his lips to see if the lipstick was staying on all right. He gave his toque a little tweak, giggled and said: 'It's still my car, y'know, and if I like I can just get into it and drive away on my own. But seeing I don't want to quarrel with you . . . and I'm sure you don't want to quarrel with me . . . '

'You don't want to break your neck, you mean,' Donny cried. 'Now Dad, be reasonable. Don't you dare try to drive that car. I'll take you, only . . . '

'All right,' Robert said. 'I'll be good. I tell you what. I'll sit in the car and nobody will see me in the dark, and you can bring the drinks out to me.'

They argued about this all the way to Lasswade, but Donny's argument got weaker and weaker. Once in the car and he'd started to drive, a sideways glance at his father reminded him so strongly of his mother that he began to think maybe they could pull it off. But not in Lasswade, where Hilda and Robert had been well known to many throughout the years. Donny drove past *The Red Lion* and said: 'I've just had a good idea, Dad — I mean Ma. There's a very good pub I know in Gorekeith where we can have a nice supper and you're not likely to be recognised.'

Donny took great care not to risk this when they walked into the pub. He took his father by the elbow and steered him to a table in a corner. The saloon bar-cum-dining room was only dimly lit, so that helped to cloak Robert's appearance, though he cursed the dim lights later on when they were eating.

But all went well at first. Donny went to the bar to get the drinks and the menu. He stood beside a tall well-built man of about his father's age, with broad shoulders, a head of thick white hair worn fairly long, and a brown still-goodlooking face. The man said something that Donny didn't catch, but they got into conversation. Donny carried a large gin and tonic to his father, and then went back to the bar to talk to the white-headed man.

Robert sipped his gin, opened the green tweed coat, felt to see that his toque was on at a suitable angle but was not revealing his ears, crossed his legs, admired the silken sheen of his stockings, and then looked around the saloon. Not a soul that he even knew by sight. He recrossed his legs and settled back to enjoy his drink. He was just about to drain it when the white-headed man who, Robert realised, had been looking steadily at him for several minutes, winked and then grinned at him.

Robert winked back in a very ladylike way, and he gave his lips a little twist.

The man said to Donny in a tone Robert heard clearly: 'Will your lady mother accept a gin and tonic with my compliments?'

'Tell him I'd rather have a pint of heavy,' Robert whispered to Donny when he came to the table and repeated the message. But it was a double gin and tonic that he got. He looked at it, gave his lips a lick, and then raised his glass and bowed to the man. 'Here's looking at you, kind sir,' he said.

The white haired man winked again. So did Robert. A second or two later the white haired man came to the table with Donny. 'My name's George Carnie,' he said, putting out his hand.

'This is my mother, Mrs Greenlees,' Donny said.

George Carnie was a retired sea captain. He had been all over the world. Now he'd come back to live at Newtongrange, where he'd been born. He ate supper with them and insisted on paying the bill. At closing time they said cordial goodnights without any mention of ever meeting again.

'What a performance, Dad — I mean Ma.' Donny said when they were in the car. 'You should've been on the stage. You'd be smashing on T.V.'

Robert giggled and said: 'I didn't do that bad, did I? I daresay George thought I was really Charlie's aunt from Brazil — where the nuts come from, y'know!'

'You're a nut all right,' Donny said. 'And so is he to be taken in by you.'

'We're all taken in by somebody,' Robert said. 'It's a part of life. You're being taken in yourself if it comes to that.'

'Ay, I daresay,' Donny laughed. 'Oh, Dad, you were a

right scream when you said: "My hubby passed on a while
back." I nearly laughed out loud, though I know it's not
funny.'
    'Of course it's not funny. I'm the one that knows that. I
miss your Ma, and I miss her more when I'm wearing her
clothes. But I felt I had to say something to George. To explain matters, like.'
    'You did it fine,' Donny said. 'You were that good I
could've kissed you.'
    'Well, why don't you kiss me now?' Robert said.
    'I'm not that soppy,' Donny said.

V

    Five or six months after that Donny had influenza, so he
telephoned his father on the Saturday afternoon and told
him there was no hope of their usual weekly outing. Robert
said it was okay, he'd be quite pleased not to go out for once,
he'd watch television instead, and he hoped Donny would be
better soon.
    In the evening, without telling Donny who was fast asleep,
Alison left him and the two little boys in charge of a babysitter and drove to Curlerscuik. She had no intention of
taking her father-in-law out for a drive and a few drinks — she
regarded such outings as 'common'. She wanted to see him
only because she wanted him to agree to handing over the
Otterheath shop and house as a gift to her and Donny, and
she had in her handbag a paper all ready for him to sign —
'To save death duties, Father. It's something that should be
done now, and it'll save money and prevent a lot of trouble
later on.'
    Alison had it all rehearsed, but she never got a chance to
make her speech. She went into the cottage by the back door
without knocking, and she gave a startled yelp when she saw
what her father-in-law was doing.
    Robert hadn't had his hair cut for over six months, and
now it was hanging over his ears and down the back of his
neck. He was combing it before the mirror in the sitting-room
and arranging curls over his cheeks when Alison opened the
door. His face was well painted and powdered, and he wore
an evening dress that Hilda had admired but seldom wore: a
stylish creation of primrose and gold silk with a high neckline
and flowing sleeves of chiffon.
    'What are you doing, Father?' Alison cried. 'What do you

mean being dressed up like this?'

'What do you think I'm doing?' Robert said. 'Getting ready for my beau to take me out on the ran-dan, of course. Will you have a drink?'

He picked up a half-empty glass of whisky and toasted her before draining the glass. 'Would you like whisky or gin?'

'Father, I'm fair ashamed of you, ' Alison yelped. 'You're a disgrace. Behaving like something in *The News of the World*. If this is what you get up to when you're on your own it's high time a stop was put to it. I'll have a word with the doctor about such outrageous behaviour.'

'I'll behave as I want to behave,' Robert said. 'And I'll have none of your bloody jaw, my girl.'

'Get thae claes off at once,' Alison shouted. 'I'll take them and all the rest of Mother's things to Oxfam before you get into any more mischief.'

'I'll do no such thing,' Robert said, taking another gulp of whisky. 'You've interfered in my life far too often, my girl. Don't think I haven't seen all you're doing to get the business completely under your control. But you're not going to succeed. I've made a watertight will — though I've no intention of dying for a while yet. I'm going to enjoy myself first.'

'Take off thae claes at once,' she shouted. 'Or I'll get a real man to do it for you. I'll get the bobby here in a jiffy.'

'Are you taking the name of our local policeman in vain by any chance?' Robert poured a fresh drink. 'Constable Paddy Fairbairn himself, do you mean? Paddy Fairbairn that couldn't take the clothes off a scabbit cat, far less a grown man. Even an old one!'

'Get thae claes off,' Alison screamed.

'You're forgetting your posh voice, aren't you?' Robert said. 'You self-centred, pug-nosed cow. You hooked our Donny before he had a chance to look around and see what he could make out of life and what fun he might have got. Well, you won't be so full of pride and highpan notions by the time I've finished with you. So there's the door. Clear out before I clash my whisky in your face — and it would be a waste of good whisky! Get out, and don't come back!'

'You auld bastard,' Alison screamed in her high thin bloodless voice. 'I'll make you pay for this.'

She was in such a temper flouncing into the car that she never noticed another car drawing up behind hers. As she drove off with much sound and fury a tall man got out of the other car, opened the door she had just banged and went inside.

Alison woke Donny out of a deep sleep and ordered him never to go near Curlerscuik again and to have nothing more to do with his father except through a solicitor. They argued about it for a fortnight. Then on the Saturday night Donny told her he was going to visit his father and was taking the two little boys with him.

Alison slapped Donny's face and stood with her back against the door, saying: 'You don't move one foot out of this house, Donald Greenlees, or I'll know the reason why.'

Donald said: 'I give you two seconds to get away from that door, woman, or I'll give you such a sock on the jaw you'll not be the better of it for a week.'

Two minutes later Alison was holding her face and yelling: 'You're a pervert like your faither,' while Donny herded the two frightened little boys out in front of him. 'That'll maybe teach you to keep your trap shut in future,' he said, closing the door behind him.

The boys sat quietly in the car all the way to Curlerscuik. Donny was silent, too upset to try to explain. He felt that would come when they got to their grandfather's. William, the eldest, was a sedate boy of seven, selfpossessed and selfsufficient. He was named after Alison's father, and he had all Alison's ways. Bobby was six, wide-eyed with curiosity. He ran ahead of them into the Curlerscuik cottage.

'What've you got on a skirt for, Grandpa?' Bobby cried, gazing at his grandfather's silk-stockinged legs.

'I'm not your Grandpa tonight, Bobby,' Robert said. 'I'm your Granny.'

'But Mammy says Granny's with the angels.'

'Granny is not with the angels, no matter what your Mammy says. Granny is here right now. I'm your Grandpa some days, your Granny other days. I'm your Granny at the top, but I'm your Grandpa at the bottom.'

Watching the child's puzzled face, Robert said: 'I'm A/C one day, D/C the next. Do you ken what that means?'

'He doesn't know anything about electricity, Dad,' Donny said. 'I mean Ma. You'll have to teach him, and he'll learn in time.'

'I'm really androgynous, Bobby,' his grandfather said.

'It's too big a word for the bairn,' said another man's voice.

George Carnie came into the sitting-room from the kitchen, carrying a tray of bottles and glasses. 'We thought you might come tonight, Donny,' he said. 'We were hoping you

would, anyway. So we're well prepared.'
'I ken androgynous is a big word, Bobby,' Robert said.
'But you'll learn what it means as you grow older. I hope
you'll learn it quicker than I did.'
'Now Dad — er — Ma,' Donny warned. 'Let him stick to
electricity in the meantime. Maybe you and George between
you will teach him and William all about direct current and
alternating current. I would do it, but I don't think my ex-
planations would be as good as yours.'
He turned to the white haired sea captain who was wearing one of Hilda's scarlet cardigans. 'How did you get here
George? I don't remember us giving you this address yon
night at Gorekeith.'
'I gave him the phone number when you were away to
the gents,' Robert said. 'I wasn't going to miss the chance
of seeing him again.'
'I'd have found you all right,' George Carnie said. 'I'm
very good at hunting out things and solving puzzles. I enjoy a
bit of jiggerypokery.'
He poured out orange drinks for the two solemn-faced
small boys, then he said to Donny: 'And what're you wanting
to drink to our future happiness, Donny m'lad? Whisky, gin,
or plain beer?'
'Well, if it's your future happiness it had better be the
best and most expensive drink you've got.'
'That'll be champagne then,' George said. 'I'm glad we
have a bottle. I bought it in case we had a wedding.'
'George and me are thinking of setting up house together,'
Robert said.
'But — ' Donny looked from one old man to the other.
'Does he know about things?'
'Of course he knows,' his father said. 'Would he be here
tonight if he didn't? Him and me are in the same boat. Don't
you worry about us, son. We'll be all right together. A/C one
day, and D/C the next. I think we'll be very happy, and we'll
give the neighbours something to talk about.'

Kenneth MacDonald

THE SILVER TIN CAN WILL VISIT YOU TOMORROW

Ray had rambled around most of his life so it was no surprise when he grew tired of working in New Orleans, packed in the job he had in the docks there, and headed up to Shreveport. He wanted to go there because the Red River went through it and he'd heard a lot of songs about the Red River Valley. He'd been seven months in New Orleans, about the usual length of time he stayed in any one place. He'd arrived the previous fall, quickly got work at the Pontchartrain Beach Amusement Park, but he got bored with that and moved on to the waterfront. The work there was harder but he preferred either the longshoremen he worked with or his own company when things were quiet. After a while, though, New Orleans got too humid and hot for him and he slipped quietly out of his room near the French Quarter and threw his bag on to a bus.

In Shreveport he hung around for a day or two wondering what to do next. He could've got work as a short-order cook, the way he usually did when things got tight, but he'd grown to hate the smell of cooking fat and only did that as a last resort. Shreveport seemed to be even hotter than New Orleans, so he decided to take a driveaway somewhere else. When he needed a change of scenery in a big way, Ray always used the driveaways. Once he'd driven one from Chicago to Denver in three days. On the way he'd stopped in some shit-hole town in Iowa and ended up screwing the girl behind the counter of a store he bought some beer in. The thought of it made him smile. He'd seen 32 American states and whenever he'd wanted to see another he'd gone to the driveaways. It was an easy way to do it and sometimes he got a good car. Once in California he'd taken a beautiful silver-blue De Soto Fireflite from Los Angeles to Fresno because the old woman who owned it was scared of freeways. Now that had been a car. Nothing fancy, just smooth and comfortable. Most of the ones he got now were economy cars, Nissan, Hyundai, junk. For that reason he always made sure to call all the driveaways, just in case they'd something classy lying there waiting to be taken somewhere. There were only three in the Shreveport book. The first said it was a quiet time and had only two going out of state, one to somewhere in Tennessee and the other to Flagstaff, Arizona. The second had absolutely nothing going out of state. The third number had cars to be taken to Crookston, Minnesota, San Diego, California, somewhere in North Carolina he didn't catch the name of, two to New York State, and one to Salt Lake City. He hung up and thought them over. Carolina was definitely out; he'd run into a little trouble there one time and didn't want to go back. New York or California he always seemed to end up going to, and he'd been in Salt Lake the year before. He'd never been to Minnesota but the drive up there was almost due north, through countryside he knew looked like one endless cornfield. For no good reason he called the first company back and said he'd take the car to Flagstaff.

It was a journey of around 1000 miles — about the same as the Chicago-Denver trip — and the man behind the counter said he'd have the best part of four days to do it. The procedure was standard. The guy was old, ugly, fat. He looked as though he was tired of handling the questions of people like Ray. When the time came for him to impart the legal details it all came out in one tidal rush.

'D'you hold a clean driving licence? Have you ever been imprisoned for a major felony relating to driving? Have you ever been imprisoned for the theft of or from motor vehicles? Have you ever been charged for any offence relating to driving other than minor traffic violations? Have you ever been refused car insurance for any reason whatsoever? Are you able to post a surety bond of one hundred dollars to be returned upon safe delivery of the vehicle? You are hereby notified that should you fail to deliver the vehicle within the aforementioned time limit, and you fail to notify the owner of the vehicle as to the reason for this delay, the FBI will be notified and your bond forfeited. Also, if the owner of the vehicle is not satisfied with the reason for a late delivery, he or she may in turn contact us and the FBI may be alerted and your bond forfeited. Do you understand these regulations and agree to abide by them? Sign here, please. Car's in lot six. White Pontiac. Have a good trip.'

At a K-Mart on the outskirts of Shreveport, he bought some beer, some taco shells, pecan pies, M&M's and a road map of Texas. The fastest route would be due west on

Interstate 20, but that went through the endless, sprawling Siamese twins of Dallas and Fort Worth. If he could get on to Highway 82, which ran through north Texas, it was a straight trip through New Mexico to Arizona. Two hours drive took him to Texarkana, on the border of the states which gave it its name, and he started the haul west.

He was in an area of Texas he didn't know. He'd worked once on a boat down in Corpus Christi, ferrying tourist fishermen up and down the shore. It had been nice down there until he'd been beaten up on his way home and wound up in hospital with a rib sticking into his lung. He took that as a sign to move on. Some people might have found the drive through a new region interesting, but Ray had been moving around too long for that. 'One grey line's the same as any other,' he told people who commented on it, 'Everybody's going somewhere and nobody's got a good reason why.' He'd travelled around America on trucks, on buses and in cars. He'd worked on a fairground trekking across the midwest and had had to drive eight hours through the night once or twice a week, watching the sun come up through tired eyes. He'd driven hired limousines full of burnt, grizzled old folks between the beaches and golf courses of West Palm Beach and Miami. As he drove, he tried to think of all the jobs he'd held for longer than a few days. Cab driver. Hotel clerk. Exterminator. Fairground barker (he'd got a raise because he drew customers by shouting, 'Okay, folks, we're particular at this here gallery, very select, only people with a dime to try it are allowed to stop'). Grease monkey. Bellhop. Rigger. Stevedore. Sharecropper. Nightclub announcer. Lumberjack. Bartender. Debt collector. Bookie. Laboratory technician. Woodcarver. Swimming pool cleaner. He'd worked in factories manufacturing golden thimbles for Chinatown bazaars, egg-boxes, printer's ink, and alarm clocks. The alarm clocks had been the worst. Every time he heard one, even now, he thought of that cramped store in Syracuse, the metallic clanging reverberating off the aluminium walls. As he drove he wondered how he had stood it the two months he did. He'd worked assembly line in Michigan, on a hog farm in North Dakota, as night watchman in a grain store in Wisconsin. 'Done about everything there is to do,' he'd say, 'Worked on freighters, worked in bars, worked on farms, worked on cars.' Sometimes people would recognise the lines from a song, sometimes they'd accept them as Ray's own, and he'd let them.

He'd left towns for a lot of reasons. He'd never been chased out by the law, although he told people he had. Usually he'd just get bored with the town or the people or the job he was doing and leave them all behind. He felt being on the move kept his mind active and free from the torpor which seemed to be the lot of so many of the people he came into brief contact with. He'd left towns because women were trying to tie him down, because it was too hot or too cold, because he'd read about somewhere else in a newspaper and thought he'd like to be there. He listened to signs. Once he was working as a dishwasher in the kitchen of a hotel in Pensacola, Florida and he began having dreams about dipping his hands into a sink full of soapy water and spearing his wrist on a sharp potato knife. He didn't wake in a sweat, but the dream made enough of an impression for it to stick in his mind for a few days. Eventually he would poke his fingers tentatively into the bucket of dishes, feeling carefully around under the surface. Once that started he knew it was time to move on. Even now, looking back at the incident from six or seven years, he couldn't figure out what it was about it that had unsettled him.

The Louisiana humidity had given way first to clear skies, but now, about two hours into Texas, it began to get grey. The road was a two-lane, without much traffic. As he thought that to himself, the song came into his mind and he rolled down the window and sang, 'Gone, Tulane, he can't catch up with you, gone Tulane.' After a while the strength of the wind coming in started blowing the M&M wrappers and taco bags around so he rolled it up. Pretty soon he would be able to stop for something to eat, but he wanted to kill as much of the journey as he could today. He'd split it into stages of roughly 250 miles. If he was past Wichita Falls by tonight, Tucumcari, New Mexico, tomorrow, and had reached the Petrified Forest by the following night, he'd be able to coast into Flagstaff in plenty of time, maybe even drive around looking for a likely place to stay before he returned the car.

The road was getting even quieter now, maybe only one car a minute. The beer was all gone and he pulled off the road to urinate. As he stood under a tree, he noticed something light in the grass a few feet away. Zipping himself up, he saw it was a Texas licence plate, WQP 544, with a little Texas-shaped black dot between the letters and numbers. His immediate reaction was to keep it, but on the way back to

the car he threw it away, realising that it would only be more
stuff to carry and that he would never have any use for it. It
wasn't as though he had a home to display it in. He started
up the engine, thought it over again, then got out and picked
it up and threw it in the back.

Every so often his attention would be caught by a sign at
the side of the road, usually for the IRA. He didn't know
what the letters stood for, but he knew they were something
to do with retirement, pension funds, something like that.
They baffled him. Various employers had sat him down and
told him about this financial plan, that inflation-linked
scheme. None of it meant a thing to him. A girl he'd gone
out with had once asked him what he thought he would live
on when he was old. He'd given her some flip answer, but
they'd both known the prospect made him uneasy. He pict-
ured himself as an old man is some skid row hotel, his vest
covered in dribbled spittle and his trousers baggy and stained
at the crotch, telling some kid about what a wonderful life it
was on the road, no ties to bind or responsibilities to anyone
but yourself. It was a dismal sight and he found his mouth
dried at the thought. The country tune on the radio matched
his feelings, so he hit the dial for something livelier to lift his
spirits. Years before he'd seen a map of the U.S.A. with different dark shades to signify the number of radio stations
there were in any particular area. Around the cities, as he'd
expected, it was virtually black, but he'd been surprised to
see a thick black band, hundreds of miles across, running
almost straight from the Mexican border up to Canada through
the midwest. A huge splodge of stations across the dial. Miles
and miles of sound. Well-served as the region was supposed to
be, though, the only thing Ray could pick up clearly was a
Dallas station which played the 'Best Damn Country', according to the jingle. Today it sounded as plaintive as the rest.
Eventually Dwight Yoakam came on, cataloguing a list of
things that wouldn't hurt. Ray liked Dwight Yoakam, he'd
even once driven for a day and a half to see him sing in a club
in Corpus Christi, but not today. Today his yowl just sounded
like a dog with its leg in a trap. He pushed the button off and
the big car hummed along in silence.

By Bonham the sky above was the colour of wet newspaper, and Ray pulled off the road into the forecourt of a
motel. He went next door and sat down at the counter of a
place advertising 'Big, Juicy, Ol' Fashioned Burgers', and

ordered coffee and food. A few seats along a tanned old man sat chewing his food and staring meditatively into space. His hands were worn and cracked but the fingers were slender and extended fully around his coffee mug. When Ray asked him where he could buy some beer, he put the mug down and chuckled wheezily, turning and showing white teeth. 'Sure. Get on that highway and keep driving, son. You're in a dry county.'

'Shit,' said Ray. 'How far to the county line?'

'Oh, ten, twelve miles west. Past a little place called Savoy.'

The news disappointed Ray, who'd been hoping to drive until nightfall then collapse in a motel, and he turned his attention back to his plate. The old man didn't seem set to converse further, but he suddenly asked where Ray was going.

'Arizona,' he said. 'I'm returning a car.'

'Pontiac.'

'Right.'

'AU 8321. Yellow plates.'

Ray looked along at the old man, who was still looking straight ahead at the wall behind the counter, his fingers tentacling the mug. 'Yeah – yeah, that's the one.'

'Live in Arizona, son?'

'No, like I say, I'm delivering the car there.'

'Where do you live?' the old man said, turning on his chair and looking at Ray.

Ray wondered what to say. He was never able to answer that question comfortably. Should he make something up, or tell the old man where he'd last lived? 'Well, I've lived in a lot of places,' he said finally.

'So've I, son. But now I live here,' said the old man, putting his cup down and looking at Ray expectantly.

'I guess I don't know where I live. Nowhere at the moment. When I get to Flagstaff — '

'A boomer,' said the old man quietly.

'What?' said Ray, leaning closer.

'A boomer,' the old man said in the same quiet tone, taking a sip of his coffee. 'Not many of you left.'

'Boomer? I, uh — ' Ray looked at him and shook his head.

'Somebody who moves around a lot, never staying in one place long, making a buck any way he can. That's a boomer. That you?' The old man looked at him out of one eye, his head cocked.

Ray thought, then nodded. 'I guess so.'

The old man turned to face him.

'Let me tell you somethin', son. I'm an old man, but I did what you're doin' for twenty years. It's a hell of a life. Don't let them tell you anything else. I met nicer folks and made more true friends when I was roamin' around than I've ever made settled, here or any place else. At first it surprised me, how good people were to a stranger, how folks'd trust you and look out for you. Lotta good people out there.'

Ray was conscious of the quiet of the place, as the old man's voice filled it. He looked around, but no-one else seemed to be listening.

'At first I followed the work. Wherever there were jobs to be had, I'd go there. I been all over. All over. But then I found I liked the weather better down here and I just kept travelling back and forwards, east to west, as much as I could. Just stopping and moving on, stopping and moving on.'

The old man turned and took another mouthful of coffee. He stared straight ahead, lost in reverie, peering back through time.

' 'Course, I'm talkin' about forty, fifty years ago. It was a whole lot easier to travel back then. You wanted to go somewhere, you went down to a bend in the tracks, waited on a freight, and hopped on. No trouble. Oh, there were some tough old boys on the railroads, but most of them, if they caught you, just said, "OK boys, ride's over. Clean up your stuff and git." There was a couple of mean ones, though. I remember one guy that worked the Union Pacific. He carried a Winchester, and with him it was shoot first, ask questions later. They were great days, though. You never went hungry. Even if you were bummin' round, if you met a hobo in the same boat he'd give you some of what he had, some Mulligan stew. Didn't matter what it was or how little he had. That was what got me friendly towards strangers, I guess. Yeah, they were the best days I ever had, and I missed them since I stopped.'

He turned towards Ray with clear, watching eyes.

'But I don't envy you, son. It's a different world out there today. When I was a kid you could say people wouldn't do you harm if they could do you a good turn. Can't say that now. Can't travel in boxcars now. Ain't seen a 'bo for a long time gone. Walk into a strange bar, you're more likely to get a fight than a drink. Kids today, don't seem to know how to handle liquor. Two shots and they go crazy. S'why I came here. No drunks in a dry place. But it ain't just that. People have changed. Always running, working, never stopping and looking around. Life's getting faster and faster in the cities. Getting so folks are too busy to even be polite, never mind friendly. Nope, it wouldn't be me. Not in this world.'

The old man went back to his cup and a silence filled the diner. His reminiscences seemed to be over. Ray got up, watching the old man all the time.

'Well, nice talking to you. Time to be moving on.'

'Yeah,' said the old man with a smile. 'Time to be moving on.'

Ray hesitated, and when it was clear the old man had said his goodbyes he paid up and left. At the door, though, he couldn't stop himself asking one last question.

'If the old days were so good, why'd you stop?'

The old man turned around and smiled an old man's smile. 'My legs got tired, son. My legs just got tired.'

Ray went outside, but the man put his hat on and followed him.

'Wouldn't plan on making a lot of miles tonight,' he said. 'There's a lot of rain in that sky. When it rains here it's like hell. Nothin' like it. If I was you, I'd check into the Ranch Motel, where your car is.' Again he looked at the sky. 'You ain't goin' far tonight. Ranch Motel, that's where to be.'

Ray said he wanted to make a start, and get some beer.

'It's your trip,' the old man shrugged. 'I wish you luck, but in a couple of hours you'll wish you were in the Ranch Motel, watching TV. 'Night, son.'

Ray watched him shuffling off and looked at the Motel's sign and dilapidated timber frame. He'd no intention of stopping in this town, least of all there. He'd wait and see what the weather was like when he stopped for some beer.

The first drops of rain tapped on the roof a few miles after a little town called Saint Jo. Over to the south, there was a pocket of clear, blue sky, but in front of him and to the north, it was a dense, murky grey. In the distance he could see lightning flash. He'd never seen anything like it. It wasn't sheet lightning, lighting up the sky all over. When it forked down, it didn't flash for an instant and disappear, it stayed visible for a second or two. At times he thought he was driving ahead of it then he saw more ahead and to the right. Out the window, the trees were shaking and straining in the wind. Even the thick grasses by the side of the road were blown almost flat, like grass by the runway when a plane's taking off. He seemed to be the only thing on the road. He'd go five minutes or more without passing a thing. All the while the rain got harder until the wipers were on full and the view out the windscreen was still a monochrome, gauzy blur. Around him the land was green and alive, but the vast sky was full of grey, greyer and more sombre than any sky he'd ever seen. The old man's words about hell came back to him as another fork of lightning cracked down, longer, sharper, and closer than any he'd seen. He was driving right into it. Suddenly the metronomic beat of the wipers was drowned out by a mighty rumbling, distant at first, then so loud it reverberated inside the car. He seemed to be right under it. Like the lightning, the thunder seemed to last far longer than any he could remember. As soon as the first peal ended, a low rumbling continued, and another almighty clap made him start in his seat. It seemed like the loudest, most ominous sound he'd ever heard. A vision came into his head of biblical wrath being visited upon back-sliding congregations, of God calling forth the sinners. Again he looked out of the windows for a place of refuge, a glimpse of lighter sky, but the land and sky were empty and bleak. As he turned his head back to the road, he saw a big truck tugging a house on a trailer coming towards him. Realising he'd swerved over the middle white line, he wrenched the wheel back to the right. The truck passed him, the house wobbling unsteadily behind it. Down his back, his shirt began to stick to his skin. He reached across and tugged a Bud from the six-pack he'd bought in Sherman.

Ray wanted to look at his map to see where the next town was, but he was scared the car wouldn't start again if he did. Grimly, he drove through the desolate emptiness, lights he didn't understand flashing on the Pontiac's dash. All he could hear was the nylon swish of the big car's tyres cutting through the rain and the hypnotic click-clack of the wipers forcing streams of water off the window. Up to the north, more lightning struck, close, it seemed, to a distant power pylon, though Ray couldn't tell if it was near or many miles away from it. Again the sky grumbled, after which there came another violent crashing from above him. The rain fell harder and harder, relentlessly battering the window, out of which Ray could see his lights illuminating flashing lines of water bouncing like beans into the car's front grill. The previous puddles had been replaced on the road by one continuous pool. In the quiet moments, Ray could hear the hiss of water being sprayed aside by the tyres. Again the thunder roared mournfully. On the dash, a very persistent orange light blinked twice then went out. The car was doing around 25 when the tracks ran off the road towards a garage. Ray pulled in and stopped. As it jolted to a stationary position, Ray realised his eyes were screwed up from attempting to focus out the window and rubbed them. When he leaned back, he felt his stomach strain and felt the muscles at his sides bunch. He'd unknowingly been tensing up along the road, and as he sagged back he exhaled involuntarily. For a few seconds he gulped in air and squeezed his stomach and sides. Down in the small of his back he felt stiff and old. He longed to get out and stretch properly, but saw the rutted ground was deep with water. Now he'd stopped he could hear the wind blowing. It didn't whistle or sigh, but seemed to gust with immense power like some unstoppable force, like a busted dam or a speeding train. Ray listened to it howl as it went under the car, blowing from behind him. Perhaps that was why he hadn't heard it before; it was moving the same way as he was. The garage door was a faded green and although it was locked, the wind tugged at it and he heard it creak, but the sound came from far away, as though the gale had carried it off and brought it back. For a minute or so he watched the raindrops splashing into the puddles. He'd hoped that stopping would show the storm was passing, but he saw now it wasn't. Wearily, he turned the key and pulled the car back on to the road.

Now Ray felt the wind pushing him along. The slightest acceleration gave the car a new power, and generally it coasted along faster than he'd remembered it. There seemed to be fewer sparks of lightning and the sky seemed to be quieter, but the rain was as persistent as ever and the sky the same deathly shade, like weatherbeaten black paint. The old man in Bonham's words of advice about the weather returned to him, and Ray resolved to stop in the next town he came to. He realised driving through the rain would eventually lead to water getting into his engine and the car breaking down. However, he'd been impressed at how well the Pontiac had handled, considering the battering it was taking. The dashboard lights still flashed now and then, but the car had driven smooth and sure. One day he wanted a car just like it. If he was going to travel the land, he wanted to do it in something like this.

He was beginning to pass more cars now, all of them with

their lights on. He took their presence to be a good sign.
Above, he noticed patches of sky not quite as grey as the
rest, but the rain still battered the windscreen. Ray had never
seen rain like it. He'd been in some storms before, but never
one so powerful, so relentless, so universal. Seems like it's
raining all over the world, he hummed, and it did. It was impossible to think that somewhere, probably within a couple
of hundred miles, it was clear, sunny even. All he could think
of was one big storm over America, roaring and thundering,
heaving and crashing down on the earth.

The sign said Belcherville was one mile to the north, Bowie
16 south. As he turned the car right, he felt the wind push it
towards the middle of the road and looked ahead for a motel
sign, a bar, any sign of life. Around a bend he passed an old
Buick rusting in someone's yard by the side of the road. On
the other side there were a couple of weatherworn shacks
before the road curved round to the left. Maybe this was the
town beginning, he thought, slowing to take the bend in case
there were any motels around it. What he saw gave him a
shock. He was on the way out of town. There were only fields
on either side of him and the road ahead merged with the
grey sky ahead. There were no buildings ahead of him.
Slowly he let the car cruise to a stop and turned it round.
Nothing. He hadn't missed anything. At the turn of the bend
he got out and stood by the car and looked around. There
was nothing in Belcherville, just a handful of empty old
houses creaking eerily in the rain, wires whistling in the wind,
and the old car disintegrating on the bend. It was horror-
movie stuff, void, dismal, too deserted to be peaceful. Ray
thought of a town he'd driven through once in Alabama.
He'd been looking at his map by the side of his truck when
two men came over and he saw the tell-tale suspicion in their
eyes. A Klan town. Belcherville reminded him of it. Sitting
on the bend he felt alone and not a little frightened, and he
drove back down to the highway without looking behind him.

Getting out of the car, even for a few seconds, had
drenched him, so he turned on the heater to dry out. When
he did, one of the lights on the dash came on again. When he
turned the heater off, the light stayed on. When he turned it
back on, it went off. It was a car, he realised, way ahead of
him.

He turned right back on to 82, the car again picking up as
the wind pushed it on. The grass by the side of the road was

long and wet, flattened and beaten by the wind and the
storm. Ray was beginning to know how it felt and wondered
if he'd ever get out of the car into a dry hotel room, clean
clothes, a warm bath, a bourbon and a beer by his side, some
food on the table. Again he rubbed his eyes. He was getting
tired now. On the circus, he'd popped bennies and been able
to drive twelve, fifteen hours without taking his foot off the
gas. He must be getting old. Now he felt tired after a third of
the time. It's the storm, he told himself, the storm's doing it.
Tomorrow will be better.

The rain fell steadily along the road, neither slackening
nor increasing, until out of the gloom a little town called
Henrietta appeared. He was 20 miles from Wichita Falls and
it was a little after 8 p.m. This would have to do. He ran from
the car into the Waggoners Motel, dropped his bag on the
floor of the dark little room they gave him, and fell asleep
with his boots on.

The following morning he looked out on a town examining
the storm's damage like a cat sniffing food in an unfamiliar
bowl. Shopowners, waitresses, gas station attendants, cow-
boys, and an assortment of old folks were wandering about
the streets, studying the damage and passing comments.
Through them weaved a crew of workmen in hardhats, going
from pole to pole putting the lines back up. As their white
truck moved from one to the next, a group of people stopped
to watch them reel in the wires, one man clamber nimbly up,
and restore them to their usual position. At the A.O.K. Motel
down the street, a bunch of people waited on the porch for
their lines to be hoisted back on to the pole outside. Obviously, the storm here had been an event, something Henrietta would talk about for a long time to come. Above, the
sky was the dull colour of a cow's udders. But the Texas heat
had dried the streets and there was no suggestion of more
rain to come. It was road weather, and after the previous
day's exertions, Ray looked forward to a leisurely drive into
New Mexico.

He stopped at a K-Mart in Wichita Falls for provisions — a
dozen beers, a half-bottle of Old Grand-dad, potato chips. He
even picked up a sticker with 'We've Got It Good In Wichita
Falls' on it and stuck it across the rear window. 250 miles of
West Texas stretched before him on the map like a red rivulet
of blood.

By Chillicothe he'd settled into a nice routine. The radio

34 KENNETH MACDONALD

fed out a non-stop stream of lachrymose country plaints and
honky-tonk choogle, the dashboard lights stayed off, the
bourbon slid down nicely. Ray tried to remember whether
New Mexico or Arizona was the state in which you could
drink openly at the wheel. In one of them, he seemed to remember, you could drink and drive legally. The only thing
illegal was to be drunk in charge of a car. He racked his
memory. Maybe it was Texas. Beside the road, the green and
yellow vegetation had given way to ploughed earth, a muddy
brown after the rain. Along the way, small pumps excavated
for oil. Sometimes as many as eight or nine in a single field.
Ray wondered whether the owner was in some Houston sky-
scraper, sitting at a desk the size of the Pontiac, or whether
he was just some good ol' boy trying to scrape a meagre living
off the land. The fields were all empty save for the pumps,
cranking and drilling. He thought about Texas. He knew
there were parts of it that were wilderness, and despite the
fact most of the time he'd spent there had been in the cities,
that was his impression of it. A big, empty place. In the north,
where he was, it was green and empty. In the south it was hot
and empty. He'd once heard a conversation in a bar down
there and a man said you could drop some countries in Europe
in Brewster county and they wouldn't touch the sides. He'd
never been to Europe so he didn't know if it was true, but
he'd been to Brewster county — it was right down on the Rio
Grande — and he knew what it was. Hot and empty.

As Ray drove through Amarillo and saw the signs for the
Cadillac Ranch, he began to sing softly to himself. The sky
was clear now, but something was nagging him. In his mind,
he knew something wasn't right, as though he'd gone to the
store and forgotten what he was there for, but he couldn't say
what. The Amarillo station played the same cycle of country
songs as the Wichita Falls one, the Dallas one, and the others
others he'd picked up. He wondered what had made people
write songs about all these places, Amarillo, Cadillac Ranch. He
liked to hear the names of places in songs, though. Made him
want to be moving. And he liked to use the mention of a song
on the radio as a conversation-starter if he was hitching. Still,
there was something on his mind. Maybe it was Amarillo. He
knew from the time he'd been there before that it sat on the
border of two counties, and that one of them was dry and
the other wasn't. He remembered because he'd tried to buy
beer on the wrong side. It had left him with unpleasant memories, so he drove through, then past Cadillac Ranch, the tails

pointing out of the earth like stems, broken and absurd. Thinking about songs always made him think of the time he'd driven into Winslow, Arizona, and the town sign had said, 'Take It Easy in Winslow Arizona', just like the Eagles song. He'd never got over it. He tried to remember the name of the song about the wind on the West Texas border, but his brain was beginning to fog over and he'd to make do with whistling the tune as he crossed the state line. It was getting towards evening, and he decided he'd stop at Tucumcari, where he'd planned to spend the night, for a coffee, then try to make it to Alburquerque before nightfall.

Dean's Restaurant was on East Tucumcari Boulevard within sight of the highway and as Ray sat at the counter, he saw that the place was just like the one he'd been in in Bonham. It was at that hour of dusk where a happy hour would've been in full swing in a bar, but in the coffee house only workers going home, women with bags of shopping, and lonely old men sat. There was the same air of sluggishness and restlessness, the same feeling that everyone there would rather have been doing something other than drink coffee, listen to the waitresses' grating high-pitched laughter and feel the evening come on. Ray drank his coffee in silence, wondering why he had started noticing these solitary people more. He knew they had existed everywhere he'd been, but only in the last few months had he seen them. He looked at a bunch of old men sitting at a table, their cowboy shirts fraying and their caps worn. They sat in silence, looking at everything around them but each other. At the counter, another old man sat in similar clothes, drinking alone. Ray wondered why he wasn't with them, what old feuds and misunderstandings prevented him being part of the table. He drove back to the highway wondering about it and wondering what his own interest in it signified.

When he checked into the motel in Albuquerque he bought a newspaper and discovered the previous day's storm had actually been the fringes of a tornado. He'd barely noticed the report, which was buried among a 'World Watch' column on the front page, beside all the local headline news. Between a story about the President's health and the Senate's decision to ease gun control, it said the tornado had destroyed a little town called Orr in Southern Oklahoma, killing four people and leaving 45 homeless. Surrounding towns were also affected, it said, and there had been damage as far south as Bridgeport and Denton in Texas. Ray had never seen a twister before, despite having driven around the south many times. He knew they mostly came in the spring and it always seemed to be that in winter and in springtime he was up north. It was always about July before he got the winter chill out of his bones. He tried to remember if he'd seen anything that looked like a tornado while he'd been driving, but he knew he hadn't been looking for one. The thought of a little town being wiped out disturbed him more than he thought it would, and not just because he'd been on the periphery of the event. Like an itch that kept coming back, he couldn't clear it out of his mind. He wondered where all the people in Orr, Oklahoma, would go and where they would be a year from now. Although he knew tornadoes were common in the south, he couldn't get used to how little attention seemed to have been paid to the event just a few hundred miles further along the highway.

The following day's drive across endless, barren, scorched New Mexico was a steady rise in altitude. It was hot here. Albuquerque had depressed him, not only because of the news about the tornado, but also because it seemed to be a mixture of new shopping malls and old Indians selling souvenirs from shawls spread out on the sidewalks. He left town and put 50 miles behind him by mid-morning, the car's automatic speed control on for long stretches. By setting it, he could drive with his foot off the gas and the speed stayed constant. It even compensated for inclines. He set it for around 60 and let it coast along.

He'd been in New Mexico before and had liked it. The high, conical mesas had always seemed to him the most distinctive form of American landscape, and he'd seen plenty of them all over the state, rising straight and massive out of the scrub and bush. Someone had once explained to him how they came to be that strange level-topped shape, but he'd been drunk at the time and had forgotten. He liked them because they looked at once identifiably American yet also like some land mass from far away in Mexico and Central America. You certainly didn't see them in North Dakota. Even when he was working up north and saw photos of the west, he only had to see some high mesa and he could smell the sagebrush and feel the hot desert air. He'd always wanted to visit a place called Monument Valley, near the Four Corners in the north of Arizona, where there were a lot of them. Cigarette ads were filmed and photographed there and it looked a still, hot, dead place, where the green brushlands contrasted vividly with the earthen, rust-coloured plateaux and the clean, pale sky. The mesas there rimmed the horizon like footstools in some land of the gods. The sight of them, even in some magazine ad with a staple through the middle, never failed to start something stirring in his stomach. 'Someday,' he'd think. 'Someday . . . ' The mesas had always suggested magic to him, Indians who believed the rock had mysterious powers, shamans worshipping in its shadow, sacrificial rites and pagan worship at nightfall, but today they suggested nothing as fascinating. Today he barely noticed them at all.

The tornado, the old man in Bonham and the bunch of sad old men in Tucumcari, the word 'boomer' that he'd never heard before yet which seemed to describe him perfectly, the deserted town of Belcherville: all of them had had some effect on him until in combination they rumbled around his head, nagging and causing doubts about himself, his lifestyle, his selfish, introspective way of living. Like the landscapes he'd driven through, stagnation and emptiness seemed to be his dominant chord. As the miles slid away and the markers flashed past, he sat in silence, his rootless life staring back at him as the white lines disappeared under the front of the car. He'd been lonely before and knew he wasn't given to fits of morbid introspection, but this felt different. He didn't feel old, but he was gripped by a sense of time slipping away. There were many places he still wanted to visit, but for the first time he found himself looking for a place to use, if not as a home, certainly as a base. He never liked living with someone else, but now felt lonely sometimes when he awoke in a room that was cold and empty. Good ol' boys in busy bar-rooms annoyed him, but more and more he wanted a bunch of buddies to drink with and know — their backgrounds, their families, their jobs, their lives — rather than the transitory friendships of the road. He knew if the car crashed there and then, the addresses in his pocket book would lead only to old associates, paths crossed once and never again, months and years ago. He knew, too, the majority of them would have trouble remembering who he was, when they'd met. Determined to chase these thoughts away, he punched on to a station playing old radio mystery plays, opened a beer and headed off the Highway into the Zuni Indian Reservation.

Ray had no particular fascination with Indian culture, but felt in need of a break from the endless highway driving.

Along the hilly, winding two-lane road he thundered, the car seeming to go all the faster because of the deserted nature of the road and land around. Near a spectacular mesa, Ray got out and looked around him. It was late in the afternoon and the clouds overhead reflected off the top of the car. The mesa, though, was bathed in desert sunshine. Standing alone by the car emphasised to him how small he was, a tiny pebble swamped by the vastness chiselled from the stone around him. He wanted to find people, an Indian village like the adobe houses he'd passed at Laguna a few hours before, but the world around him was empty. Nothing moved, and Ray figured that any sound he made at that moment would be heard only by him. Snakes don't have ears, he thought. He suddenly felt cold, got in the car and drove back towards the endless emptiness of Interstate 40.

He crossed the Arizona line later in the afternoon. He was now 150 miles from Flagstaff. He knew he should have made as much distance as possible that night, allowing more time to search for a room in Flagstaff the following day, but Ray felt unnaturally tired. He decided to give it another hour or two then stop for the night. Ahead of him, the road stretched out endlessly. Ray came over a rise and saw it etched against the apricot sky like a spoke. Absent-mindedly he looked at the speedometer and when he passed the furthest point he'd seen from the rise he saw he'd driven almost 5½ miles. He sighed and sipped on the bourbon. The sky was getting darker now, not Texas dark, just evening coming down. It was a spectacular sight, a panoramic vista of greys, pinks, violets and whites, pillows and sponges of darkness, shadow, and light spread out before him. He stopped at an Exxon station for gas in Chambers and looked out past the Best Western Motel sign at the coloured hues of the sky, the red tail lights of the freeway heading east, the weary blinking of the fairy lights on the motel chalet roofs. On his way back to the car after buying more bourbon and beer he passed the motel restaurant and noticed a large family — around eight or more — dining. They were talking quietly among themselves the way people who are in each other's company on a regular basis do: as though they all had something to tell, but not so hurried that anyone was monopolising the conversation. It was such a refined, peaceful scene, Ray stopped to look. Then a woman caught him staring and he moved on. Since he'd been thinking about Winslow earlier in the journey, he'd half-decided to bed down for the night there, but the listless

George Jones songs on the radio depressed him, and the mystery programme, which had at least distracted him, was now in the command of a repulsive agony aunt. At 8.15 he pulled into a motel in some place just past the Petrified Forest, switched on the TV, then drank the bourbon until he passed out.

The morning when he awoke was gritty and hot. Ray didn't feel hungover, but for a moment he couldn't remember where he was. For a few seconds he was without a name, a sense of place, roots, destination, purpose. Then it began to come back. He had the car to deliver. Today by two. He remembered the fat guy's words. 'The FBI will be notified and your bail forfeited.' He went into the bathroom and splashed water on his face, then drank some. It tasted warm, chlorinated, as though someone had just washed in it. Swallowing it made him need something else to drink. He sat in a diner eating breakfast and gulping down orange juice as fast as the waitress could serve it up. When he'd finished he looked out on the street. He saw the various store signs with the names of the town preceding their function, Holbrook Realty, Holbrook Val-U-Foods, Holbrook Lawn Care, Holbrook Kwik-Stop Grocery, as is the style in small towns across America. He knew that a month from now, Holbrook would be just a name to him and he'd never be able to remember the town he stayed in before he delivered the Pontiac to Flagstaff. Across the street a garage sign caught his eye. It read, 'WRONG WAY, SEVERE TIRE DAMAGE'. It was in bold white capitals on a black background. He'd seen the words before, in car parks and the like, but for the first time it said something to him. Something he'd never noticed, or which had never made any impression on him before. Wrong way. Again the feeling of persistent, unspecific doubt came back to him. He racked his mind. What was it? Why did he feel so uncomfortable, so restless? He saw the broken lines of the old man's face looking back at him from his reflection. 'It wouldn't be me'. 'Not in this world'. Again he wondered where he would be at 50. More and more he had the feeling the old man was right. Ray normally paid little heed to the opinions offered by people on his lifestyle and morals, but the dry, experienced crackle of the old man's voice, coupled with the arid, barren landscape he'd driven through, had made him turn questions on himself, on his way of life. He'd always, throughout his life, felt his travelling days would end some day, that they were simply a prelude to something settled, a sewing of oats, experiences to one day turn and look back on, but he was becoming overpowered by a sense of being short-changed, a feeling that there had to be more. He knew that most people he came in contact with regarded him as an oddball, a relic from another time endlessly bumming around. And for what? The spread of the century had turned one small American town into the next. A mall with a drugstore, a market, a burger joint, an ice-cream parlour. What was he achieving? What was he proving, or attempting to prove? Was he roaming because he liked it, or because he couldn't fulfil his expectations by staying in one place? Or was he stuck in the same routine as the guy in the assembly line, the clerk at the store, except that his was to be dogged by a powerful restlessness, an urge for going? In his youth, every new place had been a new mystery to him, a chance of meeting people, new girls to make. Now his enjoyment at stopping in a new town was checked by the weariness of getting himself there, the exasperation he knew would take over at the realisation this wasn't where he wanted to be, and the impression that this town was the same as the last, the way the one before that would be the same as the next. Other people took vacations, Ray just travelled, working endlessly here and there, scratching a living to survive. What would he do if he didn't like Flagstaff? He didn't know. Was there anywhere he could say he really wanted to go to? He looked ahead and saw a dreary life of bit jobs, drunken nights, one-night girls, grey rooms. There would be beers after work, the occasional fight, junk foods, nothing to stop him moving on, on, on. He'd never allow anyone to get close enough to him to invite him home for a meal, for fear he'd see how happy people could be in a cosy, homely setting. His nights would always be alone, drinking in a bar, working somewhere, looking for a girl. There never had been any other way for him.

He paid and left, starting out the 70 miles west for Flagstaff, but after only a few miles he stopped and stood for a minute, his mind travelling somewhere else way ahead. He flashed through some more small towns, then saw the signs for Winslow. Winslow. Take It Easy In Winslow Arizona. How many times had he seen that sign? How many times would he see it again? Winslow Arizona. A little town in the middle of a big desert with nothing in it, yet he knew it well enough to picture the town sign in his eye. He smiled, a grim little smile that he caught in the mirror. Suddenly, he stopped the car, and looked at his map, tracing his finger along the road he wanted. A few miles short of Winslow he saw it. 87, a little state highway running north off the road. He turned the car on to it. Monument Valley was almost 250 miles away, through some of the dullest terrain in the state, but Ray sighed contentedly. He thought about mesas, and bones in the red earth, and they sang back to him as he drove.

Alison Campbell

'TI AMO'

His mother, he said, was starting to complain of the smell.
'Smell,' I said. 'What smell?'
'When you're in the last stages of cancer, your skin be-
gins to decay,' he said.
His father had always had loose skin but now it had
started to look papery like the charred edges of a brown en-
velope.
'My father used to work on the railways,' he said. 'He
saw all the people being packed onto the trains for Germany.'
'Is that why you don't like Germans?' I said.
He'd told me that he went to Switzerland to work, to
Zurich. People were very rude to Italians. They were guest-
workers . . . poor and expendable.
He'd met an American woman there; the only friendly
voice around. So he'd quickly started to learn English.
Her name was Gigi and she was fourteen stone, tanned
and elegant in white bermuda shorts and lots of thin silver
jewellery.
Later, she'd given his mother a watch. An expensive Swiss
one. She had learned to speak some Italian from him, and his
mother laughed at the unmistakable accent.
'Mi piace,' she'd said, but had never worn it.
Gigi haunted my thoughts. How different he must have
been with her. I felt mouselike beside her rich exuberant
ghost.
Her pictures confirmed my image. Her skin was the colour
of peanut butter and her hair, black as Italians' should be,
was long and caught in a scarf.
Suddenly I felt as papery as his father, sitting silently at
table rolling crumbs together from the dinner bread and sip-
ping wine like a bird. He smiled a lot distractedly, and when
he stopped, the creases round his eyes and mouth stayed.
He was small and frail. I couldn't imagine him carrying
heavy packages around stations.
I tried to take in the conversation, but it was too fast. His
mother kept lifting her arm and motioning towards his

brother shouting 'Giaordano' a lot.

He was pale and sat indoors, reading the bible in the heavy dark room at the back.

I asked Rinaldo why she seemed so angry.

'Oh, she's fed up he doesn't have a girlfriend,' he said. I wondered if I should feel guilty. Did his mother think I was going to marry Rinaldo?

His mother looked like a matronly cherub you used to get on scraps. It occurred to me she would have looked a little too sparkly with Gigi's watch on.

It didn't seem to go with her print dress with the thick wrapover apron. I wondered if it was cheating, and the floral sleeves and hem were sewn onto the apron. I certainly never saw the front of the dress.

Shortly afterwards we went to Corfu.

Rinaldo drove the red car over the ferry ramp at Brindisi and we were off.

'Kerkyra,' I said, as I leaned against the railings. I tried not to be sick as I breathed the stale night air of the hot sleeping bags on the covered deck. But the clear turquoise water swished everything away.

We found the house, stumbling through a lemon grove. It was for rent and it had a well, shrouded by ferns.

I asked a friend to send me 'Teach Yourself Greek' for my birthday. I did not find it easy to learn from a book. Rinaldo could prompt me easily and cheerfully, so I reverted to Italian.

In the evenings we walked to eat. I didn't like kalamari, but the fish was thick and meaty, and for once I ate up the skin. The nights scared me, hearing nothing. There were no street lights and the blackness oozed through the shutters. There was no electricity. I couldn't even feel my way to the wall to light the fiddly paraffin lamp.

Sometimes, I'd crouch my head and shoulders over Rinaldo listening for his breathing, making sure a presence hadn't killed him silently, and was now waiting for me at the well.

Lieve walked out of the oregano one day wearing a loose dress. Her hair was ratted, and whitened by the sea. Her hands were thick and brown and she offered fresh peaches from a soggy bag.

'You're back this year?' she asked Rinaldo squinting with one eye, shading the other with a hand.

'And where is the Americano?' she laughed as if in some private joke with him.

Rinaldo smiled, too, flipping the fruitstone forwards into the ferns.

'She left me for Paul Getty,' he said, wiping his long splayed fingers on his bathing trunks.

'This is my love now,' he said, squeezing my shoulders and tippling me towards him.

'Hello,' we said smiling at each other. Lieve had a house which she rented too. Only she paid for it at nights when the owner came in through the window, she said.

We drank ouzo in her garden . . . the house was closer in to town than ours. She had one room and a kitchen, white-washed like the outside walls.

Her room was bare except for a bed and two pieces of warm orange material across it. A basket of threads, scraps and silks stood beside it. The lid had burst off and stood beside it as if poised to roll across the uneven floor.

'I really prefer women,' she said, when Rinaldo went off for bread and feta for us.

'My friend was here from Antwerp for one month. It was good. No one bothered us.' I wondered if she meant her landlord.

She sewed clothes and sold them to tourists. She made rings too, little silver bands that interwove and knotted on each other like lace.

'I sold a lot to the Americano. She liked them.'

'Was Rinaldo in love with her, then?' I asked.

'She was always joking and buying things,' Lieve said. 'She was older than him, I think.'

I could not ask any more. That was all she had to say.

I liked Lieve. I liked her steady light eyes and her thick eyebrows. I liked her unsurprised, low-key greetings when I started to come and visit in the afternoons.

She would wave towards the billycan on the stove, and wander into the garden to sew. I would make myself some coffee and look round the kitchen. The window had a small deep sill, and flowers frothed from a tiny glass jar. A bunch of oregano hung upside-down to dry.

I liked her quiet absorption in her work. Some people were quiet because they listened and absorbed what others had to say. Lieve was quiet because she was self-contained and immersed in what she was doing. Sometimes when I said something to her in conversation, she would look through you vaguely, narrow-eyed, and you knew you would have to

wait a minute until she was back, there, in the garden with
you, sitting sewing on the rickety wooden chair under the
tree. I brought things to work on. Lieve showed me how to
alter a dress into a skirt. She gave me bright silks and taught
me to do French knotting round the waist.

At our house, Rinaldo talked a little about Gigi.
'You are not LIKE her,' he would always end up saying,
as if, by emphasising our differences, I would somehow be re-
assured.

I began to visit the local airstrip, watching the fat barrel
planes take off and touch down, sometimes with only minutes
in between.

I was drawn to the runway. I hated planes and would
never think of taking anything but a ferry. But the excite-
ment of watching the pastel tourists step waveringly across
the bubbly tarmac always gave me pleasure on their behalf;
anticipation of the island they had come to. Similarly, those
same bodies roasted to a toast two weeks later, made me feel,
watching them, that I unaccountably had performed some
transforming magic rite over them.

The three of us ate in town before Rinaldo and I caught
the ferry back to Italy. Lieve carried her sandals, then put
them on in the town centre to avoid oily motorbike puddles
and empty cans. I said I would write, but ended up sending a
glaring postcard from Brindisi.

'Where *were* you?' said Rinaldo's mother as we opened
the flyscreen door of their apartment. I stepped back into the
hall and looked at the tight fawn front doors with crosses on
the corridor walls. I heard her voice going higher and faster.
Rinaldo joined in; a fevered duet of anxiety, anger, joy, I
didn't know. I only picked out Rinaldo's voice saying 'Dio,
Dio,' over again, threading its way through his mother's tex-
tured notes.

He stepped out of the flat, closing the flyscreen door behind him. He was frowning and did not look at me.

'My father is dead,' he said. 'He died in the night two
days ago.'

A week after the funeral, I went back to the flat with
Rinaldo. I had been staying with Mauretta and Black, married
friends of Rinaldo's living in Bergamo.

The day after I arrived, I asked Black why he had that
name. He said Lieve had called him that when he had gone to
Corfu with Rinaldo last year. He supposed it was because of
his black hair. He asked me not to tell his wife about Lieve.

Rinaldo took me into the back and showed me the shrouded table in the middle. The room fringed the table apologetically. Even the crosses and madonnas hanging on the walls smiled with downcast eyes.

'That was where the coffin was,' he said.

'My aunts and uncles came to see my father before the funeral. My mother was upset of the smell,' he said. 'Look.' Ducking to where he was pointing, I saw an air-freshener tablet suctioned to the underneath of the table. It smelt of pine.

I went home. It would be harder there, and I needed hardness. I had felt propelled into other people's lives and emotions. I needed to come up against some boundaries of my own.

My father died shortly afterwards. His death gave substance to the telegrams I exchanged with Rinaldo subsequently. They said things like,

'I am thinking of you, Squirrel. Ti Amo.'

The following year, we met in Milan to go to Corfu again. Rinaldo looked much thinner. He said his mother had lost weight too, and still cried a lot.

I looked in his bag for some change. (As usual, I'd come with 50,000 lira notes.) As I picked out wads of my letters, a photograph of a slim, intense woman in a yellow sheath-like dress fell through.

Rinaldo scooped it up and dealt it to me, as you would the Queen of Diamonds.

'Even she's skinny now,' he said laughing, and looking straight at me. I wondered how many other letters Gigi had written to him over the year.

'Why does she write?' I asked.

'I wrote,' he said.

'I told her about my father, and how she wouldn't recognise me, I am so skinny now.' He flipped the narrow belt of his velvet trousers.

'And she sent me this photo. She spent three months on a health farm to get like this,' he said, and flicked his middle finger, nail down, onto the photograph, sending it spinning to the ground.

Picking it up, he tore it once and put it face down in the ashtray.

'It's a lot cheaper to get slim our way,' he said, smiling with his mouth tucked in at one corner. He touched my fingers where my rings spun for want of flesh.

Suddenly, I felt old, pale, and very tired of winter.

Robin Fulton

HOMAGE TO A GARDENER

Why call them 'weeds? Look —
Dandelion fields. Willow-herb hillsides.
Lupin embankments
(primitive blue, predating the hybrids).
Even in gardens
nothing is quite tamed. Take chrysanthemums
— 'gold-flowers' to Greeks —
disintegrating nostalgically
in autumn suburbs,
shreds of mellow colours on misty days,
outlasting shrunk leaves,
surviving even the first rimy dawns.

Father would have said
'A bonny sight,' not bothering to add
'but . . . ' He might have said
nature is too prolific, impatient,
refine, select, prune,
wait, outwit frosts, earwigs, north winds, south winds.
Each plant gave its all,
concentrated itself, to one stem, one
gigantic blossom.
Cut, they shone from October to Christmas,
autumn suns de luxe.
Thus far nature gave in to art. He let
neither win outright.
He saved from real gold's perennial death
the colour of gold,
a ripeness that would not refuse to die.
He saved from nature
something choice, more-than-nature, incarnate.

NOT YET

Cornflower thicket,
long past the season
of blue thronging heads.
Ash-pale petals leave
tawny after-blooms,
many-pointed bright
stars, tissue-thin, tough;
back-lit, the silver
of much-weathered wood.

Pull them up? Not yet.
The last miniature
cobalt survivors
who arrived too late
hang on. I watch them
as if they were frail
unwritten gospels,
rare first-born from whom
much might have been hoped.

CLOUD AND SEED

White solitary evening cloud
bulging like a city adrift.
Hard not to admire you. Yet not
one pin could dance on your soft crown.

I watch you float, from ground-level,
between us, a silhouetted
row of stalks with withered-in, black-
dwarfish, hob-nobbing dense pin-tops.

Extremes meet. The vigorous dead
crowd round me just before my birth,
just after my death. I'm both young
and old. Both cloud-big and seed-small.

AUGUST 1920

Surprised? Of course — to find clouds
so unhistorical, white
and quick; and hedgerows chock full
and loud; and murmuring corn
about to yellow; cool pale
about-to-ripen Pippins
— sweet Cox's, Golden, Ribston;

and children knowing not much
and adults knowing too much
ambushed by summer's fulness
and wishing it would stop short
and hold its blue, its bright green;
and not a trace of brown tint
that makes our photographs sad;

and Over There, where so much
had stopped short, somehow still far
away, 'abroad,' and far back
enough for those with sad cause
to count to say 'It's two years
or three since then,' the war gone
to ground beneath a tight nerve;

and further north than these dales
in Edinburgh, May Scott
(who married William Fulton)
not yet a widow; her son
my father John a month less
than twelve; in Thurso, not ten
quite, Margaret Macpherson;

the certainty of my flesh
improbable as dog-rose,
convolvulus or speedwell
deciding: 'That's enough. Let's
stop short and keep our sap moist.
The grandson, old, shall smell what
his father's father smelt, young.'

THE FIRST SIGHT

As when the sun breaks through thick cloud
and our eyes wince and find shelter
among shades, so
at the first sight of your fresh grave

I tried not to look. I listened.
In the church across the river
an evening psalm was unwinding;
the river with its soft voice spoke;
up the hill around your own church
the sycamores were loud with rooks.

It's the first sight that won't let go:
as when the sun in a picture,
made relentless
by art, unblinking, stares and stares.

CAN'T STOP

I've been rushing away from your death
ever since then.
I wanted to stop still by your death
with the patience
trees spend on one part of a landscape.
I still do. I
am not without that kind of patience.
Caught in a dream
endlessly un-dreamlike, the landscape
hurries past, must
follow the timetable to your death.
Wrong way! Too late! I'm on the wrong train
rushing away from, not to, your death.

Andrew Greig

THREE POEMS FROM THE HIMALAYA

1 Desire

Between one expedition and the next
we buried the tiny Buddha's bones
upright, with respect, at the bottom of the garden.

We were driven
back to the mountains
on the crumbling verge of tears.

Between the highway and the ditch,
thirled to desire, the restless West
is pushing to its limits —

no one said we are too old
to die young, too young to retire
as we left Lhasa behind.

2 Arrival

We're back again
with our tents, our trash
and more. Be arrogant:
we animate these mountains.

(Whether a stone does or does not
fall when we're not here
is a toy metaphysic
fiddled in spare moments
like headtorches or letters from home.)

Mal flicks his lighter
and an avalanche roars into life —
we have come to assert
everything fits
that it might do so.
This is the true scale of things:
the entire mountain mirrored in our shades.

All day snow sank in the billy,
was boiled, drunk, peed, replenished
as we passed the mountain through us.
Night came on, meaning something
in the presence of witnesses.
Unblinking stars and lightning,
the darkness is lit
at a depth we can rely on.

3 Interlude on Mustagh Tower

In these high places we are melting out
of all that made us rigid; our ice-screws
hang loose on the fixed ropes to the Col.
Monday in the Himalaya. The clouds are down,
our objective is somewhere but obscure,
let it soar without us for a day.
We lounge in thermals on the glacier,
brewing and shooting the breeze, the improbable
project of conversation between the living.
Our laughter rings across the ice. Why not?
None of us will die today, that's immortality
you can taste and pull on in a cigarette,
sweet and rasping, the way we like it.
Steam rises from the billy, Sandy pours;
it is true high, worked for, that we pass
hand to hand between us with our brews.
Men on ice, going nowhere and laughing
at everything we cannot see but know
is there — in the cloud, on the Col,
a hand of some sort is tightening our screws.

Gordon Meade

THE POTTER'S WHEEL

What would you have me be,
A lump of clay upon a potter's wheel?
Already, I can feel my bones dissolve,
My porous skin give way.

And what would you have me do,
Be both the feet that turn the wheel
And the hands that shape the bowl?
Already, I can feel the pedals underneath
My soles, my fingers wet and cold.

Yet you would have me be
And do it all. Be four, you say,
The clay, the wheel, the potter, and
The bowl. I stand outside myself
And feel myself revolve. I am the motion
Of the pedals, and the fingers' deft
Resolve. The bowl nears its completion,
And, for an instant, I am whole.

LUG, QUEEN OF WORMS

Beneath the sand
Something stirs.

With coiled
And wormy turnings
She is knitting herself
Into the bank.

Her casts
Glitter in the sun.

The sea-god wants
To beat her glitter out.

She burrows deeper
Down into the rock
Of the sea-floor establishing
Her head-quarters there.

The rain-god wants
To wash her glitter off.

She houses herself
On the weather-chart
Planning her movements
On the same map.

The wind-god wants
To blow her glitter away.

She looks out
From the storm's eye
Watching the battle going
On all around her.

Slate-clean.
The beach waits
For her to raise
Herself again.

NAMED DOGFISH

Born Squalid
Under the sign of Leo
In a Northern rock pool.

Born Rough
Hound, not Dolphin,
Loved, but lowest of the low.

Born Sandy
Dog, but more Wolf,
More Tiger, in your own element.

Just hatched
From a mermaid's purse,
Your dark anchored horny womb.

You're four inches
Long and your creamed underbelly
And warm brown-speckled back all

Point to
Shark. And your blunt
Pencilled snout confirms your legacy.

An eating-machine.
A ripper of nets if needs be.
But lover of your young, they say.

And you're just
Waiting. Eager and relaxed.
Flexing your perfect fish form.

Trying out
Your darts and turnings.
Growing into your length of death.

In under an hour
You'll be part of it all.
The legends and the facts.

Catcher and caught.
Sold as rock salmon on
The fishmonger's iced slab,

Or, clumsily
Dissected by first year
Students in a zoology class.

An hour. Two feet more.
And how many kills away
From that? You don't care.

All you can feel
Is the North Sea's boom
Through rock. And now, can

Hardly wait
For that last inch
Of water to pour over the pool's

Rim to let you in.
To life, more life,
And death quick when it comes.

THE DANCING HEN

I remember Jimmy Duncan
And his way with animals.
How he loved to show us
His dancing hens.

How it meant him holding
Them by the neck, while
He rendered them feminine
With a pair of rusty

Pliers. How his hens
Would dance, and sing.

And I remember Netty Duncan,
How she'd walk for miles
To find the right tree,
To chop down. How one day,

Her electric saw slipped
Her hold, and danced along
Her thigh. How she walked
Three miles back to the farm,

Her hand held tight against
A severed artery, the saw
Tucked underneath her arm.

Andrew Fox

BATHSHEBA (AFTER REMBRANDT)

You rise at dawn
    when
his parchment comes, light the candle and read the king's
                request,
                poised on the woven gold of the counterpane,
unable at first to make out the delicate
    Hebrew script
with its elusive turn of phrase.

                The king tells how
            your body moves under
        the folds of a blue dress,
ocean blue like the mild
voluptuous
breakers; compares the feeling that calls him to
                the particular mystery
of a woman and the ache which
    draws a salmon
back to its native river: the salmon blind in its
            delight. 'I do
        not care if death will follow. You
    are the destination I carry inside.'

'But sir,' you will remark
to the officer who climbs the stair, 'what about
my child? I listen to him cough at night,
worry in case his breathing
is interrupted.'

The guards shoulder their pikes
in the yard below. Wax collects in a brazen saucer. Calm
odalisques walk barefoot in the frost. The king
beguiles you with the private voice of his desire:

'Bathsheba, Bathsheba, come to me naked
    under your blue dress.'

Alistair Mackie

IN THE BATH

Deid-done wi the affairs o state
I let this shargert landscape stew
in scaudin watter. My twa een
patrol la république.

Aneth this skin and bane I hear
the workin fowk o the cells,
the nerves o the tribunals,
fell doomsters for the 'oor.

The highways o the arteries
faur the horses' hooves hemmer,
and blottit warrants tally up
the deid-leet for the blade.

Aye, bleed has been the best soap.
The state's been scoured o lice.
Nearhand. Look there, see
on the sides, the orra scum.

I'm dwaumin surely. I can jist
mak oot a horizon,
a porcelain horizon.
White, white.

Ach, Racine, that line o yours . . .
'Le jour . . . Le jour n'est . . .
Le jour n'est pas plus pur
que le fond de mon coeur.'

I work for an absolute white,
a strategy like snaw.
Whit heid shall nae be smoored?
He scrieves on the draft —

'The people's will maun be whettit
to cut clean.   Though they stink thegither
like pish-hooses, I need
their scythes and bloodlust.'

I'm doverin in this steam.
Decrees can wait.   I hear
the far-aff burrin o the drums
Wha's speirin for citizen Marat?

The washer-wife lookt in.
State papers, wee rafts, were shippin
bleed and watter
at the starn.

The reid dawn o the tricolour
was dribblin owre his briest.

David Kinloch

A HARPSICHORD WINTER

In memory-foam insocks
for our added comfort,
steeped in personal footbeds,
we hear a woman with breath
like a scythe proclaim
from her economy of straw

that music must be cut for wood
and burnt to keep the nation warm.
She heralds a harpsichord winter,
crisp, beyond panes, as a rainbow
hard to believe in.

Chopsticks are the order of the day;
in every county chairmen grate
keyboards like Parmesan on open fires
and sonatinas become economical with truth.

Scarlatti's minims fall like black snow,
cremated Buxtehude is tinder
to her power plants: a virtuoso
at the harpsiberg of State,
the icechord of her tonsils
trills with uncut nails
upon our ivory necks.

She plays us with fingers
of coruscated frost,
weaving our blood
through the concupiscible lattice
of her pleated skirts.

W.N. Herbert

THE ANTHROPOLOGICAL MUSEUM

The attendant can't resist the thumb-piano;
across the afternoons' chasms he has become
competent at recalling a half-way culture:
rheumatic rhythms, unrheumatic gropes
at a rope-bridge, like the fraying hair across
his white scalp, are rasped by the deep burr
of a fireside accent in which he tells a girl
'that's made of intestines' . . . I follow, looking at
papery eskimo vests in some confusion . . .

'mye hame dila' . . . 'ghost mucus': a stone tusk;
a leathern belt is worn by girls during 'tsaranche'
. . . 'active flirtation', dangling with 'iayoyi':
incantations to prevent conception . . . seed capsules
of *martynia sp.*: a charm against snakebites, on
the principle of 'the doctrine of signatures' . . .
they are walnuts with fangs, twin-hooked like
the poison teeth of serpents. . . . *All praise ye the Word,*
ye things without sound: a soft, eccentric smell
fills the museum, as of the leaning stances
of old scholars, looking into drawers of barbarity.

Being thus collated, tidily heaped, ransacked
by a kind of logic and our eyes, the memory
of other eyes, the symbols are rubbed clean
of symbolism, seeming like
those details in dreams that convince us, though
we can never remember them.

A cave in Australia is filled with moths, which
the aboriginals feed on: a nutty flavour . . .
at night they flood the sky like soft stars,
revising constellations . . . 'och' is Swedish for 'and' . . .
I follow, looking at madonnas carved by cannibals,
muted ghost-scarers . . . a child passes through,
dislocating myths, snapping islands' moorings:

'what are weapons?' . . . it is like a modern translation
of the Bible, in which one continually expects, as
the tablets crack, an aeroplane to pass over.

'Although the Indians understood
the stone arrow-heads had once
served a purpose identical with those
they had themselves once used
they insisted they were thunderbolts,
and mentioned they were always found
in the vicinity of lightning-storms.
In this they resemble the dog
who, often forgetting where he has
hidden some bone, will instantly recall
on passing the site, and cannot be
distracted from its recovery . . . '

What are the links between the distant things
and you, these caches of other countries
buried in their cases, that are all the ways
I feel myself approaching you?

The attendant lathers his air with
a Tibetan Buddhist gong, calling us to
our slow departures . . .

ARIADNE ON BROUGHTY FERRY BEACH

Ariadne sleeping in the stomach of the strand
curled in her turtleshell of purple silk
surrounded by declivities, the left hollows
of youths and maidens, the close dip that was
her lord, the sandstuck embers that perfumed
the dark she's dreaming in, that sticky net,
curled like a coracle on
the shipabandoned bay.
                              Something like a beak
is wakening in her upper jaw, the skin grins back,
something like a hairy branch is stabbing from
her ribs, her belly bloats and blotches like
a drowned dog, a starving child;
tarred and caulked, blackening her dreamy flesh
rolls a little, crackling legs and spitting hairs
quivering, airpained; her lids balloon
as eyes split into eyes split into eyes.
                                    The vine
of metamorphosis has taken her,
the divine tree grows in her and out of her
as Dionysus smiles and wipes his chin, stirring
the silk with a tipsy foot, leaving her
to wake to her desertion
to the reflective lap of waters.

RELUCTANCE

Perhaps tomorrow you will come
and I can start to know you.
Just now I can't quite say your name
as though you were a rare tree.

Whatever you were clawing for
through the glass, rain's blind hand,
you can now let go from your
desires, like that unclenching cloud

that sent you from it, with
this message of your bright thirst.
It will recoil into my hands, with
its own messages, for my desire.

Out there, the sour perfection of
chestnuts is spat on the cabin roof
like slow-thinking gunshots, rolling
like a trim, lackadaisical thunder.

In here, we make love in whispers,
hastily catching our accents' strangeness-
es up like honey on a twisting spoon,
to keep them from darkess, our only

neighbour. The season presses on us
like syrup as we float, bottled in
a silence like giant fruits, crushing
ourselves against the bed's palate.

What you have regarded as
stillness, resolves itself into a faint
eddy, as the light swells over this
body, and there are no objects.

It is as though the world is headless,
but the gouting is outside; here
there is only the lolling of light
over bodies, the strange swirls

of speech that feels itself thick and
unnecessary; we move, and rest.
There's no need to adjust the curtains,
the sheets, our hair, our bodies.

What has stopped is only visual,
not moral. The connections loose
their grips on the monuments and
slap lightly on your stomach.

Things begin to replace themselves
against my skin; wool and thorns,
the spider's parachute, this wine
I'm sitting in. My throat becomes

a hypocaust, and I wash my hair.
Gradually, pavements come into focus
and the rain returns, as if to make
dimensions more definite in grisaille,

but blundering graciously as usual.
Only you have immersed yourself in
everything, beyond my sharp touch,
and trees are your headless memorials.

These spoons and pots I handle
warily, as though not to disturb
them, make them count down
my touches to the last touch,

are responding bluely to you, as
you grow more grand and huge
accidentally catching me in your hem
and sweeping me from the day.

PICTARESQUE

Boccionean ower thi sillery
Tay-
brig, girdirs chappin thi skeh
lyk a haurd-biled egg, uts
yowk turnd black i thi shell,
thi quhite o thi waatir no quite
richt-
ied by thi san-banks
joukin thru,
obese Nessies flechd wi seals
thi sehz o money-fu
seal-sheppit pursis,
breengin thru thi staishun wi
jist eneuch time no ti see
thi gentilman's boags:
big eneuch fur ettins!
Goad's dentures, aff-
quhite! a poasitive Orfeo's thrappil
o piss's sangs thuv knoakit
doon . . .

Mony-a-thief, Carsnootie
(wi Buddan scuddan by),
an Haar-broath whaur a chartir wiz . . .
an Monta Rosa, thi Grampiuns' ribs ahent,
an whaur wiz Lunan Bay? th'eident loom
o Scoatlan's memry, thi Noarth British
Teleclionic oaperaitur
is stackin thi legs back oan
drucken oactapi —
                    FuturaBallan
thi cummin o
Gibbonic gressis, lalalalain intae
thi lacuna nae
readir o Catullus evir saw,
noan-Tibullan mains:
a row o fenceposts wi
a craw oan ivry wan,
less a parlament than

68   W.N. HERBERT

('Quamdiu centum cives . . . remans . . . '?)
a dey at thi raceis; hoodie-bookies wi
binoaculars trennd oan
coos scattrin lyk grecht wud roackin-hoarsis
in ex-classical silence . . .
('erint . . . erunt . . . everit?')
an therr's thi sea again
Mare Whitdjecryum, wi a wee
mist-ankilt Eifful Tooer oan ut
drehan oot
a moneyliss Monet, an here's
an 'Aiburdeen o thi harns'
whaur aathin's yet
ti be seen tae be bein,
ti be beamd past bothy-brenns an
iley-
mous a message tae toarn-bunnitirs ivrywhaur:
'feel thi pulse o thi warld's still in
this dulse-furnackit wrist, an hear
a sang nae mair repulsive than
gulls' dulcet tones — oor toon's stane
can boonce licht aff
thon guilliemoattult lift, thon
unlaunchd satellite o Scoatlan's turnan
fiss, birlan lyk anithir mune abune
aa fuddils furlan in wir thocht,
an aa oor mane sall be is

bring yir thocht intae
wan grippie-fist, wan nexus, wan kangil
fit eneuch tae spang ut oot
tae aa hurehzuns, an past, an purge aa gaps!

THE MAN IN DUNDEE MUSEUM

Yirth wiz owre waarm tae wauken'um;
noo he's bared lyk breid, an aeon's auldirs.
Banes dreh as whalirs' tack
tak color fae thi clart
as meh skin micht fae thi sun
eftir a lang, hasky saturaishun.

Thi geegaw of fleesh seems fuleish
aside'iz ribs splent bangils,
thi jiggirs o lorn in ma veens
gurthie and garish
by shaddas lyk pebbils
i thi lunkirts o'iz een.

Whit giff-gaffs cud fankil thi tendons
o sic sandman's fingirbanes?
thochts in thon skull'd be
dreh oats inna beakir,
an whit luvs werr cradilt in
thon pelvic arc ur foondirt noo in sand.

Naomi Mitchison

A MATTER OF BEHAVIOUR

I am not one for making distinctions between one sort of person and another. And besides, there are matters of behaviour which I myself, as a teacher, have tried to establish. You see, Elsie was a Tinker -- that made her different. It was no use talking about regulations. The fact was that mostly all the tinker children came to my school in winter, maybe two terms, but then they would be on the road again, all summer, everything they had learned from me forgotten. Then in August, when it came to a new start, away behind all their own age. It was hard for the tinker children, right enough, though they were healthy apart from scratches and rashes that their mothers were not bothering themselves about, and maybe they were learning another set of things on the roads the travellers took, deer and birds, a fox or maybe a pair of weasels running the road, what's called wild-life these days. But could they put it in writing? Not they, so they'd be laughed at. Not by me, but by the other children, for no child is kind by nature.

But as for wee Elsie, her mother was dead and her Dadda only wanted the boys off on the roads with him when it came to the end of April and the good weather calling at them. So Elsie stayed with an old auntie that had the use of a shed and a row of kale and two cats. She barely missed a day off school. When I saw she could read to herself I gave her a few old picture books that I was throwing out and soon enough there was a tink reading the best in the class.

More than that, she was trying to keep herself clean, which was more than the old tinker wifie did. The way it was, my children would never sit next the tinks. It was the smell off them, you understand, wood smoke and little washing, with no soap. But if you lived the way the travelling folk used to, you'd not have much chance of looking a bath in the face. Mind you, it is different today; many of them with the smart caravans, the same size and make as the tourists' or better. You'll not see a woman lugging away between two barrow handles the way I'd seen them when I first took on a

single teacher school with a roll of twenty dropping to fifteen, away in the west. No, it was different altogether in
those days.

But Elsie managed to wash herself and her school clothes,
though they were nothing great. But I found her bits of
decent cloth she could work with in the sewing class. She
learned to knit and I unravelled an old jersey of my own, a
New Year's present, but too bright altogether for me. But for
all that Elsie was slow at her writing. She persevered, yes,
that she did, and she picked up arithmetic, so long as it was
about real things, and indeed that's how I feel about it myself. Once she was in Standard Two she made friends with a
few her own age, two from the Forestry houses and one,
Linda that was, from the Post Office. Respectable families
and they'd ask her for tea, or rather their mothers did, maybe three or four times in the year, and pleasing themselves
to feel they'd been good. But all the same they never let it
drift out of their minds that wee Elsie was just a tinker.

She grew up to be a handsome figure of a girl, so she did,
with that bright hair that most of the travellers have, and
bright blue eyes to match it. I'd seen less of her once she
went on to the Grammar School at Oban, and left on the
stroke of fifteen, for the old woman was getting less able
to do even the bit of cleaning she used to do and when her
father and the boys were around it was Elsie who had to
wash and mend their clothes and see to their dirty heads and
all that. So it was hard on her. She would come over to me an
odd evening and I could see she'd been crying.

Well, the years went by and, as you know, I married and
we moved around, first to Dumbarton, then to Glasgow itself. But I'd enough friends around the village that would be
pleased to see us both, and my own wee Ian when he came.
So I kept up with the old families I'd known and I saw Elsie
turn into a fine young woman, even if she had no time for
anything beyond what she had to do, and then suddenly she
was married.

This would have been in the early sixties, with things
brightening up and all of us sure the bad times were past.
There were only a few at the wedding and the old wifie was
safe in the kirk-yard, but Elsie's father had smartened himself up with a red rose in his coat and so had the one brother
who was still about. I liked the look of the bridegroom. His
mother and sister were there and doubtless wondering what
like of a lass was coming into the family. Truly, I was afraid

the two tinks might make a scene and that would be hard on
Elsie, but they were scared to say much. They were fou
drunk by the evening, but the others were well away by then.
I went to the wedding myself. I thought it would have
been kind of nice if one of her school mates, Linda or Jessie
perhaps, had been there to see how bonny she looked, poor
Elsie, but none of them came. (Linda was courting at that
same time and married the next year. I was at her wedding
too, but it was a bigger affair, with a two-tier cake.) It was
only strangers or part strangers in the church, come just for
the taste of a wedding. Elsie was wearing high-necked white
and I wondered was it a bought dress. Her hair showed flaming
under her veil and I didn't wonder a man would fall for her.

He seemed a very decent man, a welder from a steel
works, and his folk pleased that I had come and at my
present of a set of tea cups, the same I'd give to any one of
my old pupils if I'd been to the wedding. They went back to
one of those small towns that were springing up, Edinburgh
way, but not for long. The year after they moved to Corby in
England. She wrote to me from there. I think she was a wee
bit scared to be out of Scotland and not always understanding what people said to her. I was kind of surprised to hear
from her, but all the same I wrote back and the next year she
wrote again, asking me if ever I was in the south could I not
come over and see her.

I thought this hardly likely, but as things turned out my
husband was sent south to a branch his firm was setting up
in Kettering and that was only a bus ride from Corby. I remember it well, a beautiful, rich countryside, parts of it
Buccleugh land, so what were the Buccleughs doing this far
south was beyond me. There were well-doing villages, pretty
old cottages and gardens packed to the gate with rose bushes.
But Corby itself was given over to steel, rows and crescents
and long streets of workers' houses and all that was left of
the old village not knowing itself in the middle of them.
There was a great chimney, alight with flames from the fur-
naces below; you could see it for miles. They called it the
Corby Candle.

There was a Scots club and pleasant enough to be among
ken'd folk, even if they were from the far ends of Scotland.
They would have concerts and that; time and again there'd
be a hundred folk standing to sing Auld Lang Syne. But some
were terrible home-sick, worst the ones who had come
from towns along the coasts, whether it was Peterhead or

Campbeltown. They missed the sea sorely, here in the very middle of England. But the fishing had gone down and the money was away better down here. There were others from Wales or Cornwall or anywhere at all, but it was the Scots there were most of, and who made up the best part of the clubs, the Labour club as well.

So Elsie met me and took me back to her house, talking all the way. It was a modern house, in one of the crescents, two bedrooms and a smart bathroom. And almost all the furnishing bought: a lounge suite, the kind you'd see advert-ised, a table with a pot plant, new kitchen stuff, only she'd brought her old kettle and her griddle, for you'd not get one in England. But she had an electric iron and there were my tea cups, not a chip out of them. Everything was kept shining and a biscuit jar, I mind that, which they'd won in a Labour Party lottery. She showed it all to me, piece by piece, and told me not one bit of furnishing, not even the suite, was on the never-never, but all paid for. 'And nobody knows I'm a tinker!' she said and when I laughed and said she shouldn't be ashamed of that, she clutched my hand and said 'You'll not tell!'

So I said no, no, and laughed a bittie and then she took me out to her wee garden in front of the house, all newly planted with small rose bushes that still had their labels on. They'd a drill of potatoes and a few cabbages at the back. Her wee girl was at play-school -- yes, they had that and all — but there was a baby boy in a pram out among the rose bushes, asleep, with a soft fuzz of orange. I said to her, laughing 'I see he has your colour of hair' and I can still hear her saying back 'I could wish it was black!' And her husband, just coming back from work, had dark hair. They were that friendly, both of them, and I went over there from time to time, with my Ian who was about the age of her wee girl. She talked sometimes of the days she'd been at school — she'd still got the books I'd given her — but not much about the other girls, only a mention of Miss McSporran who had been the infant teacher and well liked by all my pupils.

But then, as you know, my husband was moved back to Scotland and we settled down in Hillhead. I remember the last time I saw her she had a big stomach, but full of content and looking forward. So the years went by and I sometimes thought of Kettering and Corby and wondered how the friends we'd made were doing and sometimes we'd send cards. But mostly I was glad to be back in Scotland with my husband

and my own two, both shooting up taller than myself, and
Ian talking of what he'd be doing after University. For my
own part I was doing supply teaching, but I had begun to
lose touch with my profession. And indeed, teaching in Glasgow is away different from teaching in a village.

And then, in the late seventies and eighties, the bad times
came on us, with the yards closing down all along Clydeside
and where were the orders going and the men on the streets
not knowing where to turn, and all the anger breaking. And
not us alone, but industry everywhere, what our forebears
worked for and built up, coal, steel, shipping, the great com-
panies that had seemed to be there forever. It seemed strange
to me, since we had won the bitter war with Japan and tried
and executed their Generals, that now they could be the ones
who had all the factories, or else it was the Germans who had
them, while our men who had fought, the older ones, in that
war, were now thrown out with nothing but their old medals
and the dole. What had gone wrong?

At first it did not hit us and our friends just so hard,
though salary rises that my husband had expected just didn't
come through. What we felt most was the terrible price that
everything was, the way you had to pay a whole pound for
something that was only worth what used to be half a crown
in the old days. And then, well, everything got worse. But
you'll know that. At least I had my two educated.

The works at Corby went. The steel industry was cut
down so that it was hardly there; we didn't know what
worse would follow. How had it happened? It seemed we
couldn't make steel as cheaply as other countries, or it was
not the kind that was wanted. We couldn't understand. Only
we knew it was a matter of money, not of men working. And
when money talks there's no place for people, for ordinary
men and women, the like of Elsie and her man.

Well, it seemed that there could be small industries starting up here or there, maybe taking over premises in a small
town and not doing too badly, at least for a few years.
You've heard of T.T. and McV? Yes, well they started up
somewhere west of Bathgate, on some waste ground there
was, and it seemed there were jobs going. A few of the Corby
men heard of it. It was nothing like what they were used to
and you wouldn't see the furnace men going, but those
who'd been on the lighter side and willing to take training,
they might have a chance. At least they'd be nearer home.
The wages were nothing near Corby, but better than the dole.

Yes, it had come to that. They cursed the Tory Government and this man MacGregor — but no Scot! — who'd been put in charge of the steel industry, but they went up to the new place for interview, remembered to say Sir, and were taken on. Elsie waited to hear. They sold most of the furniture, the best bits, the ones they'd been proud of, the lounge suite, the Hoover, the washing machine.

Well, I know the rest of the story by hearsay. He started work. For a while they were in one room, not easy to keep decent. And then they got half an old house, a bike ride away. The two older children, the girl and the boy, started at the new school; the girl was well up in Secondary by now and promising well. But the third child, another wee boy, was still at home. There was no kind of pre-school in those parts. The nearest was a bus-drive away and most likely full up, let alone she couldn't afford the bus fare. She tried to feed the children well and her man best; that's the way it is for most of us women.

Well, she went to a jumble sale. The children kept growing and had to be clothed. Some of the jumbles were away better than you'd get at the shops, anyway the shops where Elsie could go. The wee one was with her of course, he was a red-head the same as his brother, though it's not a true red but more of an orange. You'll know it, I'm sure. There's always a bit of snatching at the jumbles, and so it was this time. It was just bad luck that she met with an old school mate and they knew one another. Yes, they met across a boy's jacket and Linda — for it was her — said 'Ah, it's you — you dirty tink!' and a man behind said 'What, playing tinkers' tricks on us!' And poor Elsie ran out of the sale with nothing, just hauling the wee one, pulling him along crying, and maybe the good folk walking past would have stopped and scolded her, and when she got back in she saw that her purse was gone out of her pocket.

So she put the wee boy into the bedroom with what toys they had and half an orange, and herself went into the kitchen, turned on the gas and put her head in the oven.

That was how the two children back from school found her and had the sense for the boy to run to the corner and ring the police — and lucky the 'phone was working. The ambulance men found the two children practising the artificial respiration they'd learned at school — and they'd turned the gas off. And it all came in the evening paper and I happened to read it. It was only a small piece and I only read as far as the name because I was waiting for my Peggy to come home before I'd put the kettle on and I wondered could it be Elsie. But the next morning there was a photo in the paper of the two children and I could see that the girl looked like her mother. I knew they'd been in trouble, that the man had lost his job in Corby, but she hadn't written to say where she was. No, she'd have been ashamed. But now the shame was worse. And now I was ashamed too, that I hadn't got round to writing and finding out how my old pupil was doing.

I rang the paper and got her address, saying I was a friend, and the very next day I made my way over. I remember once when I'd visited at Corby, my own Peggy asking me 'Is she really a tink?' and I said 'Yes, and I'm telling you who the tinkers were. It was they who made the weapons for the High Kings of Ireland that came over to the west of Scotland: all those beautiful swords and shields!' For that's one of the Tinker stories, though who's to know what's true and what's not? But I felt I had to get another picture told and believed, even if it wasn't the right one. Maybe it is and would account for a lot; in the old days, before my time, the tinkers really made and mended all kinds of metal things and were more welcome then than they've ever been since.

So off I went and found poor Elsie lying on a lumpy old sofa they had, wrapped in blankets and the big girl, allowed off from school, making tea and keeping an eye on the wee boy. I'd brought some cakes and we all took our tea together. I could tell from what the girl said that her father had been in a terrible taking, coming back from work to find his wife carried off to hospital and the two children, though they'd done well and the paper said so afterwards, all to bits and no tea made.

The next time I went over she was getting on fine and ashamed of what she had done, but she told me how that name that Linda had thrown at her had been that sore on her, she had just felt that nothing else she could ever do would be any good. Nothing would ever get the bad name off her back and it came out that the boy had been called a tink at school. Nobody at Corby had ever said anything against them, but now when they came back to Scotland — and she burst into tears, the poor thing. I could have sorted that Linda who had thrown it at her, and both of them my pupils. Sure as I'm a living soul, Linda would have seen that story in the papers, but not a cheep from her. Most like she'll have forgotten Elsie's married name, so there she'll be sitting at her ease. And me forgetting Linda's married name, I'm not able to get at her! But I'm hoping that someone calls her something worse than a tink, this side of Judgment Day.

Alexander Fenton

KIPPER'T

It wis on a Wednesday, the secont o' Mey 1923 tae be exact.
I min' 'e day fine. We ca'ed three loadies o' corn intae the
barn in 'e mornin', an' syne we threesh, an' aifter wir denner
we ca'ed in 'e lave, 'ere wis nine loads in be the eyn o' 'e day.
I min' 'e loon wis grubbin' 'e siderigs, gettin' 'e grun ready
for shaavin neeps. Its funny 'e wye ye min' things files. It wis
a caal day, bit it turnet oot aafa fine, an' fin we wis at wir
denner 'ere wis six aeraplanes geed ower. 'E road roller wis on
'e go on 'e road ootside tee.
    I geed up tae hae a look at it an' hae a news wi' the road
boys. There wis ay a bit o' funnin wi' 'em, especially Willie.
His faither wis a fairmer up 'e road. 'E wis an' aafa shy kinna
billie in 'e or'nar' coorse, bit eence ye got tae ken 'im, 'e wis
aa richt. 'E kent an' aafa lot o' 'is sangs, I min' eence I hyowet
neeps wi' 'im for siveral days an' 'e sangs an' 'e verses nivir
divallt, God 'e wis jist a richt divert. Bit gin ony strange body
wis aboot, nae a squeak wid ye get oot o' 'im.
    'Is day, though, 'e wis aafa soor on't.
    'Aye, Willie,' I says.
    'Aye,' he said, short like. He widna richt look at me face.
    'Caal kin,' I says.
    'Aye.'
    'Did ye see yon aeraplanes? 'Ere wis six, ye ken!'
    'Nu',' he said.
    'Aye, they geed ower jist aboot an 'oor syne, ye couldna
bit hae seen 'em. Ower fae 'e Geese Peel han', across 'e Howe,
an' oot o' sicht ower Mains Hill. Ye'd a' been a bittie abeen 'e
Smiddy at 'e time.'
    Willie niver spak, bit on till 'e machine, ettlin' tae gee't a
shofelfae o' coal. I ay likit 'e smell o' traction ingines an' road
rollers, a kinna sulphur an' stame, ye micht say. The ither
lads hid been doon 'e road afore Willie wi' the wagon, pittin
in a fyow patches far 'e surface hid been sookit wi' snaa. He
wis im leen drivin', back an' fore back an' fore ower ilky
patch, an' syne ay haad on tae keep tee till 'em.
    I walkit roon 'e roller a bit, fine pleaset wi't tickin' awa

there like a clock, an' Willie up on 'e platform be noo wi' eez han' on 'e wheel. I gaed roon be 'e front an' took a look o' 'er, an' I jist happent tae notice a kinna damp bittie, aa 'at ye'd ken a reidy colour, on 'e front o' 'e big roller an' in ower 'e rim o't.

'Fit kinna mark's 'at, Willie,' I shoutit up till 'im. Willie spak. 'Oot o' there!' he roared, opened 'er up, an' aff 'e set alang 'e road chook-chookin' aa the machine wis able. Wisn't 'at a queer kinna thing noo? I'd niver kent 'im like 'at. Ah, weel, I hid tae yoke Bobie tae get in fit wis left o' 'e ruckie, an' fit wi' biggin' on 'e cairt, an' chasin' a rat fin we'd gotten doon till 'e foon, Willie geed clean oot o' ma heid again.

'E neesht day it wis jist 'e normal roon', odd bits o' jobbies, sortin' 'e pailin', gaitherin k-not girse an' openin' dreels for tatties. Northies socht a shot o' ma shaavin' machine tae get 'is girse-seed in. Him an' me wis aye reel gweed at neeperin'. I nivir thocht tae mention Willie till 'im though, bit on 'e Friday I'd an eeran doon till 'e Station, seein' aboot a new tablie comin' frae Aiberdeen wi' 'e cairrier, an' I got a bag o' coal tae tak hame. I cam on een' o' 'e road-lads in aboot for coal tee.

'Aye, an' far's Willie 'e day?'

'Seek.'

'Seek?'

'Aye. 'E bugger niver took 'e machine richt hame on Wednesday, left it at 'e fit o' 'e brae, an' 'e hisna been oot o' eez hoose since.'

' 'E wis fairly a bittie queer like fin I sa' 'im. Oh weel, I hope 'e'll be aa richt. Tell 'im I wis speerin' for 'im gin ye see 'im.'

'Aye.'

Willie, peer breet, 'e bade be 'imsel' bit 'e wis ay richt tidy.

It wis a special pleasant evenin' an' I took a danner' up be Northies. He'd gotten a new mull in nae lang seen, an' an ingine tae ca't. Fin we wis gettin't riggit 'ere wis some pipe missin', aye, the exhaust, ye ken, an' for a start we wis like tae be smored. He wis sayin' it was aa richt noo. I spak aboot Willie till 'im. North Pitties is a high set fairmie, gey caal in 'e winter an' ye canna get up 'e road for sna', bit it has a gran' ootlook an' there wisna a lot Northies didna see.

'Oh,' 'e said, ' 'at's queer 'at, I some thocht it wis 'e roller 'ere wis something wrang wi'.'

'Foo 'at?'

'Weel, 'e ither day I jist happent tae see the reek o't aboot
'e Cross. It wis stoppit a gweed lang time, I couldna mak oot
fit it wis deein'. At ae meenit I noticet 'e reek wisna jist 'e
usual, it hid a kinna ily black appearance, an' 'at laistit for a
filie or it stoppit. Fitiver it wis, it m'n 'a redd itsel' up, for
nae lang efter she wis haddin doon by the smiddy.'
    ' 'Ere'd been something tae upset 'im, surely. He wis in a
richt ill teen. An' I haard 'e left it at 'e boddem o' 'e Brae an'
niver feesh't intill 'e depot.'
    'Weel-a-wyte!'
    It wis aboot a wik ahin 'at, jist a fearfu' time o' sna' an'
sleet an' nae growth in 'e girse. Northies wis doon offerin'
some neeps if we couldna get 'e stirks oot, an' dyod we hid
tae get 'e twa loadies fae 'im, for 'e stormy widder nedder
upplet nor divalled. I'd tae lowse fae drivin' weeds an' I wis
jist gie'in Bobie a rub-doon in 'e stable fin a mannie come
roon 'e nyeuk o' 'e close wheelin' eez byke.
    'Weel, fairmer, ye're in 'e lythe.'
    'Aye, ivnoo.'
    He'd on a blue kinna cape, an' 'e turned 'e byke half in
throwe 'e stable door tae haad 'e saiddle oan got weet fin 'e
took it aff. Nae that it widda maittert. 'E legs o' eez breeks
wis gey sypit onywye.
    'Sic a day.'
    'Aye.'
    'I'm 'e bobby fae Inverurie' he said. 'I'm prosecutin' an
offeecial investigation.'
    'Are ye, though?'
    'Aye. It wis aboot a young lad 'at wis on 'e go aboot a
week seen. Did ye see ony strangers on 'e road?'
    'Na, de'il 'e een, 'ere wis jist 'e road-lads I saa. Fit kinna
lad wiz 'e?'
    'Oh, it wis a Gairman. He cam in by me speerin' about
arky-ological sites, nae things I ken muckle aboot, bit I tellt
'im tae gang tae see the circle o' steens at Aquhorthies. Weel,
'e managet 'at an' boy, 'e wis fair trickit, syne 'e traivelt back
an' speert foo tae get tae Auchterless, 'ere wis some steens 'e
wintet tae look at 'ere, forbye there wis appeerently a Roman
camp somewye aboot. Losh, I doot 'e Romans widna hae
geen aboot biggin camps if 'ey'd come in 'is widder. A queer
kin' o' wye he spak, "sank you, sank you," he wid say. Ye'd
fairly min' on 'im gin ye'd spoken till 'im'.
    'A Gairman? Ye'd think they widna hae 'e neck tae show
'eir faces hereaboot.'

'Oh weel, 'e wis a weel-mainnert lad. Haad awa fae 'e wye 'e spak, 'e lookit jist like wirsel's. A "stoo-dent", 'e said 'e wis.'

'Weel, I've seen naething o' 'im. Bit hiv ye nae trace o' 'im ava?'

' 'E got 'e bus tae come in 'e road, an' somebody saa 'im comin' aff o't aboot Linshie, bit aifter 'at nae hide nor hair o' 'im. I've been up at 'e steen circle on Mains Hill, an' 'e's nae at 'e back o' a steen 'ere. An' 'e's nae up at 'e Roman camp, or at least nae tae be seen if 'e 'is, I geed richt up 'e hill ower 'e burn tae this cairnies 'ey ca'd 'e Fite Steens, bit na, na, neen o' yer Keyser's bairns an' 'eir jackbeets there.'

'Imphm. An' fit'll ye dee noo?'

'I'll try 'e places farrer doon 'e road. He michta gotten as far as Turra, ye ken, an' syne teen a bus again tae Banff or back tae Aiberdeen. Bit 'e hisna been seen 'ere, for eez freens hid been expeckin 'im a fyow days back. It wis 'em 'at reportit this lad wis missin, Will-helm Joehannin' 's eez name, appeerently. Weel, I'll haad on. Ye'll let's ken if ye hear onything.'

'Aye.'

Ah, weel, we got ower 'e gab o' Mey an' a day or twa efter 'at we got 'e beas' oot, an' even tried 'e horse on 'e girse aa nicht. 'E Mrs an' me wis socht ower tae Feithies on 'e aifterneen o' 'e Sabbath an' we geed ower 'e hill on wir bykes tae see 'is new wireless receiver 'ey'd been lashin' oot on. Damn't, it played meesic an' aathing, bit whot a begeck we got fin we haard o' wir ain districk on 'e news: a general call for onybody tae let 'e police ken if 'ey'd seen a "Gairman student, said tae have been studyin' arky-ological sites, last seen in 'e viceenity o' 'e fairm o' Linshie, Auchterless, on the efterneen of Wednesday the secont of May, when he descendit fae the bus an' appeared tae set off along the Turriff road. The missin' man wis aboot 5ft 10 wi' close-cropped dark hair an' kinna thick glesses, an' cairried a leather bag on 'is back. Anyone havin' information as to his present whereabouts should contact . . . " an' so on. Wisna that winnerfae noo? A rale ferlie. It was a spik for a day or twa.

Nae lang ahin 'is, 'e Mrs geed up tae the Aalyoch tae see a freen' an' get 'er tea. I bykit up for 'er in 'e evenin', an cam off ma byke at yon steep bit abeen the smiddy, an' walkit by 'e Cross. Jock Mull hid 'e placie jist abeen 'e Cross an' 'e happent jist be dargin' wi' a spad at a big steen in 'e corner o' 'e park there.

'Aye, Jock.'
'Aye. Ye're on 'e ran-dan.'
'Aye. Jist awa up for 'e Mrs. She got a hurl up till 'e Aal-yoch wi' 'e grocer.'
'Oh, aye.'
'Wis n' 'at a queer thing aboot 'at Gairman — I heard it on 'e wireless receiver at Feithies. Ye didna see 'e Gerrie yersel'?'
'Na.' Jock pit doon 'e spad, an' cam closer till's. 'E wis a gey canny lad, niver hurriet. 'E took a packetie o' tebacca oot o's pooch, rowed a paperie roon't, syne stuck it in eez moo. 'E ripit in eez pooch again an' brocht oot a wee boxie 'at hid some broon paper in't. 'Is hid been soakit in saltpetre an' driet oot. 'Ere wis a fleerish in 'e boxie tee, an' a bit o' flint, 'at had a bonnie orange colour. Jock tore aff a bittie o' 'e broon paper, an' held it abeen eez smoke, syne k-nackit 'e fleerish anest 'e flint an' up 'e sparks flew, gweed fat sparks, an' God it wisna seconds till 'e broon paper took and the reek wis fleein'. Aifter a fyow puffs, 'e says:
'I doot 'ere's something nae richt.'
'Is 'e wife weel eyneuch?'
'Na, it's naething tae dae wi' me. It's Willie I'm baddered aboot.'
' 'E road-lad?'
'Aye. Ye ken me an' eez faither aye neeperet, we've been richt gweed freen's. An' Willie vrocht a lot about 'is place tee fin 'e wis a loon. 'E wis like a sin till's, it wis jist a rale disappintment fin 'e left 'e fairm. He wis 'at bashfae, 'e'd niver think tae tak over 'e place aifter eez fadder, 'e'd jist niver 'a' managet it. I widna like tae see onything happenin' till 'im.'
'I ken. I haard 'e wis seek, like, bit fit wid be ahin't? I spak till 'im 'oan day 'e geed doon 'e road wi' 'e roller an' I kwidna get a richt wird oot o' 'im.'
'Well, its been badderin's a lot an' I dinna ken richt fit tae think. Bit atween wirsel's, min, 'at roller affair wis aafa queer.'
Jock wis needin' tae teem eez crap. 'E wis een o' 'is gaant kinna lads, it didna maitter fit 'e ate, ye'd a thocht it jist geed throwe 'im. 'E'd a dark kinna skin, an' aye 'e bonnet on's heid. Fin 'e took it aff tae gie eez baildy heid a claa it wis like a fite meen shinin, wi' a rim o' hairies abeen eez lugs. 'E'd shave aye on a Sunday tae redd 'e wik's stibble, jist 'e plain kitchen soap an' 'e cut-throat, an' bilet water oot o' 'e iron kettle. Nae 'at 'e wis muckle o' a han' for 'e kirk, it

wisna for 'at 'e wis shavin, it's jist 'at 'e feck o' 'e men hereaboot aye lik't tae mak 'emsels mair decent at 'e onset o' 'e
wik. 'E'd aye on a shaftit weskit an' a sark buttoned up till
'e neck, hait or caal 'e niver wore onything different, haad
awa fae an' aal' kwite in 'e rochest o' widder. I widna winner
gin 'e sleepit in eez sark, bit 'ere's nae doot 'e took aff 'e
draaers an' breeks for 'e'd twa lassies an' a laddie. A richt fine
lad, Jock, jist a gem, 'ere's mony a mart we'd been at 'egidder
an' we'd maybe hae a gless o' 'e richt stuff aifter, bit neen o's
wis drinkers an' we didna gang teerin' aboot makin' a ka-rant
'an feels o' wirsel's like some lads 'at bade nae 'at far awa
fae's. I niver thocht ye kwid lippen richt on 'at fowk at took
ower much.

Ah weel, we wis rale gweed freen's, an' I c'd see 'ere'd
been something in eez heed for a filie, 'e'd maybe seen 'e
Mrs gaan up 'e road an' some thocht I'd be by later, for fit 'e
wis deein' wi' 'e steen wis o' nae God's eese whatsoiver.

Appeerently, on 'e day I've bin spikkin' aboot, 'e'd been
sittin' in 'e kitchen haein' a fly-cup. 'Ere'd been some wird
aboot comin' in wi' sharny beets, so Jock'd lowsed 'e pints
an' slippit 'em aff, though there wis mair wird syne aboot 'e
bitties o' strae 'e wis spreadin' ower 'e linoleum, for 'e'd
fresh straed eez beets 'at mornin' in 'e byre. He wis parkit at
'e fireside, on 'e aal widden airmcheer wi' a wee faalin' doon
bit on ae airm, jist fine for haddin' 'e cup, fangin' in till a
shafe o' breed clairtit wi' rhubarb jam. 'E jar wis a bittie oot
o' date an' 'e jam hid granulatit, bit neen 'e waar taste for aa
'at. Ye c'd aye knack 'e sugarie bits wi' yer teeth. Gin it
hadna been for 'e reeshlie noise inside's heid, he'd a haard
'e roller seener. In 'e normal coorse ye could hear ony vyackles
comin' ben 'e road, an' ye c'd peek oot o' 'e fower-peened
gale winda tae see faa it wis. Jock kent 'e maist o' 'em. 'Is
day, be 'e time he heard 'e chuffin, 'e roller was in 'e halla an'
aa he saa wis 'is black reek yoamin' oot o' 'er. Him in 'e
middle o' eez piece an' 'e beets aff, 'e kwidna jist rin oot for
a look, sae he jist chaaed awa an' sookin in sups o' tae throwe
'e trailin' edges o' eez mowser. Weel, aye 'e reek appeared an'
begod there wis a lad cam in tae sicht in eez park for a meenit,
till 'e nyeuk o' 'e wa' blockit 'e view. 'Ere wis a black bag
ower eez shooder, gey heavy like. Jock thocht e'd come in
by, sae 'e wytit for 'e knock, bit na, na, an' it wisna lang or
'e boy poppit up again, still wi' 'e bag bit it was rowed up
anaith's oxter, an' 'e wis gaan at a gey lick. Jock thocht it wis
Willie, though he wisna richt sure. 'E got 'e beets runkit again,

an' oot tae see fit 'ad been g'n on. 'E saa naething aboot 'e hooses, nor roon 'e back. At 'e eyn o' 'e steadin, neesht 'e horse-gyang far 'e horse traivelt roon an' roon an' dreeve 'e mullie, 'ere wis 'e tail-eyn o' a hey-soo, stannin' still a fyow feet high, bit it hid been aa connacht wi' watter an' 'e hey was black an' fool lookin', nae eese for feed. Jock noticet 'ere'd been some disturbance at 'e side o't, 'e same's a gweed lump hid been haaled oot an' biggit up again. 'E steed a file an' lookit, bit canny lad 'at 'e wis, 'e didna interfere wi't. Syne 'e steppit ower 'e park, followin' the feetprints in 'e dubbie grun', as far's 'e road. Be 'is time 'e roller wis gone. 'E hid a look aboot. 'Ere wis some kinna black marks on 'e surface, an' a special big patch 'at hid been weel battered doon jist aside 'em. 'At wis aa. 'E lookit up 'e road an' doon. It wis jist as teem's it ay wis. As 'e turned awa tae haad back till 'e close, a glint o' something catchet eez e'e on 'e patch. Wi' a closer look 'e saa it wis a cornerie aff a roonaboot bittie o' gless, like a glesses gless. It coulda catched a tyre o' a byke, so 'e pooched it. 'Ere wis some fite bitties amon' the tarry steens tee, bit withoot eez specs 'e couldna mak oot fit 'ey were.

Jock wisna fit ye'd caa supersteetious or onything like 'at. Aa 'e same, 'e didna aathegither like stannin' 'ere, an' 'e didna like 'at disturbance at 'e hey-soo, bit 'ere were something 'at jist widna let 'im look ony mair. 'E geed hame tae see till 's horse.

'At nicht Jock didna sleep as soon's 'e wis ees't till, curled up atween 'e wife an' e' wa'. She wis aye first up in 'e mornin' tae get 'e fire goin'. She c'd fair rattle 'e poker ower 'e ribs o' 'e grate an' if ye wisna waakent fin she startit, ye widna be sleepin' fin she wis deen. Fowk ay took a teet oot first thing tae see fa's lums wis reekin'. It didna dee tae be late in 'e mornin' or 'ey'd be sayin' fin ye foregaithered at 'e mart or 'e smiddy or 'e souter's shop — 'Aye, Jock, I doot ye wis some latchy 'is mornin', I didna see yer lum reekin' fin I lookit oot.' No, it did not dee. Bit 'e wife wisna bad at gettin a spunk till 'e paper an' 'e kettle hotterin' for a cup o' tae 'e time 'e porrich wis beginnin' tae bubble.

It wis a restless nicht for Jock. He wisna exactly dreamin', bit 'e aye min't on 'e black bag 'at Willie'd been cairryin'. 'Ere wis nae doot wi' 'im noo bit fit it wis Willie 'e'd seen. 'Ere wis a kinna shape aboot 'e bag, near han' human if ye let yer fancy go a bit, an' fit wye wid Willie quarry aboot 'e aal hey-soo? It wisna mowse. Ay at nicht Jock took a take 'e

wye o' 'e midden afore gaan till eez bed, an' hid a look at 'e
sky an' 'e meen an' 'e stars, notin' 'e airt o' 'e win' an' fit wye
'e cloods wis blaain', an' God 'e first nicht aifter 'at, 'e set oot
withoot thinkin', syne 'e picter o' 'e bag cam intill eez heid,
sae nae farrer a step did 'e tak bit roon till 'e back o' 'e hoose.
It got tae be 'e'd hardly gang oot o' 'e hoose at aa, except for
deein fit hid tae be deen amon' 'e beas', an' back in as seen's
ye like. 'E eence or twice 'e'd been by 'e eyn o' 'e steadin 'e
hey-soo wis ay 'ere, an' aifter the caal o' 'e gab o' Mey, fin it
cam warmer widder, 'ere wis aa ye wid ken o' a queer smell in
'e air, like a hen 'at hid dee't an' lie'n ower lang oot o' sicht
in a dreel. 'E got richt wirkit up, an' though 'e said niver a
wird at hame, 'e wife hid startit tae look at 'im gey queer.
    Weel, 'is day the Mrs geed up till 'e Aalyoch, the van wis
in by Jock's an' her wi't. Sae 'e kent far she wis gaan an'
she'd mentiont 'at I wid gie 'er a con-voy hame later on. Of
course, be 'e time I'd got aa 'is tale oot o' 'im, I clean forgot
far I'd been gaan, an' losh, didn' 'e cairrier nae appear on 'e
road an' 'e Mrs wavin' oot o' 'e windae as she geed by.
    'At's my kail throwe 'e reek 'e nicht,' I says.
    'I'll be gettin' some wirdies tee, I doot', says Jock.
    Weel, aifter 'at I socht tae see far 'e roller hid stoppit on
'e road. 'Ere wis a big patch o' rolled metal. I'd better e'en
than Jock an' richt eyneuch 'ere wis a lot o' fite speckies, an'
fit ye'd a thocht wis a bunch o' black threed stickin oot at ae
bit. I took 'e pint o' ma knife an' scrapit a bittie. 'E fite lum-
pies wisna hard, there wis jist nae doot at all, it wis bitties o'
been, an' queerer'n 'at, 'e black threeds wis stuck till a bit,
though aathing wis aafa clortit in' tarry stuff.
    It wis enyeuch tae blaik a body, an' I kwidna jist let
masel' think fit it wis aa aboot. Nae mair c'd Jock. We baith
turned awa an' walkit back till 'e spad. Bit I begood tae min'
on 'e wireless receiver, an' on 'e Friday paperies, an' 'e news
'at wis ay in 'em — 'missing boy's parents' distress . . . re-
ward offered for information . . . ' Fit 'e hell hid bin goin'
on aboot 'e Cross?
    Jock wis mair easy like noo e'd spoken. We didna discuss
'e maitter, though. I'd ma ain beas' tae see till, so I whuppit
my leg over 'e saiddle an' shoutit, 'weel, weel an',' an' left
Jock stumpin back ower 'e park.
    In 'e neesht months, I'd see Jock noo an' aan bit we spak
nae mair aboot 'oan thing, an' said nedder echie nor ochie till
onybody else. 'E Gairman loon wisna fun', an' 'e papers are
nae lang o' drappin' a subjick gin 'ere's nae richt news in't.

Fit I did notice, though, wis Willie. I saa 'im eence on 'e road an' spak, bit 'e pey'd nae heid. 'E'd walk up as far as Pitties, syne 'e'd turn an' gang back tae Turra. Appeerently 'e'd niver been hame tae see eez fowk since 'at day in Mey. Nae doot 'ere wis something far v-rang. I didna like tae see Willie like 'at, him an' me'd been thrang afore 'is. An' aye Jock's story hung in ma heid. I kwidna forget 'at black bag, likely for coal, an' fin I wis up 'e park ae day 'e picter o' 'at black, ily reek cam back intae ma heed. Aye, it wis eerie. I wis beginnin tae get some glimmerin's o' thochts, nae 'at I wis seekin 'em, ye ken, bit 'ere wis nae haddin' 'em. I widna winner gin Jock'd 'e same ideas. Onywye, I didna ken, for withoot a wird o' agreement ye c'd see we wisna g'n tae spread 'e tale aboot. An' Jock did naething aboot 'e soo, there it wis left tae stan', nae bit fit 'e hey hid been sair connacht afore onywye.

Doon aboot Turra, I haard 'at Willie'd nivir geen back till 'e roller. 'E'd left it in a richt mess, appeerently the fire was half chokit an' full o' bits o' run metal 'at 'e fite eisels hid meltit. 'E road boys hid got 'er clean't oot, though.

Weel, we got 'e crap in an' hairstit in fine order, an' syne intae the plooin, an' 'e pullin' o' neeps eence 'e beas' wis teen in. 'E New 'Ear cam, an' 'e sna' fell, an' meltit, an' froze, an' 'e roads took an aafa batterin'. Jock cam in aboot ae day. He spiert if I'd come up by a meenit. I bykit up wi' 'im, nedder o's sayin' onything. 'Ere wis some saft spots on 'e road, ye felt 'em as 'e tyres geed ower 'em. I min' comin' hame fae 'e skweel, I'd fin a placie like 'at an' I'd press't wi' ma beet, an' see 'e driblets o' watter comin' up atween 'e steens, an' syne fin ye stoppit pressin' it raise again. Aye, a thaa aifter hard frost an' sna' fairly howkit 'e roads, an' laddies' beets helpit 'e holes on a bit tee. An' begod, it wis jist 'e aal patch Jock took's till. 'E tap surface wis aa lowse, an' fin I scrapit wi' 'e tae o' ma tackety, jist a hale mush o' fite beenies an' black hair cam intae view. It wis a God's mercy naebody'd been 'ere before hiz. Jock took a quick look 'at's, an' I took a quick look at him.

'Fess yer spad,' I said, 'an' a guana bag.' I steed by 'e patch, haadin on tae my byke, ready tae look 's if I'd been sortin't gin onybody cam by. 'E road wis gey quairt, though, sae it wis aa richt.

'Flype open 'e bag,' I said tae Jock fin 'e cam back, an' I up wi' 'e spad an' skimmed aff as mony bits as I kwid, ay feedin' 'em in as Jock held it. 'Ere wis nae earthly doot fit we hid — a mannie's heid, fair crushed tae murlicks, an' 'e only thing 'at c'd 'a' deen't wis 'e road roller. I begood to jaloose fit micht 'a' happen't. I some doot it wis 'e Gairman lad. 'E'd likely come on Willie wi' 'e roller, an' speert 'e wye tae the steen circle on Mains Hill, or something like 'at, an' Willie, bein' sae bashfae an' maybe nae unnerstannin 'e queer wye o' spikkin, wid 'a' grinned a bittie oan answert. 'E lad widda likely persistet an' Willie widda geen on till 'e machine tae start 'er up an' get awa. Maybe 'e lad wis walkin' alangside shoutin' up at 'im, tryin' tae mak 'im unnerstan', an' I've nae doot 'e trippit an' wowf wi' eez heid anaith 'e big roller. Mercy what a thing tae happen. Ma stamach wis grippit up wi' 'e thocht, an' mair sae wi' gettin' a glintie o' fit Willie'd felt like. 'E'd been clean terrifeet. A lad wi' a heid in a splyter an' nae doot richt aff at 'e shooders, an' Willie 'e caase o't, fither 'e likit or no.

I rakit amon' 'e metal wi' 'e nyeuk o' 'e spad tae gaither ilky bit an' get it baggit. Jist as weel we hidna fun't a 'ear ago, bit time hid deen its usual job an' aathing was pickit clean. We trampit doon 'e patch as weel's we kwid. Neen o's said onything.

I min't again on 'e black reek, an' on 'e meltit brass I'd haard o' in Turra, an' on 'e mark I'd seen on 'e roller fin Willie got sae angry wi's. Claes an' bag an' aa must 'a' been burnt in 'e fire box o' e' roller, 'at widda been 'e caase o' 'e ily reek. Peer Willie, what a job. It wid a teen a fyow splashes o' tar tae cover 'e bleed tee. An' syne 'e'd gotten 'e corp intill a coal bag, an' cairriet it ower Jock's park. I didna think we no't tae look in 'e soo, 'ere wis nae doot fit wid be 'ere.

'Ere wisna much spikkin atweens. We geed up tae Jock's place an' I geed 'im a han' tae harness 'e horse intill 'e cairt. I plumpit 'e bag intill 'e boddom o't an' we geed roon till 'e aal soo, wi' a fork apiece. It wis gey mucky stuff, 'at hey, aifter lyin' for mair 'n a 'ear. We wis ees't eyneuch wi' deid beasts, bit it wisna agreable fit we wis 'at eynoo. We forkit awa till we'd won weel intill 'e heap, 'e hale o't stuck 'egidder an' comin' aff in flat layeries o' black stuff. Ae layer turnet, an' man I hardly like to say fit wis 'ere, a black body wi' aa 'e sap clean oot o't, fairly flattened, like a cat I eence saa 'at hid got stuck in anaith 'e couples o' an aal hoose far 'e thackit reef hed fa'n in on't. Jock took ae look.

'Kipper't,' 'e said. We got it on till 'e cairt, alang wi' 'e aal hey an' 'e guana bag wi' 'e bits o' eez heid, an' up tae the quarry at 'e heid o' 'e hill. It wis oot o' eese, bit fowk dumpit

aal rubbish in't. We howkit hyne doon amon' 'e rubbish, cow-
pit in wir load, an' happit it weel again.
Nae lang ahin' 'at, Jock retired an' meeved till a hoose
aside Turra. He's deid noo, peer breet. An' Willie wis got in a
dam. 'E wis aye a tidy lad, an' 'e'd faal't up eez jaicket an'
laid it ower 'e hannle bars o' eez byke.
A hullock o' 'ears on, I wis hyowin' wi' 'e souter's loon, a
learnet kinna lad, a body ye c'd spik till. Aathing cam intae
ma heid, as we workit ben 'e dreels in 'e gushet-nyeuk. Ma
hair wis gettin fite, be 'is time. I min' on 'im lookit 'at's, jist
as we come doon aside 'e burn, fin I speert, jist on 'e meenit
— 'bit wid 'ere be a God?'

Iain Crichton Smith

THE SCREAM

The play lasted about an hour and took place in a small theatre off the High St in Edinburgh. The story of the play was not complicated. A prison had been burnt down in the night and there was an enquiry as to who had done it. The cast was as follows:

The Governor — an idealist who hated brutality.
The Governor's wife — who supported her husband as an honourable man but was also sex-starved.
Two brutal guards — one tall and one small. They had ill-treated the prisoners, made them bend down and eat their own excrement. In the presence of the Governor, however, they always appeared reasonable and respectful, having only the welfare of the prisoners at heart!
There was a cleaner who appeared at times dim-witted but at other times could discuss Marx: a homosexual prisoner who was beaten up by the guards in a scene of great cruelty: the man who headed the enquiry who was an ex-communist, drank a great deal and was in love with his secretary, a not particularly good-looking girl of great idealsim: and finally a boy who had left Cambridge and who found himself plunged into 'real life'.

The audience liked the play. It started slowly and then built up to a claustrophobic denouement. But the enquiry didn't discover who had burnt the prison down.
The part of the homosexual was acted by Jeff Coates, a young actor from Cambridge. In the pivotal scene he was fitted up with electrodes while the two guards tortured him.
One of their lines was 'the poof of the pudding is in the eating.' For the two guards were intellectuals too, clever, cunning, able to switch from viciousness to calm collected discussion especially when the Governor appeared, the Governor tortured by moral doubts whom they despised.

After all what was a prison for but to convert criminals to goodness by torture? Jeff Coates was changed by the play. At first he had not liked it very much. He thought the dialogue at times brittle, its poeticisms brilliant but perhaps esoteric. But gradually it took a grip of him, he felt himself inside a world of almost total evil. At coffee breaks he would speak only to the Governor and never to the guards. In the crucial secene he screamed a high piercing scream though of course it was only a pretence of torture he was suffering. At times however he felt he was being really tortured. The trouble was that he was really a homosexual and that made it worse — or did it? He couldn't make up his mind. Was it indeed worse to be a real homosexual in that scene? (Also in the play he was attacked by prisoners.) He sometimes felt that the two guards really hated him for neither was a homosexual. They made comments about his walk and these comments he accepted as belonging to the play. The women in the cast befriended him more than the men did, though of course he was not interested in them sexually. In the scene where he was being tortured he felt real hatred emanating from the two guards as if they were his most bitter enemies. Of course he had experience of being beaten up in real life, particularly in a public convenience in London, about two years before.

His scream was real, he thought, because it came from the centre of his being. And yet it was happening in a play. These men didn't really hate him, he told himself, they were merely acting, they obviously had to act as if they hated him. The Governor too in real life was stingy, sarcastic, embittered, not at all attractive. The two guards in real life were not at all intellectual: in fact he despised them. For he himself had read Artaud on the Theatre of Cruelty. The stage became very small each night. It shrank. Every night he waited to be tortured. It was almost as if that was the reason for his existence.

As time passed he became more and more solitary, arriving late, leaving early. He didn't want to see these contemptuous eyes nor did he wish to listen to the banal conversation of the guards. The scream was taking a lot out of him, he had to prepare himself for it, it shattered his whole being so that if there had been glass near him it would have shattered. He didn't wish to discuss the play with the others since in his opinion they didn't really know what it was about, they did not know what suffering was. Of course none of them had ever suffered except in fantasy. That at any rate was what he thought. He himself had suffered, especially on the day that his mother had discovered him in bed with a male friend of his. That was the worst. Her whole face had disintegrated: he would always remember that moment.

O none of them had really suffered. He himself had suffered, however. He was the one who was in the prison. The suffering was disguised by talk about morality, about Marx, but nothing could disguise the torture. And his scream, was it real or not? For after all he wasn't really being tortured. In fact the two guards used to make a point of asking him over to take coffee with them. He was probably making a mistake in thinking that they hated him.

And he loved acting. He had acted many other parts as well as the part he was acting in this play. That was the awful and marvellous thing about actors, that they took on themselves the pains and sufferings of others. They brought to audiences the calmness of art at the expense of their own tortured spirits. He had acted kings, drunks, and most especially the dark blind figure in THE ROOM, by Pinter. And in all these instances he had sought determinedly for the meaning of the text. When he was acting the part of Creon, he had thought, This city of Edinburgh is Thebes, we shall show it its plague, though there was in fact no appearance of plague in Edinburgh's theatrical facade, with its green light shining about the castle at night.

To be an actor was to be a healer, a doctor. And the scream waited for him every night. In fact he had become obsessed by it.

He stayed in lodgings on his own. Every night he left the theatre and walked to them through the throbbing festival city, through the slums of the High St. After the scream he strolled through the streets, emptied of emotion, solitary. And he thought, the guards are at least uncomplicated. They are brutal, they have assessed the world as it really is. They had no imagination, they could not put themselves in the position of the weak, nor did they want to. He found himself hating them in return. Why had they taken these parts unless they were in a deep way suited to them? And this in spite of the fact that such an idea was stupid.

And as for the governor, he despised him. The governor had never protected him. There he was tortured every day while the governor stood around like a moral priggish Brutus and the guards like Mark Antonies ran rings round him. They would spring to attention while prisoners bled in the cells. O how they laughed at that poor tortured libertarian in the burnt prison under the open sky! Who had burnt the prison? Was it perhaps the governor himself? Or his wife? Or the cleaner who could discuss Marx? And every night his own high scream was the peak point of the play. It rose to a crescendo, then died away to a whisper, to exhaustion. And the audience winced (or perhaps they loved it. Who could tell?) But none of them was unaffected. He saw to that. And when the play was over and the audience had left, he and the other actors would have their coffee and discuss the effectiveness of the night's work. And it became more and more demanding to create the scream. It wasn't easy to scream like that every night.

One night he waited behind till the others had gone. Then he went out into the street. It was a Saturday night and the air was mild. All round him he sensed the delirium of the Festival. There were lovers strolling hand in hand, there were men in strange colourful costumes, the world itself was a theatre. It was Romeo and Juliet he saw sitting on a bench, it was the old woman from CRIME AND PUNISHMENT who staggered drunkenly down the street. The city was a theatre at which the plague had not struck.

He walked with his usual mincing walk. He had never been conscious of it himself but he had been told of it. Actually he was still wearing his prison clothes for he hadn't bothered changing. Well, why shouldn't he? One night he had seen a tall man in a black gown walking towards him on stilts, with a skull instead of a face.

He now entered a street which was quite dark. The council was dimming its lamps in certain areas even during the Festival.

And then they were there. There must have been about six of them. They were wearing green scarves and they were shouting. They owned the street. They were like members of a crowd in one of Shakespeare's plays, perhaps JULIUS CAESAR: but they were really vicious. It might be that their team had lost. Who knew? He and they were in the dim street together and they were marching towards him. Perhaps he should run? He thought about it but he didn't run. They were chanting. Their heads were shaved.

Poof, they shouted, poof they shouted again. They danced around him. Poof in his theatrical clothes. And they with their shaved heads on which Union Jacks had been painted. (One light in the alley like a spot light showed this to him.)

It had happened before. It would happen again. Those without imagination were upon him. The animals with their teeth.

Poof, they shouted, bloody poof. And then they were on him and beat him to the ground and trampled on him. And his glasses fell off and cracked, he could feel that. He looked upwards but he could hardly see them. All he could see was a kaleidoscope of colour. And he could smell the smell of alcohol. And then he screamed. And as he screamed the high piercing scream they ran away and left him in a quick scurry.

And he lay there on the street alone, listening to the noise they made as they left, and he thought, That scream, was it different? Was it different from the one in the play? Which was the real scream and which was the unreal one? The prepared or the unprepared? The, as it were, artistic one or the real one? And he thought, the artistic one was the real one. This was only an accidental one. This was not the scream of art, this was the one he had attracted by walking like a poof and taking that lane which he should not have taken and continuing to walk towards them as perhaps he should not have done. Had he been trying to learn more about the artistic scream by this one? He felt naked in the dim street without his glasses.

He would have to make his way back to his real landlady. And with his real face. And put ointment on his real bruises.

He staggered a little as he stood up, coming out of the scream. Everything was silent around him. No one had heard him. There had been no audience. How therefore could his scream have been more real than the theatrical one?

How?

Tim Neil

A CHRISTENING

He has been sleeping in the hills, having been moved out of the city the night before; his clothes are negligible, so old and so worn as to be on the edge of existence, as is their owner. He stumbles towards the city with the sunrise, drunk now on memories rather than alcohol; his last drink was two days ago; but because he has been, on average, drunk for the last two years, he behaves and thinks as though he still is. A trail of spittle has recently been wiped from his chin. His shoes are incongruous and new, having been given to him quite recently at a religious mission for the destitute in the city. If he can remember where it is he will sleep there tonight; if he cannot he will sit in a park somewhere in the city, telling passers-by his stories until, at nightfall, the police take him there. Perhaps it will mean another conviction, but this is immaterial to a man whose name is different every time he gives it to the officers. It is an understood thing; the officers know his face and know that if they have had the same name twice it is only by accident. What his name is or was they do not know; neither, we may probably presume, does he; and the fact that, were they to find it out, they might solve one of their cases of disappearance, does not interest or excite the police at all. Only the people of the mission think seriously of rehabilitation. Some of the alumni of the flophouses are indeed to be seen, clean-shaven and shabbily but cleanly dressed, in chapels around the city, but these are not success-stories. Few if any of these now live under the same name they were born with; few if any of these can put their names to a history of more than a few years' duration; many will prove not to have sufficient stamina and will disappear from the straight and narrow before this year, or next, is over and done with. Christmas breaks their backs. They attend the mission celebrations and stand around afterwards, a cup of tea or coffee in their hands, thinking of drink or something stronger, and the pale ghosts of cocktail conversations flicker over the room as the Father passes by, smiling. It is hard to have much to say when one's name has no solidity. It is a difficulty these people confront daily in their jobs as dust-men, lavatory cleaners and dishwashers, or nightly as assistant night-watchmen; they clutch their brooms, mops, dishcloths or torches not as tools but as tickets. At the Christmas cele-brations they swap names and occupations, and stand as anyone might stand at a cashdesk or till; they expect some-thing in return for what they have just given, and they receive nothing. They are aware, some dimly, some sharply, depend-ing on where the room that has been found for them is, of families and names that mean perhaps a little more than an occupation. Some time after Christmas or New Year they may pass a liquor store with their pay (always in cash, too little for a cheque and never a bank-account to pay it into) freshly put in their pockets; and then the room, wherever it is, stands empty again, and if a name could be shed then another would be found cast off on the pavement.

He enters the city by accidental stealth, through one of its stranger suburbs that still remembers agriculture and can be entered by methods other than roads. Let us be precise: he enters by falling from a field over a garden fence, and by walking up the garden path under the amazed eyes of a gar-dener. The master and mistress are still asleep and the gardener it too old to protest loudly. There is some purpose in his movements and it is not by accident that he follows the path and then the road towards the centre of the city; for his sense of purpose is largely composed of a sense of direction. His sense of direction is by no means flawless, and this is not a part of the city with which he can remember being familiar; he takes wrong turnings, on occasion he walks in the wrong direction altogether, and so, although he arrives at the city's edge in the early morning, and although it is only another six miles to its centre, he does not arrive there until after mid-day; and from there he travels like a pinball, avoiding traffic, to the central park by roundabout routes. In parks people are more generous; they seem to remember older forms of charity and drop small change into the hands of the sufficiently im-portunate; in reality the destitute is a form of litter that one pays to disappear, rather than go to the trouble of picking it up and putting it in a bin.

He sits on a bench beside a young couple and offends them, although he smells hardly at all: the night's fresh air has neutralised much of the filth. He sits for a while in the heat that seems to pour off all of the concrete in the city and into the park; signs announce that the grass must not be walked upon, but the grass is in reality not there to be trampled. It died after the first two weeks of summer. Unlike some of his colleagues, he has not forgotten how to read, or how to bother; he reads the sign; he perceives that it is only indirectly meaningful, not because he knows that there is no grass to speak of, but because he is dimly aware that he is precisely the sort of person the warden will expect to find sprawled in some forbidden part of the park at sunset; at sunset, he will become officially litter; and the police will come with what is officially a black maria, but is in reality a dustcart, and take him away to be recycled, or at least re-clothed.

After a few minutes he turns to the young couple, who are still sitting there, unwilling to be offended even if they actually are, and says to them: I was a businessman too, once. There is no businessman nearby for comparison, but this is not important; it is important to talk, and to tell a story; it is not important that the story is true, or even the same every time; he is not a journalist, but a novelist of an impermanent sort; the story can very well be someone else's, but unlike the novelist he attaches his unreal claims to it only for a brief period, and always in any case he attaches a pseudonym, and if it is his own name it is not so in any valid sense, but only by a failure of imagination or a success of memory. I was, he adds, waving at buildings that are clearly residential, over there. Nothing big you understand, nothing big. I went bust, my partner ran off with the money. Ran off. The young couple admit their offence at last, stand up and walk away: he sits on the bench still and looks at the sign. The story might be true, but he has already forgotten it.

It is the end of the day, and it has been neither a particularly good day nor a particularly bad one. By about four o'clock he had, in the only one of his pockets that remained still without a hole in it, enough money for a bottle of whisky, whisky of the cheapest sort, whisky that one suspects is nothing more than an impure alcohol, stained rather than flavoured, the sort of whisky that has 'finest' on the label, the label dirty and printed on cheap paper, the bottle thin and easy to smash. It is in the same pocket that had held the money now, half empty, and of course he is not drunk yet, nor will he be on the contents of this bottle; it is not enough; its taste makes his spit acidic and perhaps even discolours his teeth, but it will not make him drunk.

He has left the park, not deliberately, but because in order to find a shop selling liquor so cheap that he can afford it he has had to walk too far away from the park to return to it before dark. He is sitting now in one of the cheap parts of the city, on the doorstep of a derelict house. This is the part of the city where crime is meant to be rife, but he is too obviously the owner of nothing to be attacked; he can sit and drink in perfect safety. It is sunset. There are cars passing: old cars, mostly, cars that have been inherited rather than bought, or cars that have been stolen from owners who preferred to claim the insurance; cars that have been made up from the remnants of other cars, impossible cars, Fords with Volkswagen wings, Renaults with Fiat roofs and bonnets and engines so old as to be almost mythical; and there are some new cars, but none of them come from around here; this is one of the roads out of the city, and they are taking it. Some of these drivers have heard that there is a revolution about to take place, and they are driving out into the country to avoid the worst; they will be back in a few weeks, when the new government has settled in, and they will return to their homes and offices without danger; they drive through this derelict district in perfect confidence; this is not where revolutions come from; this is where the poor stay and the self-made men depart from, occasionally and largely by accident. All the same they drive swiftly and keep their windows wound up. There are no revolutions here but there are plenty of bricks.

From where he sits the sunset is visible, not directly, but reflected in the windows of the building that he sits opposite. He drinks with his eyes upon it, drinking now for no reason other than that he is thirsty; there is nothing that he is escaping, there is nothing in particular to forget that he has not already forgotten; he is thirsty and no other sort of drink will do. The sunset in the glass is imperfectly reflected; the window is so old that it contains lead and has flowed, and so the sunset has slipped from a vague semi-circle into the approximate shape of a pear; it is an inappropriate splash of colour and its presence here is inexplicable. Everything else is dirty or broken or simply old; the fabric here of both things and people is threadbare; here there are frightening mimicries and hopes — doorsteps carefully cleaned, Christmas clubs, hire purchase. He sits and neither applauds nor condemns such activities. He does not even notice them. It is possible that he will be the last person in the country to become aware that there is a revolution happening or about to happen, even though he is sitting drinking in the city where it will begin.

He raises the bottle to his lips and swallows; the liquid is acidic and he winces; somebody walks past while the bottle is raised, a man in his thirties; he does not notice and lowers the bottle, pushing it after several attempts into his pocket. He will have nothing to eat and nothing further to drink tonight unless he moves. This is not a place for charity; charity rarely pays visits; charity begins at home. He stands up and walks away uncertainly in the direction of the city, leaving the sunset in the window without an audience; it has lost very little; he had not even recognised it as a sunset. He walks slowly, his coat swinging with the weight of the bottle; it bumps occasionally against his hip as it swings; at the corner of the street he stops, takes the bottle out of his pocket and finishes its contents with a single swig; he throws the empty bottle over a wall and it smashes. The evening air is clear and cool. He turns around the corner of the street and sets off once more.

Once again he travels slowly; but there is less traffic, he spends less time turning away from roads in constant use; he moves, perhaps, faster than he had in the morning. He walks up a long street, steeply sloped, walking away from one of the city's smaller parks. It is already shut; he stopped for a while when passing and looked over the fence at its large ornamental pond, a few imported ducks swimming around or standing on the shore. At the opposite end of the pond from where he stands, there is a statue, of whom he has no idea. It is an old statue, a hundred years old, a hundred and fifty, more, of a well-dressed hero. A man, possibly, of famous liberality, or of philanthropic virtue — perhaps he paid for the park himself and his own statue also; or perhaps his friends or inheritors or allies commissioned it; or perhaps this man has been in some sense stolen, and his statue stands signifying nothing he would have countenanced when alive. It is too dark to read the motto. There may be no motto; there is writing, certainly, but it may be simply his name and the dates of his birth and death. Perhaps it is not even a good likeness. It stands, implacable and subject to indignities: there is, inevitably, pigeon-shit on the shoulders and lichen in the crevices; it stands open to wind and rain, although there is admittedly little of the latter in this country, hot as it is. He turns and continues to walk up the street, passing now through a cleaner, more affluent area. The buildings are white, their lines generous, their windows sizeable and well-curtained, the pavements clean and empty: dinner is being eaten. He moves up the street oblivious of the proximity of good food and wine, passing parked cars of expensive marque and recent construction and not considering theft; the windows are newer, made without lead, but they reflect not a sunset but the houses opposite and him as he walks up the street, oblivious of a reflection that many others would study as they passed to ensure that they are looking, so to speak, themselves, and themselves at their best. He cannot even be said to ignore his passing before several mirrors, since he does not even notice their existence. It is possible that, were he confronted with his own reflection, he would attempt to shake its hand or tell it a story. He walks up the street to the crest of the hill on which it is built, and sees the rest of the city laid out before him, large, well-lit, grand, expensive; it is early in the evening and certain parts of it will still be populous. He rests for a while. If he finds nothing he will at least be found himself, by the police, and taken to the mission. He crosses the road and walks down another street almost the image of the one he had just walked up. There is another small park at its foot, containing another pond and another statue, perhaps it is a statue of the same man, but it is too dark to see, and he had not taken in the likeness of the other anyway.

It is well after midnight. He has had little success, but enough; a glass of wine from an embarrassed restaurateur, a little money from an older woman alone at a cafe table on the pavement, enough for a double vodka of the cheapest brand on the shelves of a bar down a sidestreet. This is enough, but the parts of the city that are normally full during the evening and night are tonight half-empty. He does not ask himself, or anybody else for that matter, why; or he did not, because he has now fallen asleep in the doorway of one of the more expensive shops on one of the most prestigious streets; it is a good place to fall asleep. It is not a place he will be allowed to stay. If the police pass at all they will almost certainly move him on. He has been asleep for half an hour or more, and the police have not yet come by. Instead there is a woman walking down the street, early middle-aged, not well-dressed but not badly, her hair loosely gathered in a knot; she is window-shopping, or just walking, an unfashionable person walking past things that she has by now almost certainly missed irrevocably, barring a win in the national lottery or a sudden and unexpected inheritance. She has seen his legs protruding from the doorway. During the day or under any

other circumstances she would almost certainly have simply
walked on with the rest of the passers-by; but tonight, perhaps, unobserved and already stopping on a street she might
normally feel almost obliged to walk straight down, tonight
it is possible that she feels invisible. She stands quietly and
looks at him. The light is falling almost directly on his face. It is small,
almost chinless, heavily wrinkled, covered in stubble just
thick enough to be called a beard, and the eyes are shut. It
is the face of a monkey; it is the face of an unambitious gar-
goyle come down from its parapet, drunken somehow, to
sleep. It is wearing a thin coat, a shirt the colour of which is
not discernible, black trousers and a pair of plimsolls still new
enough to be generally white. The shirt is open, the skin beneath dirty and strangely corrugated until she realises that
she is looking directly at the ribs. They rise and fall without
rhythm. She looks at the leg, the trouser rucked up around
the knee and the sock absent, and sees that the fat of the calf
has been stolen somehow as if by the performance of an
operation executed without cause or reason, leaving the bone
and muscle and the sinew open to the naked eye, the skin so
ineffective as to be transparent: perhaps this is not a man but
an anatomical exhibit. He wakes up, or at least appears to,
his eyes opening. One of them shuts again, and the two study
each other without recognition for a short while, three, four,
five seconds, before she turns and walks away, frightened or
at least discomfited, from this man in the process of becoming invisible. His even and empty stare has reminded her of
herself; she walks away; he falls asleep again. Half an hour
later the police arrive; one shakes his shoulder, another stands
a few feet away from the door; they stand him up, he struggles
a little for the appearance of things and because his own in-
tentions are not entirely clear to him, and because he has
been dreaming — he says to one of the policemen as they
bundle him into the car, my hat, where's my — but they
laugh and push him, not too roughly, into the back seat; and
they drive off, not to the mission; not tonight; tonight they
drive him to the police station.

He wakes perhaps an hour later, in a room which is a curious
hybrid of shower and office. There is a desk in one corner
with a chair on either side; the walls and floor are tiled; there
is a sort of bench, covered in imitation leather, in the middle
of the room; there are taps and hoses. He takes none of this

in; he is aware only that the police have not taken him to the mission, unable to forget that the mission should be his ultimate destination, and so he sits and feels himself to be in transit; clearly something is happening; it does not matter what, they will take him to the mission in a little while. He is naked and sitting in a corner of the room; his head lolls back and forth; he appears drugged, his body limp, folded in unlikely places, one hand lying palm up on the floor; his legs splayed, his penis ridiculously shrunken, his eyes apparently sinking into his skull. A door opens and a policemen looks around its edge and studies him reasonably closely. 'It's all right; he's still breathing,' he shouts over his shoulder. 'He stinks.' He steps into the room, small, compact, well-exercised and well-fed. Another follows. They stand just inside the door and contemplate their catch. They suspect, both of them, that this damaged little man is by no means one of the revolutionaries that they have been detailed to question. But he has been brought to them for questioning nevertheless, and there is an undeniable need for bodies; there are quotas to be filled; they must be seen to be doing their jobs if they are to keep them, and at the same time it is wise not to be too successful, or there will be an equal and more unfortunate need for revenge when the new regime is in place. So they look at him; they study him closely. Holding their noses, they have ransacked his ragged clothes for some hint of sedition, and have found nothing — nothing at all, not even identification, no names at all other than that of the manufacturer of his jacket. Methodical, they have taken the name and will question the owner of the company concerned at the earliest opportunity. Now they walk across the room towards him; one reaches for a hose, the other turns on the tap, and they play cold water at high pressure across his naked body, and he opens his eyes at last and turns to face the wall; they hose his back; he struggles without agility or success to avoid the water; they hose his legs, his stomach, his chest, face, crotch and backside; they turn off the hose and the short one kicks him accurately in the kidney. The other helps him to his feet and gives him a blanket, and they take him to one of the seats beside the desk and sit him down. The taller policeman switches off all the lights apart from one that shines full in the little man's face; the shorter policeman sits in the chair on the other side of the desk; the taller policeman leaves the light switch and takes up a position behind the chair on which the little man sits, and in the darkness behind the thin shoulder he quietly unloops a truncheon from his belt. He shivers; his eyes are open wide; he has forgotten the mission and is afraid, clean and almost sober for the first time in two years. 'What is your name?' asks the sitting policeman; he poises his pen above a form; briefly he toys with the idea of dispensing with formalities, of a summary execution. He is afraid himself. Whilst he waits for an answer he attempts to tot up the number of people of this sort with whom he has dealt in the past few days. Perhaps it is enough. His wife need never know. The little tramp says nothing. He quivers and shakes; his eyes dart back and forth like an animal's, but without a spark in them of life, hope or mischief. 'Name?' the policeman repeats; he is in a hurry. The truncheon comes to rest on the thin shoulder. 'Name,' says the policeman once again, no longer as a question, but as a threat. The tramp feels a sudden stab of pain in his upper back. There is an echo in the tiled chamber. Namenamename the policeman appears to say each time. He struggles with names and attempts to pick one that seems correct, that has a feel of veracity, that is the truth; it seems to him that it is the truth that is required, but the policeman in front of him asks too quickly and too often, and the policeman behind him hits too often and too hard; the truth is impossible to come by, it is a commodity in distressingly short supply, he mumbles out a lie and the sitting policeman, satisfied, writes it down; and then he says, 'What is your address?' 'I have a wife,' he says, but it is irrelevant, although it may be true; 'We will deal with her later,' says the policeman with the pen. 'Address?' He is confused. At the mission they never ask for his address, they know he has no address; 'I have no address,' he says; the policeman behind him hits him just behind the ear. 'Address?' mouths the sitting policeman, inaudible; there is a ringing in his ears and a little blood trickling from his nose. He must have asked again; there is more pain in his shoulder. He mumbles out a number and a street. The policeman at the desk looks up at the policeman standing behind the chair. The latter shakes his head. He strikes the tramp across the neck. The sitting policeman leans forward; he looks disappointed. 'There is no such number on that street,' he says. 'Your real address.' The tramp does not understand; he shakes his head; he does not understand that the facts must be, not true, but plausible; his mouth hangs open, his eyes become, if anything, duller than before. He continues to shake his head until there is a sudden, and considerable, pain beneath his left shoulder blade; he becomes aware that the blanket has been removed. Behind him the standing policeman scowls; he moves his left hand in circles like a man cranking a recalcitrant car; he jabs the point of the truncheon into the lower back and twists. The tramp blurts out another address, another nonsense; by sheer chance it is a real address; the policeman takes it down, he lifts his pen from the paper and says, 'Occupation?' The tramp has achieved a kind of understanding — 'Businessman,' he says; but what is good enough for the city parks, what suffices for a penny or two, is not good enough here; the policeman snorts. 'You?' he says. Two blows descend on his upper arm; he feels something break, something tears, something has snapped to make it do so; the standing policeman pulls his chair back and lays the head of his truncheon just above his left kneecap. 'Roads,' says the tramp. 'I sweep the roads.' 'Better,' says the policeman. 'Roadsweeper,' he says, writing it down. He looks up at the tramp. 'Your wife's name?' he says. The tramp says nothing. The truncheon descends on his knee, twice. The tramp enters a new place in his mind as white as the room in which he is sitting as the kneecap breaks and the muscle begins to contract; there is a kind of freshness there and a kind of clarity; his gaze rests on the papers in front of the policeman and he understands that there are a great many questions to be asked, a great many more; far too many. He raises his right arm and points at the forms. 'You fill it in,' he says. His voice surprises; it fills the room — it seems to enlarge it, to throw back the walls and raise the roof; dumbfounded, the sitting policeman looks up at him; the tramp, who has a name now, and an address, and an occupation, and an admittedly anonymous wife — things he has not had in years — appears to look back at him; he appears to have made a sort of discovery, he seems to be breaking the rules, he seems to be pointing something out, making an accusation — that questions provide their own answers perhaps, something that even those who ask the questions suspect only infrequently. The policeman is frightened and embarrassed; the tramp's answer makes him, in a curious way, the subject of his own authority, the one who should be interrogated; something must be done. 'No,' says the policeman, consciously ridiculous; 'you ought to.' He says it quietly. It is not a point that one should need to insist on. The tramp shakes his head; he appears to be disagreeing, but in fact the whiteness of the pain is growing and he shakes his head because there is nothing else to do, because he has bitten his tongue and blood is filling his mouth.

But he appears to be disagreeing, and before the policeman at the desk can stop him the other, behind the chair, strikes him with the flat of the truncheon across the temple. The proceedings come to an abrupt halt: the tramp falls off the chair and lies on the floor; for a moment he twitches, his mouth making slight noises, not of pain but departure; he lies still; more blood than comes even from a tongue pours out of his mouth. After a minute the policeman at the desk picks up his pen and papers and goes to the door; he opens it and shouts for an orderly, to whom he gives the papers. The orderly glances at them, takes a white plastic tag out of his pocket and a pen, writes the name on the tag, then crosses the room and fixes it around the wrist.

To that extent the interrogation has been a success.

Outside the room now, the shorter officer lights a cigarette and walks towards the stairs, climbs them, crosses a hall and knocks on a door. Inside there is sitting a man of some importance, middle-aged but still, at least apparently, fit. 'Yes?' he says. 'Another one just died under interrogation,' says the shorter officer. 'What did he tell you?' asks the senior officer, looking out of the window, toying with a paperclip. Dawn is breaking, early as always in summer. 'Very little,' he replies, his cheap cigarette sputtering and popping as he draws upon it. 'His name, address, his occupation, and that he had a wife.' The senior officer shakes his head. 'Then he was a fool ever to have involved himself with the reds,' he says. 'A married man has responsibilities. A married man cannot afford politics.' He pauses. 'Still,' he continues. 'His name and address, you say. And a wife. It's early. She should still be asleep. Send out a car and some men and bring her in.' Tired, he closes his eyes and draws his hand, flat, down across his face, which is still relatively unwrinkled; the obligations of authority have caused him, over the years, little discomfort. In a couple of hours he will go home himself. 'Yes, sir,' says the other, the cigarette in his hand burnt down to the filter. He turns and leaves the room, walking over to the duty desk and passing on the orders he has just been given. In a matter of minutes a police car leaves the building, and he steps out of the doors for a breath of fresh air. The light in the east is already quite strong, but for the moment the glow from the streetlamps lies like snow on the pavement and parked cars. Looking down, he can clearly make out the number on his chest; tired and depressed, he notes that it is positioned, curiously enough, where a convict's number would be also. He looks out at the dark street, and is uncertain of the true nature of his employment.

Robert Crawford

SCOTLAND

Semiconductor country, land crammed with intimate
    expanses,
Your cities are superlattices, heterojunctive
Graphed from the air, your cropmarked farmlands
Are epitaxies of tweed.

All night motorways carry your signal, swept
To East Kilbride or Dunfermline. A brightness off
    low headlands
Beams-in the dawn to Fife's interstices,
Optoelectronics of hay.

Micro-nation. So small you cannot be forgotten,
Bible inscribed on a ricegrain, hi-tech's key
Locked into the earth, your televized Glasgows
Are broadcast in Rio. Among circuitboard crowsteps

To be miniaturized is not small-minded.
To love you needs more details than the Book of Kells —
Your harbours, your photography, your democratic
    intellect
Still boundless, chip of a nation.

OSSIANIC FRAGMENTS

It's rumoured in Rotary circles that uranium's been discovered
    in the shrunken heads
Of Fiona Macleod. Bonnie Prince Charlie's
Broken out again with Jeanie Deans and Mendelssohn
But we're trying to control things. They're disguised as one
    another.

Already we've rounded up a lot of the landscape, but only
Because the mountains kept getting themselves in the wrong
    order
And so were caught out. We had good maps. The financial
    and anthropological implications of all this
Could be catastrophic. Professors J. MacDougall Hay and
    D.K. Broster

Have been called in as consultants on the question of the
    infrastructure
Of *Roamin in the Gloamin*. They're convinced these Hebrides
    could still constitute
An advanced geotechnology if they set their mind to it,
But there's still near-hysteria over those gelid scotch pies.

It's all in my report with the Lochailort co-efficients and —
Oh, forget it. We've a free factsheet about how
To be abducted familiarly through an interwar remake
Billowing under a 40 watt Celtic Twilight that's curtained
    the Solway

In a haar brimming with small print from the notes at the
    back of *Redgauntlet*.
If you get into trouble, hum the tune of *Dark Clouds*
*Weave their New Tartan Ribbons in the High Bald Hair of
    the Cuillins*.
Those kyles are so sadly non-viable.

BURNS AYONT AULD REEKIE

(Burns speiks)

Forspoken still in Embro, Scoatlan's douce
Sly Purgatoary o thi randy yuppies,
Ringin blak forst o closes ayont whilk
Ma wurds sky oot wi Coancoard's soanic bangs
Abune thi Mekong, Murray, Mississippi,
Ah bide hamschakelled in a pokey hoose
Dreamin o Adiroandacks, Perth, an Err;
Ah scrug ma bunnit tae thi bourachin toon
An speir oan luve. Ah'm graith, an ken ma graith,
Grapplin wi rift o leid that loups an jouks
Seantacks oar keepirs, yit can aye git claucht
Unkennin, sae thi makar, strenyeabill
In Embro kens thi dawtit wurds, wee divans
Idled fae haun tae haun, an gies them aw
Oot tae thi warl by bein gi'ed tae Scoatlan —
Nae penny-brydal, yon, but a rig-adown-daisy
In whilk thi Mekong, Murray, Mississippi
Clyde (aye, an Foarth) cowp mickle charpin wattirs
Intae ane spendrife spattil that gangs doon
Wi kingle-krangle gliffs, but dawchs thi laun.
Glogg-rinnin wattirs hooch in spait an vanish,
But Scoatlan glisses, e'en Embro glisses. Eneuch!

Ah waant yon guid aucht that's weet as olours, rerr
As spluntin acors thi Mojave — mair thumblickin,
Prollin thumbs hurry burry aw owre yi, wi nae
Hurkle-durkle; stramash o reists an shanks,

Loup ourweillin inventars o loo:
Loofs, lonyngs, skirdoch o orising, red.
An mornin a poddasway, ayont thi hairst-rig,
A souple, souple dawn.

BURNS BEYOND EDINBURGH

(Burns speaks)

Injured by immoderate praise and conjured up in Edinburgh,
Scotland's respectable sly Purgatory of randy, upwardly
mobile young people, stone-hard black frost of enclosures beyond which my words skim out along the horizon with Con-
corde's sonic bangs above the Mekong, Murray, Mississippi, I
endure defiantly like a cow whose head is fastened to its fore-
legs, in a cramped house, dreaming of Adirondacks, Perth, and
Ayr; I cock my bonnet fiercely on my brow to the congested
town and anxiously inquire after love. I'm unembarrassedly
ready, and know my equipment, struggling (as when catching
salmon) with hearty, free conversation of language that leaps
and evades lines lined with baited hooks, and keepers, yet can
always get suddenly laid hold on without knowing, so that
the poet rich enough to have his goods seized to pay bail in
Edinburgh knows the fondled words, small wild plums passed
idly from hand to hand, and gives them all out to the world
by being given to Scotland — no wedding at which the guests
pay money to contribute to their entertainment, but an
ancient kind of dancing on the grass at weddings in which the
Mekong, Murray, Mississippi, Clyde (yes, and Forth) upset
great grating waters into one spendthrift spate that goes
down with loud, confused, angry sudden shocks, but moistens
the land with dew. Slow-running waters cry excitedly in spate
and vanish, but Scotland shines, even Edinburgh shines.
Enough!

*I want that good intimate possession that's wet as herbs liked
by swans, rare as running after girls at night across the Mojave
— more making of bargains by licking thumbs, licking and
striking thumbs in confused hurry all over you, with no sluggishness in bed; disturbance of restive waiting insteps and legs,
leap exceeding inventories of love: palms of the hand, narrow
passageways, flirting of arising, spawning place. And morning
a garment whose warp and woof are silk, beyond the couple
who reap together at harvest, a supple, cunning dawn.*

. . . Yon again wiz thi swiffin-sang fae froe,
Thi Burns-sprach oozin fae thi daurk peatpoat
Ah ken's ma muse, hauf weet cunt an hauf leid:
Fae yon bricht hybrid aw thi warld tots,
Peat-moss o Goad, slivery weddir-gaw
Whilk Embro fowk baith lust oan an deny.
Either they caa ma mou a midden-dub,
Oar a demanit thought-bane, prettified
Fur printit towels. Daft rammishes an gowks
Witter oan an oan as if thi nemm wiz Tam
Aikenheid, no Tam o Shantir, as if aw
Wir ramskerie leid wiz jist ane dour stane baa.
Muck-wreistlin Scoatlan, durt's yir histoarie,
Naishunlet aye oabsessed wi kickin baas —
Yi scum yir makars oar cute-gralloch thaim — Ach!
Can yi no see yon hallanshakerlik muck's
Thi stuff that burns fae ma ain peat-claig buiks?
Muckle rairin o thi leid, synthetic leid,
Ane smeek o whilk can taw thi shurg o thi hert,
Is whit's become mair Scoats than onythin
Bicause it's neivir circuat aboot
By peught white-livers, bibliobams, oar proafs.
It mudges oot, lik froe, lik Noah's arks,
Row-chow-tobacco in thi tweddlin goab
Coammun as muck, as shurg hit by thi licht
An sae transmoagrified tae a tunnakil,
Sumhin tae werr inside yous that burns oot
Fae Aibirdeen tae yon Tasmanian Highlands
Oor cri de coeur, wir Ultima Thule o low.
Ah am yir Burns. Ah am in Embro noo,
Phoanin thi warld, dialin an dialin
Thi future o this laun aye vieve wi sang.

Day coups, swaagin,
Simmer-flaws pasperin thi milkmaid's path
Whan the pap o thi hass, eefauld as a rock-doo,
Shaks sangs ayont thi earny-couligs.

In yon king's weathir Ah tak yir haun
By thi pirliewinkie an get yi up tae thi taing.
Oor boadies mell lik thi raise-net fishing,
Lik a kindlie tae Adam's wine.

. . . That again was the whizzing-song from sperm, the Burns-speech oozing from the dark hole from which peat is dug, which I know is my muse, half wet vagina and half language: from that bright hybrid all the world moves with short, childish steps, God's place from which peats are dug, slevering rainbow above the horizon which Edinburgh people both lust after and deny. Either they call my mouth a hole into which a dunghill's sap is collected, or a demeaned merrythought of a fowl, prettified for printed towels. Thoughtless people driven by violent impulses and fools struggle on and on as if the name was Thomas Aikenhead, not Tam o Shanter, as if all language lustful as a ram was just one drab stone ball. Mud-wrestling Scotland, dirt's your history, nationlet always obsessed with kicking balls — you strike your poets on their mouths and prevent them from speaking, or you disembowel them to make them cute — ach! can you not see that suspicious-looking muck is the stuff that burns from my own books that are places built to hold peats? Great roaring of the language, synthetic language, one whiff of which can suck dry like a baby the wet, gravelly subsoil of the heart, is what's become more Scots than anything, because it's never encircled by asthmatic flatterers, bibliofools, and professors. It moves out, like sperm, like boat-shaped clouds, loud, complex game of winding, unwinding, and hugging in the mouth that weaves a cloth where woof vertically crosses warp, common as muck, as mud struck by the light and so transfigured into a garment whose nature has been forgotten, something to wear inside you that burns out from Aberdeen to those Tasmanian Highlands our cri de coeur, our Ultima Thule of desire. I am your Burns. I am in Edinburgh now, phoning the world, dialling and dialling the future of this nation always quick with song.

Day spills over, fluttering like a bird's wing, ground mists that rise from the soil on a hot day turning the Milky Way to samphires, when the uvula, honest as a wild pigeon, shakes songs beyond the tumuli. In those exhalations rising from the earth on a warm day I take your hand by the smallest finger and go with you up to the headland. Our bodies grow intimate like that kind of fishing where part of the net rises and flows and subsides with the tide, like an ancestral claim to water.

Ah amnae cummin toawards yi, Ah'm muivin awa
Doon thi lang perspective. Ah leave yous wi thi leid.
Ah'm stuck in Embro, tea-coasified, deid in Err —
But vivual acors thi hail gloab. Ah've sprang ma trap.
  Ma leid
's in thi spittle o thi livin an atween thi sheets o thi
    dictionars.
It's growin oan thi green screen an amang thi peeg-
    girrin blasts,
Forthens an here. In Glesca an Embro, fae Dundee
    tae Rugglen,
Oan thi Solway, in thi Boardirs, amang too'ir bloacks
    an japanese larches,
Tongue it an dawt it, tak it an mak. Mak luive.

Fae thi drouthy taing heich abune thi flistricks
An fae Embro tae, fae ticht, daurk vennels
Thi sang hails oot, rid, rid lik auld bracken,
Shairp lik whin an deid lik a geantree
Afore spring in this land o Burns.

I am not coming towards you, I am moving away down the long perspective. I leave you with the language. I'm stuck in Edinburgh, turned into a tea-cosy, dead in Ayr (Air) — But alive across the whole globe. I've sprung my trap. My language is in the spittle of the living and between the sheets of the dictionaries. It's growing on the green screen and among the heavy stormshowers, far in the distance and here. In Glasgow and Edinburgh, from Dundee to Rutherglen, on the Solway, in the Borders, among tower blocks and japanese larches, tongue it and fondle it, take it and create. Make love.

From the thirsty tongue of land above the submerged ledges of flat rock rising just to the surface of the water, and from Edinburgh also, from narrow, dark alleyways the song gushes out, red, red like old bracken, sharp like gorse and dead like a wild cherry tree before spring in this land of Burns.

(Thomas Aikenhead was hanged in Edinburgh in 1693 for blasphemous speech; the merrythought is a bone between a fowl's head and neck, sometimes used like a wishbone. The above English translation is close, but not literal, and occasionally tries to bring out the wordplay in the original Scots. Though the name Burns clearly looks towards burning, the word in Scots may mean waters or streams, as well as being the name of the poet.)

CROWD

Slow motion disco where everybody sings different tunes
And dances among shops; personal stereo of journeys
Tangling through June at the corner of Bath Street and Hope
    Street;
A drunk is a boom box, a teenager screams like a hearing aid,
    traffic
Burps and stutters through the democratic noise.
People say 'What?' not 'Pardon', they say 'Hey!' not 'Excuse
    me'. They head
For bargains, phones, ticket booths, children, bunches of
    flowers.
You can only see part of their chests which say words like
    RELAX,
GUINNESS, and I HIKED THE CANYON. They're labelled
    at buttocks and neck.
They dodge among cars, they push through fences, they crowd
So close they're going to shake hands with trees or dismantle
    buildings or squat
On the steps of the Bank of Scotland. A kaleidoscope
Of white noise, a fur of ecstatic static
Rubs against us all and spills, darts, juggles, chooses
As its totem a truncheon of water. Group dynamics
Are obeyed except on Saturdays. Pigeons shit and skid. People
Flirt, bobbing; they must be moving to an unseen orchestra
    of fiddlers,
They must be pamplonaing, they must be giddy, they must
    be late for the beginning.
What are they saying? Something about goats, about fission,
    about cheap carpets,
'Och, no fish n chips, can yous no find a guid chinese?'
Something about offence, reticence, negligence, innocence,
    bridies,
Something about the condition of Cuba. Why are there no
    lost children?
How do the cars know where precisely to go? Why are there
    not collisions
Where old ladies bash boys like dodgems, where carrots
    splatter, where
A horde of Airdrie supporters run amok? 'Whit dae ye mean
    cannabis?'
And all this happens at precisely four o'clock.

William Montgomerie

CITY BOY

Two things I have never seen:
A kingfisher flying,
Nor in a woodland green,
With mast and chestnut lying,
A squirrel red or grey.
Nor have I ever heard
On any summer day
Or night, that laureate bird,
The nightingale. How much
I have seen throughout the year!
What things await, when such
Are still to see and hear?

Glasgow

FERRY TO FIFE

Through the round porthole
in our attic bedroom
waking we watch
the Northsea's edge
slide down the rising sun
slowly

Eyes free to fly
with the white gulls
of memory

of the little ferry to Fife
on Sundays
of the walk through Tayport
to the sanddunes
to lie in a hollow
out of the east wind
in hot sun under a blue sky
all of summer days
till the last ferry
we missed only once
to be rowed home
for half-a-crown each

in our heads our only luggage
a nesting eider
in a hollow place
whose head we had stroked
gently

WOMAN IN A YELLOW CHAIR

In Merano
we shop in the quaint Via dei Portici
buying for the mountains
these soft Tyrolean boots

In the public gardens
a waitress in white blouse and black skirt
brings bottle and glasses
to our table under a magnolia

We sip our wine slowly

Oggi un Concerto

White aprons bring
coffees and icecream
Starched bows have left a ticket
quietly on every table

From warm promenades
the middle class
stroll in sunny gardens

Heute ein Kurkonzert

I snap in colour
Woman in a Yellow Chair
with red tablecloth
blue umbrella
a quiet grey woman drinking coffee

Trentino (South Tyrol)

William Neill

THE INNIS-CHANTER BALL

Mo chreach 's a thanaig, Willie,
but whom do we have here
dressed in the noble *feile*
in the summer of the year? . . .
'Tis the Innis-Chanter *Ceilidh*
that requires that kind of gear.

But I *live* in Innis-Chanter
and I think it is a sin . . .
though no *misgeir* and no ranter
that they just won't let me in
to the dance and song and banter
and the wagging of the chin.

Ochoin a ri, a bhalachan,
such things are not for you . . .
to dance the *Righle Thulachain*
from ten till half past two . . .
with laughter and with frolicking
and big drams of the *stuth*.

Ma bhios na silver buttons *ort*
and *sgian dubh* and hose,
they'll serve you drink until you burst
but you're not one of those
from Chelsea or from Chislehurst
and can't look down your nose.

The Hampstead Highlanders are these,
who've come up for the ball;
none of your teuchters, if you please . . .
No Gaelic in the Hall . . .
amidst the fun and naked knees . . .
at all, at all, at all.

DAURK AN LICHT

Weirin on nou, I wauken ilka morn
et hauf past fower intil an oorie quait,
kennin repentance micht be faur owre late
tae skail the skaith I've dune syne I wes born.
I'm nae Caligula, ye ken, I'll no adorn
the scartin o ma yeuks wi graunder state,
but I mind cantrips mak me gey an blate
tae tell the Unco Guid an thole thair scorn.

Anathema hings owre ma lyart heid.
Socratic sairmons anent 'dreamless sleep'
gang oot the wunnock et yon dowie time.
Maybe I wull get raistit whan I'm deid.
I birk up syne et dawin's cheerie peep:
Hell's aw taen up wi skellums deid langsyne.

AULD DEIL, NEW DEIL

Yon hoose wes biggit for a royal geit,
auncestor o His Lairdship that's jist gane.
O geits or leeshensed bairns he faithert nane,
but sate ahint the writhin wrocht-airn yett
wi nocht tae dae but guzzle an keep het.
Lest o the line, he wes maist timeous taen,
strang drink an foostie phaisant wes his bane.
His yirdin roosed nae wanwordie regrate.

Some weel-aff birkie's bocht the Muckle Hoose;
a browster's brat ettlin tae be a laird,
wha luks asklent at aw wansillert men.

He's keep on the same flunkies, I jalouse;
saumont an fowl in the auld gemmie's gaird.
Auld Nick's awa, but Clootie's hame again.

Tom Berry

NIGHTWATCH

Sleepless in a hotel lounge
I nightwatch
the cold spring dawn,
wind swinging lights
over rainslick streets
beside canals.

Over in the Rijksmuseum
the mindmagic
of the painter from the Rhine
hangs freshly varnished
behind protecting glass.

Ruffed men with guns and dogs
brushmarked into time;
a light signal exploding
across centuries of peat smoke
into days of jet trails
lifting up and out from Schiphol.

Landscape below
seen with a Mondrian eye;
blocks of tulip primaries
and lines like peat markings
draining through mists
over low country
to a sleepless sea
watched night and day.

Isabella Walker

EARDLEY PAINTING

Withered stalks in abstract fields
rank, coarse-grained, straight
from the shoulder.

Let others woo in velvet gloves
lovers of caressing sands.
Here it is
take it or leave it life
grey seas, elemental, rock lashing.

Come let us love
the hard cold creel way
wave-breaking-wave
gut strokes, lightning slashing
white spume, mind tangling
grit clinging, Eardley painting.

Tom Pow

THE CHILDREN OF THE RUSSIAN FAIR

I

This morning huge pale toadstools poke
through the rivermist. Once again the tents and the awnings.
Can it be a year already? A whole year? And so soon
that I must face their children again?

Dribbling in loud and late over the frozen fields
yet still arriving muddy, they refuse all correction —
the closest to contrition, when they huddle before me
muttering darkly, averting sullen, sexless faces.
It's then I catch it — their air of sour-sweet
animal ordure, of thick blue grease and cold sweat.

On Friday afternoons, at their worst, they fidget
interminably, swivelling round on already polished pants,
winding themselves up (I suppose) for the roundabouts
they must take command of come night — threading their way
between fantastical seats with feline agility —
never missing a kopek.

'Is there something wrong with you,' I address
the darkening room, 'that you find it
impossible to sit still?'

II

The slow fizz of their bottled mirth hits me long before
I have finished and they have turned to each other —
even the quietest — drenching the room with laughter.
'Did you hear that?' they shout. 'Did you hear that?'

And they are off, clambering through the broken slats;
trampling all my beloved young seedlings back
into the mire: or whirling torn images around themselves —
little dervishes, their chiffon head-dresses catching

the last of the winter light. The room echoes
as they dunt each stricken metaphor to see
where it can most easily be broken.

Like a distant uncle, who by sheer chance
has stumbled on the perfect gift, I almost love them now,
as I watch them skip away into the dark November evening —
back to the mechanical poetry of roundabouts,
to mongrel puppies and rancid stews.

Their delighted chant still warms them:
'Did you hear him? Did you hear him?
Kak krasnaya krasnaya rosa.
Kak krasnaya rosa.' Crows flapping
in a winter landscape — 'kak kak kak.'

Ron Butlin

PORTRAIT OF A SHADOW-SAILOR

At thirty-five years old
he's halfway round his lifetime's only world
— quite at sea. (*That*, at least, is true).
By day he plays the captain and the crew
whose rank and medals have been tattooed on
— gentle pinpricks cutting to the bone.
At night he lies and listens: the crow's nest sways
almost audibly above, and weighs
out silence for the darkened scene below
— letting the slightest measure only, flow
into his sea-crazed mind.

Tightening his grip upon the helm
(in 'lock-position') the shadow-sailor calms
approaching storms by will-power. He reshapes
the cliffs and waves according to his maps;
their tears and creases mean what he decides
in terms of shallows, hidden reefs. He prides
himself upon a life's experience
of reading charts long out of date: he glides
across the wind-scarred surface, making sense
of every ocean-contour (this one hides
a bogeyman within its childish scrawls,
and that one traps a god). Such reverence!
In these deserted sea-lanes he collides
with ghost-ships — their slow and soundless passage falls
shadowless across his decks and hull.

Sea-wraiths and the demons who preside
upon the ocean-floor advise him; coral
(saturated with the sudden cries
of drowning men) signifies their power.
These are his familiars; their histories
are his; their voices he alone can hear;

their silence is the elemental measure
of despair.
          Thus his world has taken shape:
a place of terror, clashing rocks, the hiss
of cross-run currents, undertows to rip
his soul apart . . .

          His log's kept neat for he believes that this
— i.e. the mastery of words, and clear
calligraphy — improves the truth. His fear,
therefore, must complement the sentence-structure
or be dropped. Each entry's much the same;
new page, top left: 'The heat, the chill, the heaving
sea beneath are everything I know
— yet sometimes I can sense a tide whose flow
runs greater, and carries to a farther shore.
Too briefly, then, I glimpse and recognise
what lies beyond this shadow-sea, these shadow skies . . . '

          As evening falls he watches ocean-colours
and the sun dissolve into each other,
letting their transparency reveal
the night sky and the ocean-floor:

          The heavens' slow creation and destruction
the shadow sailor takes into himself,
letting constellations drift at random:

— until he's made, of stars and minerals,
the darkness his imagination spills
unearthly light upon.

Lorn Macintyre

BLACK CHERRIES

My great-aunt Kirsty died, aged 88, in the Blessed Heart
Nursing Home, Glasgow, last year. Not that she was Catholic;
her husband Tommy had been a shareholder in Rangers football team. But Kirsty seemed to feel safer with the Sisters;
the odour of sanctity mixed with disinfectant?
It was an expensive place to end her days — four hundred
a week, and that didn't include the physiotherapy to try and
get movement back into an arm at least after the stroke. I
visited her once. There was a peephole in the door so that the
nuns could keep an eye on her without disturbing her. The
room had quality fittings, a private bathroom she couldn't
reach. You couldn't make out what she was saying.
To finance herself in the home she'd sold her Clarkston
house to an insurance company in a complicated deal that
would let her go on occupying it for the rest of her life. She
never got home. There was enough capital left to convey her
in some style to the south side cemetery, and then, after a
proper interval, to add her name to Tommy's ostentatious
stone.
I was left the contents of the Clarkston house. After
Tommy's death (a coronary; he was pushing 17 stones) she'd
decanted from a twelve roomed place on Great Western Road,
looking straight into the Botanic Gardens, to this four apartment semi-detached bungalow. The best pieces had had to go
under the hammer because they'd never have gone in the new
door. (Tommy had 20 suits and yards of shoes). There had
been some good pictures, some bought abroad, but they had
to be sold when Tommy's business began to go.
I was glad to get a couple of hundred from a second-hand
man to clear the place, but I kept some of the personal effects.
At one time Tommy had been one of the richest men in Glasgow. Not of the Burrell class (who was?) but loaded enough
to go abroad every year with Kirsty.
There were dozens of albums of photographs, but I hadn't
the space or the interest. My side of the family had never
really approved of Kirsty's marriage, since Tommy had the re-
putation of being a crook. It's a pity I wasn't able to identify

some of the people in the photos: my mother says that Kirsty
claimed to have helped make the Riviera fashionable, and had
seen Scott Fitzgerald water-skiing.

In Kirsty's bureau drawer I came across a marble-coloured
exercise book. Black Cherries was written in fancy italics on
the flyleaf. I thought it was a recipe book, but something
made me flick through it.

It was an old cash-book, but the debits and credits columns
had been used as a diary for 1927. 'At Port Vendres.' It had
been heavily corrected, with question marks and 'no, that's
not right' written in different inks in the margin.

It was always known in the family that Kirsty could have
done better for herself. Her postcards (before my time) were
the kind you kept. I suspect that Kirsty left this diary, to see
what I would do with it. Put it into the black sack with
the other stuff, share papers of Tommy's long since cashed
in?

When I started publishing short stories, then a novel, she
wrote me a note, saying she was following my career with interest, and that we must have a chat sometime. Instead, she
left me her story Black Cherries to destroy or get published.
My changes are minor.

At Port Vendres: Sunday 22nd May 1927
Our third night; only the menu's changed. He's sitting in his
corner. I have never seen finer, whiter hands on a man. He
tugs a black cherry from the stalk, splits it with the blade,
then puts half into his mouth. He holds the other half between thumb and forefinger, as if he's offering it to the
empty chair opposite. Then he closes his eyes and eats both
halves very slowly.

What a sad face. Has his wife left him? That's what I said
to Tommy before we came down to dinner. The name Hotel
du Commerce gives it away. Of course we could afford something much better, but I want *atmosphere*. (This place reminds
me of the boarding-house Mummy used to take us to at
Rothesay; a room filled with the tang of sea).

I smile at this stranger; he smiles back. He must be in his
fifties; almost bald, with a fleshy kindly face. He could be my
father. Tommy and I never converse while he's eating. He's
got the determination of the self-made man. Bones are
sucked. His trouble is that he never relaxes. Imagine, trying
to send a telegram to his foreman on a Sunday; another building his firm's demolishing. At this rate there'll be nothing left

of Glasgow.
He's folding his napkin carefully. I smile as he passes and
he nods. The table looks so sad, with the sprig of cherry-
stalk lying on the plate between the two empty chairs, like a
little bit of burnt-out lightning.
I ask Tommy if he minds me going out for a cigarette. He
shakes his head because his mouth's full of cherries. He'll eat
my share too, then wake in the night with indigestion. I
worry about his heart.
I go out onto the balcony. He's standing staring out to
sea, smoke rising above his shoulder. I light up too. But I'm
nervous and I spill the matches. He comes to help me pick
them up. We're all fingers together; his are so soft; immaculate
nails. (Tommy has half of Glasgow under his).
'This is kind of you,' I say. He has to help me up by the
arm, my flapper's dress (bought, Paris) is so tight.
'Just a little accident.'
'I *knew* you were Scottish,' I say, using the last match to
light my cigarette. (I fit mine into a holder; it's healthier.
Tommy's a forty a day man; his fingers are filthy).
'Which part of Scotland are you from?'
He looks anxious. 'Glasgow.'
'That's where I'm from too,' I tell him. 'North or south
side? I know — you're south, like me.'
But he's turned away, to look at the sea. 'The colours
here are amazing. It's difficult to tell where the sea stops and
the sky begins.'
I know why he doesn't want to talk; he's watching for
the boat bringing back his wife. It won't come. He looks
abandoned. But what business is this of mine? (Tommy gets
on at me for worrying over stray dogs in France).
'The tobacco here's become so harsh since the Americans
took over production,' he says. 'My tongue's been swollen
up; that's why I'm on these cigarillos.'
'Take these.' I hand him my packet of Craven A. Tommy's
got a whole suitcase full in the bedroom. He's no respecter of
customs.
'No, I'll persevere with these,' he says. Then: 'Did you
have some of the black cherries?'
I'm taken completely by surprise. 'No,' I say, but I can't
tell him why not. What is a 25 year old doing following a
man who could be her father out of the *salle à manger* of a
rather rundown Port Vendres hotel? (Tommy's calling this
my Bohemian holiday).

'I don't like cherries.' What else can I say? I gave mine to
Tommy so that I could follow him out.
  'That's a tragedy because they're so big and juicy. I
wonder if they would keep in the post' (he's looking out to
sea as he says this). Then: 'I've got a letter to finish. *Bonsoir.*'
  When I go back in Tommy's devoured all the cherries. It's
a wonder he didn't chew the stalks too. This is the worry; a
sixteen stone 35 year old man on top of you after such a
meal.
  After he falls asleep I go through his suitcase and find this
account book. I tear out the few pages he's done calculations
on. I've never done anything like this before, but I have a
feeling I should keep a diary on this holiday. Tommy mustn't
see it, of course.

Monday 23rd May
Wind shrieking all night, turning the net curtains into that
crazy dancer we saw on top of a table — *nothing* below her
white dress — at Antibes last summer. What else but an American? But even this gale can't get the better of Tommy's snoring and grunting. He must be trying to push over a building.
  I'm lying thinking about the mysterious Glaswegian in
the corner extolling the virtues of black cherries (can cherries
have *virtues*?) Maybe he's a buyer in food, looking for goodies
for a Glasgow restaurant. But he doesn't look the commercial
type.
  I would say that he's been at this hotel for some time, the
way he goes to his table. But by the time we get down to
breakfast he's been, or not eating it; his napkin seems to be
folded exactly as it was last night, like a little white envelope.
  It's still very blowy, but I want some fresh air, and we
could just bump into him. I've such a job keeping my dress
from going over my head. Tommy doesn't want to walk; he'd
rather sit in a cafe and — would you believe this? — price a
demolition job for Glasgow? I'm not going to complain,
though; I've got my mysterious Glaswegian (I reckon from
his hands that he's a musician) to find out about.
  I try to hurry Tommy down to dinner, even tying his
shoelaces for him. He insists on wearing his white double-
breasted suit, which means we have to find a cleaners every
second day. But he won't be hurried; he says it's like bringing
down a building. Rush it and accidents happen.
  He isn't at his table! I'm trying to see if it's a new napkin,
which means that he's gone. But if I move my chair Tommy

may get suspicious. What a pity my Glaswegian isn't here, because there are black cherries again. I can have some tonight,
though I'm watching the door as I pop them into my mouth.
They seem bitter.
I go out to smoke on the balcony, leaving Tommy with
my cheese. He's like a giant white mouse nibbling and splut-
tering. (God, he'd better not read this!)
I feel very lonely, standing there at the railing, staring out
to sea. Has he gone in search of the occupant of the other
chair? Will two of them come back to share the same stalk of
black cherries? Maybe I read too many novels, but you need
a bit of romance in Glasgow. I have a husband who comes
home late.
Oh not tonight. Tommy making love is a demolition job.

Tuesday 24th May
Doze off and you miss the night here, it's so brief. I'm back
lying in the light of an August dawn in Glasgow, waiting for
Daddy to come up and kiss me before going off to the war.
I'm frightened of the squeak squeak of his new boots. They
must hurt.
Then I hear a crash on the stairs. Burglars! By the time I
wake Tommy, they'll be miles away. Besides, he'll just say:
it's not our business, as long as they haven't pinched anything
from this room (especially the tenders he's pricing).
I open the door very quietly and peep out. It's him, going
downstairs, laden. Now where on earth's he off to at this
hour? Sneaking away because he can't afford to pay his bill?
Tommy's still snoring, but I'm getting up. Off with the
negligee (another present from Tommy; transparent of course)
and on with cool white cotton.
I run downstairs in my bare feet, out into the street, but
there's not a sign of my mysterious Glaswegian. When
Tommy comes down to breakfast (after I've smoked five
cigarettes) he announces: 'I'm going to hire a car and drive
along the coast.'
I'm aghast: 'But it'll be blazing hot; we'll both get sunstroke, and you know you're too stout.'
'Not if we take simple precautions.'
Oh God, does that mean that he's going to buy a straw
hat? It's not that I don't want to see the sea and maybe go
for a swim. It's Tommy's driving: last year in a village near
Cannes (name best forgotten) he ran into the local market.
Strawberries went flying everywhere, down my dress, into

the car. The gears were squelchy. The whole car had to be stripped down.

Fortunately there isn't a car for hire today in Port Vendres. Tommy's perspiring so much that we have to sit in the shade of a cafe. He soon nods off; safe enough for me to take a stroll by myself. Did I really only marry him for his money; because he swept up our crescent in an open imported American car, boasting that he had fifty men on his books? Wasn't I too young?

At dinner the mysterious Glaswegian is back at his corner table. Pea soup; dover sole; aubergines; roast beef; followed by red instead of black cherries. They look delicious, but I'm frightened to take one in case he's watching. There are some people you don't deceive.

He's certainly enjoying them, splitting them with his knife, keeping them in his mouth a long time as he looks at the empty chair. This time I go out first onto the balcony. I'm beginning to think he's gone straight up to his room, but here he is.

'How is your tongue?'

He looks surprised. 'I beg your pardon?'

'Your tongue; you were having trouble with American tobacco.'

He laughs. 'Oh I've solved that one. I spread it in the sun to dry out the sauce they saturate it in. But I'll stay on these cigarillos just now.'

Here we are chatting, when we haven't even exchanged names.

'I'm Kirsty Boyle.' My hand is the first out.

'Mackintosh'; a slack grip.

Tommy comes shuffling out, white suit spattered with cherry juice.

'Mr Mackintosh is from Glasgow,' I say. 'This is my husband Tommy.'

In a row I had with Mummy before my marriage she called Tommy an oaf; I thought it was the strain of Daddy and the war. Tommy grunts and nods as he makes for the nearest chair.

'You look pale, Tommy,' I say. 'Shouldn't you go and lie down?'

'You have to be very careful with the cherries; make sure they're properly washed,' Mr Mackintosh tells him.

'What do you want me to do? Go through to the kitchen sink with them, then take them back to the dining-room? I pay for service, even in a dump like this,' says Tommy, tapping the chair arm.

He shames me every time in public now. Some people think he's my father, and though it's a slight, I don't speak up.

'I must go and finish a letter,' Mr Mackintosh says, taken aback.

'Tommy, why must you *behave* like that?'

'It was a bloody stupid thing to say about washing the cherries.'

'Mr Mackintosh has been staying here for some time and knows.'

'If you think this place is dirty, let's move then — *tonight*. You know I prefer bigger places. I like to be near a casino.'

'No, no.' I mustn't sound too hasty. 'I like the atmosphere here.'

Tommy falls asleep as soon as he hits the bed, which is a blessing. It's like a wall falling on one. Strange: as I write down Mr Mackintosh's words, I can hear his voice clearly, as if he's dictating.

Wednesday 25th May

I haven't shut my eyes. I've been lying, deliberately looking at the window and then at the little diamond watch Tommy gave me when he demolished a whole street in Glasgow. I'm up at six thirty, dressing very simply (white cotton for coolness; sandals). Then I sit on the bed, waiting.

I sat like that in Glasgow, until the light faded, day after day. Mummy kept saying: he'll be home any day now, you'll see; but he never came.

When I hear the click of his door I count to twenty. Then I go downstairs. He's about a hundred yards ahead of me, an easel under one arm, folding stool under the other. One leg seems to drag. I want to run up, to take the box of paints, he looks so pathetic, but that would only make it seem that I'm spying on him. So I let him get a little further ahead, but not out of sight.

We're leaving the village and it's getting very hot. My toes are on fire in the dust and I'm wishing that I'd worn shoes. In the heathaze Mr Mackintosh seems to be shimmering as if he's about to explode, easel and stool sent flying, his straw hat spinning away.

We're walking close to the cliffs now, past the old forts.

When he stops and sets down his stuff, I slip behind a rock. It's no use; I'm too close. I must give him time to get ahead, except that I could easily lose him here — and myself. Now he's taking off his jacket and folding it carefully, before he sets up his easel. He looks much younger, in his green corduroys. He's settled on the folding stool and has a brush in his hand.

I can't see the painting from this distance, so I count up to 100. Then I begin to walk forward as casually as I can, with my hands behind my back. But I know I'm taking too big strides, as if I'm stalking something. I don't want to startle him, so I cough as I get closer. The brush stops.

'It's Mr Mackintosh, isn't it?' (God, that sounded so forced).

He stands up. (This man is a gentleman; if Her Majesty herself came into a room Tommy would remain on his backside; he only rises to shake hands over deals).

'Don't let me disturb you; I'm only taking a walk before breakfast.' Then: 'May I stay and watch?' (I'm making such a mess of this).

'By all means.'

I'm standing at his shoulder. His shirt collar's worn beneath the straw brim. I would like to touch his neck. But when I look at the brush I get a shock. What on earth's he painting?

I lean closer. Like grey jagged tombstones all piled together. I look beyond the paper on the easel. It's incredible, I would never have seen those rocks, with the sea beyond, like that. How has he managed to compress them into such a small sheet, and still show their power?

'I'm suffering from a green disease; I should have painted the big grey rock first.' At least that's what I *think* he said; he was really muttering to himself.

Are these buildings in the background? But I don't want to lean any closer. It seems to me that my breathing could disturb that brush. I stand, or rather lean in silence, as if I'm not there.

Mackintosh; I'm going to have to be very careful here not to show my ignorance. I don't recall hearing that name in Glasgow. Mind you, Tommy wouldn't put a penny into paintings. (Not that he leaves walls standing to hang them on. His idea of art's the dirty magazines he buys in Paris).

How am I going to do this?

'Mr Mackintosh — '

'Ye-s.' The brush dabs.
'You're obviously a professional painter.'
'I don't know what you mean by professional.'
Neither do I. He must be able to feel the heat from my
face. Why don't I just go instead of making a fool of myself?
(That's the advantage of men like Tommy, they're easy to
handle; no deep subjects).
'It's your livelihood,' I say.
'Not yet, but I'm hopeful.'
Now what does that mean?
'Yesterday the wind kept blowing the easel down. Today
— *look*.'
I bend till our faces are almost touching. What I took to
be part of the painting are hundreds of tiny crawling insects,
all different, some with shimmering wings.
'I like to give them the chance to get out of the way of
the brush.' He blows gently. 'Otherwise they become fossilised
in the paint; that's too close to nature; a still-life Cézanne
would never have approved of.'
I nod; I know that name. I took Art in school. I could
have made something of it, but Tommy's big American car
came up the crescent. I was good at embroidery, but it
couldn't be both marriage and college.
'I need good weather because I'm hoping to have an exhibition soon,' Mr Mackintosh says.
'In Glasgow? Tell me when, so I can go and see it. Will
they be for sale?'
He shakes his head. 'Definitely not Glasgow. If it comes
off it'll be in London at the Leicester Gallery. They'll all be
for sale; that's what an exhibition's for. But it all depends on
the weather.'
Is this a hint for me to go away? Not that Tommy will
wait for me for breakfast; more likely to eat mine.
'How long are you staying?' I ask.
'Indefinitely. The climate suits us — despite the none too
gentle zephyrs.'
Us? 'Oh — you're here with someone.' Question or state-
ment?
'My wife. She's in London just now, having electrical
treatment.'
I've read about that; wires stuck to the skull; shocking
pain. The poor soul; so that's why he looks so sad, with a
mental wife. That's why he's got to finish the paintings, to
get money for her treatment.

There are some conversations which you have to let come to a natural end. I go back to the hotel, but I don't feel like breakfast. When I tell Tommy that I've been for a walk to clear a headache, he nods, his mouth stuffed with food. He always demands bacon and eggs when he's abroad, making himself understood with sign language; an open mouth. (You should see him ordering snails).

We sit on the balcony, but a south wind's getting up, flapping Tommy's newspaper, which irritates me. Probably his easel's been blown over. I can see him struggling with it, painting the rock (who would buy such a subject?) to pay for his mad wife's shock treatment.

He comes back about lunch-time, lugging his equipment. I go up to our room, hoping to meet him. I stand outside his door. The one opposite is open; the foot of a bed.

Rosa the *patronne* comes at my back.

'Cette chambre est déjà prise.'

I don't understand what she means.

'La femme de ce pauvre Monsieur Mackintosh est à Londres.' She clasps her heart with both hands.

At least, that's what I *think* she's saying, she speaks so fast. But I don't want to let her go till I find out more. She's trying to tell me how much in love they are; that's why the door's left open, so he can see her bed.

'Monsieur Mackintosh est un artiste.'

'Oui, oui,' she nods vigorously. 'Mais (finger wagged) il est aussi un gentilhomme.'

I suppose (with what one reads about Picasso) that there is a distinction.

'Madame Mackintosh — elle est' — damn it, I don't know what I want to ask, so I hold up my hand level.

'Ah, très grande, et elle a une chevelure magnifique' (shows with her hands.) 'Comme une Comtesse.'

I picture this tall beautiful woman with a weak head. It gets sadder and sadder. I'm trying to muster my appalling command of the language (Tommy thinks that everyone should speak English on the continent) but a bell goes, and the *patronne* plunges down the stairs.

Tommy is threatening to hire a car again. I suppose I must let him, because the more he hangs about the hotel, the more he eats. (The white suit's almost too tight). Anyway, here comes that south wind again (I wet my finger and hold it up), so Mr Mackintosh is going to have a struggle with his painting.

We get a car, but the garage insists that Tommy wears goggles because of the dust. He now looks like a very large frog. He goes too fast along the coast road for me to take in anything. When he was courting me first in Glasgow, I used to think it was daredevil, the way he overtook even trams on Great Western Road; now I think he's just dangerous.

Do I any longer, did I ever love this man, I ask myself as the Med blurs by. I'm now beginning to dread going back to Glasgow with him.

Dinner tonight; lamb with haricots. My carnivore husband is in ecstasy, his napkin tucked into his neck, his plate heaped with slices of meat. Mr Mackintosh seems to be enjoying his also, but he eats as he paints; slow, studied.

I go out for a smoke before I get drenched in gravy. The sky is clouding over; I really should go up for a cardigan.

Me: 'Did you make any progress with the Rock today?'

Mr M: (lighting his cigarillo). 'It got windy about midday, but I'm fairly pleased with the morning's work. I went for a walk up to the Fort this afternoon; the genista's wonderful.'

Me: 'Genista?'

Mr M: 'Broom. It seems to have appeared suddenly, as if by magic; so yellow, such scent. I'll have to tell my wife about it in the letter; it's a great pity she's missing it.'

Me: 'Have you any news of how she's getting on in London?'

Mr M: (sadly) 'No letter today; probably tomorrow. But I think the electrical treatment's working.'

But how can she write him sensible letters if that's what she's getting? Poor soul; he writes, telling her everything that's going on (including the inquisitive Glasgow woman with the gluttonous husband) but she can't take in a word because of the volts.

Me: 'It's wonderful what they can do nowadays.'

Mr M: 'She would never complain; I hope it's not painful.'

Me: (not convincing) 'I shouldn't think so.'

Mr M: 'It's supposed to stimulate the heart.'

So that's what the *patronne* meant when she clutched her left breast! Not love (that's inherent), but a weak heart being treated. That means I can go on talking to him, without being frightened of saying (*asking*) the wrong thing.

But he obviously senses this because he puts out his smoke and says he's got to go and finish his letter 'to my wife. It turns into a kind of a chronicle; a bit of writing, a bit of painting and so on. Incidentally, how *do* you spell chronicle?'

I think I get it right.

Mr M: 'That's a pity; I've been spelling it with a y instead of an i.'

Me: 'What does it matter, as long as your wife understands?'

Tommy's drunk far too much tonight. He seems to get heavier every day. This bed is going to give soon. I mustn't let him drive Mr Mackintosh's words (he said a lot today) out of my head before I can get them down in my chronicle. Why do I feel they're so important?

Thursday 26th May
I wake in the dawn, but it's dull, drizzling; no sound of the artist afoot. Mr Mackintosh is in the dining-room. There are only the three of us, and Tommy is dumb and droopy with a hangover.

The maid is explaining something to Mr Mackintosh. I listen very hard, trying to keep up. Today's Ascension? Un fête? Mr Mackintosh looks very glum.

Mr M: 'Pas de courrier?'

The maid shrugs.

Because it's not walking weather we go into the lounge. Mr Mackintosh is reading the News of the World, with the Despatch on the table. This pleases Tommy no end. He offers Mr Mackintosh a Craven A in exchange for a read at the Despatch.

'Help yourself,' says Mr Mackintosh, but refuses the cigarette.

Tommy spends the morning in the stock exchange page, which means that I can't speak to Mr Mackintosh. It's maddening. I try to will Tommy to fall asleep, but when it comes to money he's wide-awake. Ask him to read a book, though.

Mr Mackintosh goes out and I don't see him till dinner. Just as I'm about to follow him out Tommy says: 'I want to go to a casino tonight.'

'We're not going near one,' I tell him angrily. 'The last time you lost thousands of francs.'

'That's French money.'

'It doesn't matter; it's still too much when you convert it into our money.'

'But the business is doing well,' he says. 'And there's another big contract coming up which somebody in the Corporation told me I would get.'

'Go tonight and that's us finished,' I warn him. But people

at the other tables are beginning to look at us, so I hurry out. Too late; Mr Mackintosh has had his smoke and gone upstairs. I pick the warm stump of the cigarillo from the ashtray. Damn Tommy; if he puts a hand near me tonight — why am I writing down what *he* says?

Friday 27th May

A glorious dawn; not a breath of wind. I hear him go out at seven, but I've been up, dressed, for a good hour, looking at Tommy lying there, with his loud mouth even when he's sleeping. Mummy was right; a great mistake. I should have done something useful with my life.

Since I know where he's going there's no need to follow him so fast. By the time I arrive he's painting.

Me: 'The Rock will soon be finished.'

Mr M: 'God willing, if I get a few more days of this weather.'

I stand behind him, making sure I don't cast a shadow.

Me: 'If you'll have your show in Glasgow instead of London I'll bring all my friends to buy your paintings.'

The brush hesitates.

Mr M: 'I'll never show a picture in Glasgow. I doubt if I'll ever set foot in the place again.'

Something very bad obviously happened to him in Glasgow: but how to put it without prying?

Me: 'That's very sad, when it's your home city.'

Mr M: 'It never showed me much — '

Let a few seconds pass; hold your breath.

Mr M: 'I'm quite pleased with the way this is shaping.'

I can't ask him about Glasgow again.

Me: 'Will you teach me to paint?'

It's not an impulsive question. I've been thinking about it for most of the night. It's a way of going back; that's what Daddy would have wanted. I'll make Tommy stay out here for a few more weeks, or else leave me here. Then? Back to Glasgow, to college.

Mr M: 'I can't teach anyone to paint because I'm still learning myself.'

Me: 'I could pay you for lessons.'

Mr M: (shaking his head) 'It wouldn't be fair on either of us.'

The conversation appears to have come to a halt. I'd better leave now, before I spoil his painting. But I'm close to tears as I go back through the hot dawn, carrying a sandal in each hand. I suppose I've always been used to having my own way. But I really would love to work with him, sitting beside him, with my arms and feet bare in the sun while he leans over, touching my drawing with his gentle hand, showing me where I've gone wrong.

I sit on the balcony of the hotel, dozing off because I've been getting up so early. I'm back in Glasgow, waiting for my father to return (he volunteered for the Commercial Company). Every time I hear the letter-box —

Someone's shouting. I dash into the hall, thinking that Tommy's dropped dead! Mr Mackintosh is standing there, laden with his painting equipment. The *patronne*'s pointing with three fingers up the stairs, shouting: 'voilà sur le lit!'

Is it a mouse? He puts down his things in a heap and hurries upstairs, pursued by the *patronne*, still shouting. She emerges, clasping her hands.

'Une lettre! Une lettre de la Comtesse!'

I'm half-way up the stairs. Suddenly I feel jealous, thinking of him sitting up there, devouring her letter. Tommy has never sent me one in his life; not even a card. He saves his calligraphy for a scrawl on demolition contracts.

After lunch I go back out onto the balcony. It's a bit overcast, but still warm. At about four I see Mr Mackintosh going out for a walk. I feel like running after him. Then I do something I'm ashamed to put down on paper. I go out into the hall, making sure the *patronne*'s not about before I tip-toe upstairs.

The door of Mrs Mackintosh's room is still open. It's very neat, all the clothes put away, nothing on the dressing-table. I expect she's taken her toilet stuff to London with her. I would like to look at her clothes but I'm afraid the wardrobe will squeak. The room seems rather cold.

There's a photograph of two people on the wall. I have to kneel on the bed to see it. It's him, younger. How handsome he is; dark hair, stylish swept-up moustache (almost like some of the *gigolos* we saw in Italy several summers ago; Tommy had another word for them) and his tie a huge floppy bow. He looks so free, at ease, not like he is now.

She's standing close to him, between them a kind of panel (a painting waiting to be hung?) of tall figures and what looks like foliage I'm certain I've seen somewhere before. The way it flows, it's very different from the Rock.

She's taller than he is; beautiful; auburn looking hair. I love her dress. (She must be an artist herself, maybe an

embroiderer). I could stay for hours on my knees, looking at
them, but I'm terrified the *patronne* will come up. The way
she talks, this room is a shrine.

It's so tempting to open a drawer and find out who he is,
once and for all, because they both look *distinguished* people.
(I certainly don't mean socially; not that you could take
Tommy anywhere in Glasgow). But I daren't touch anything
in here.

At dinner I compare him with the photograph above our
heads. He's still a good looking man, though more reserved in
the way he dresses. He has this peculiar habit I haven't mentioned before. He gets a full bottle of wine with every meal,
and drinks it down to exactly half, which he leaves. The next
meal it's a full bottle again. Surely the *patronne*'s not charging
him for a full bottle each time? (Tommy can drink down two
bottles at each meal, and drain my glass. He's also got whisky
upstairs. I think he's getting heavy on it).

Cherries (red) again tonight. But he doesn't touch them!
He's rising, nodding as he goes out. I give him five minutes.

Me: 'Are you all right?'

Mr M: 'You're lucky, not eating these cherries. They've
been overripe; I've had an upset stomach for a few days.'

(Tommy's been stuffing them; it's a wonder his gut's
not fermenting with all that drink and food).

Me: 'Does that mean work on the Rock has stopped?'

Mr M: 'No, I've managed to keep going; I must get it
finished for the exhibition.'

Me: 'Will you stay here all summer?'

Mr M: 'No; once my wife gets back, we'll go up to Mont
Louis when it starts to get really hot. We do that every
summer.'

Me: (surprised) 'How long have you been out here?'

Mr M: 'Let me see — since 1923.'

Me: 'Lucky *you*.'

Mr M: (going quiet again) 'I wouldn't say that. It's getting
chilly, isn't it? I hope this doesn't mean a change.'

Me: 'We'll both pray hard for sunshine so that the Rock
can be finished.'

Mr M: 'If I got the whole of tomorrow — '

But here comes Tommy. Well if he thinks I'm going to
the cleaners again tomorrow he's mistaken.

Tommy: 'These cherries are terrific; I don't know why
you won't take them.'

He's going to embarrass me in front of Mr Mackintosh,

telling him how I eat cherries in Glasgow.

Mr M: 'They've certainly upset me.'

'And you're the one who went on and on about washing them,' Tommy says, shaking his head. 'You're havering, Mister; I've been eating them every night and there's nothing wrong with me.'

At that moment I wish that Tommy was standing under one of his own buildings. Why do I come to the continent with such a savage?

I make my resolution as I lie in bed, having persuaded Tommy to have another nightcap of Johnnie Walker instead of his conjugal rights (such rights are usually one-sided, weighted in favour of the man.) Since Mr Mackintosh won't teach me to paint, I'll sell the diamond watch in Port Vendres and buy the Rock from him. Obviously he won't part with it before the exhibition, but he can put my name on the back and have it sent to Glasgow to me. By then I hope to be independent of Tommy.

Saturday 28th May

A lovely morning; he goes out at 6.30. I must give him an hour. But he's not there! I *can't* have come to the wrong place; there's the Rock, the buildings behind it. Did he take ill on the way? But I would have met him.

Of course I didn't see him leave the hotel. He may have taken all his things and gone because he thinks I've been pestering him. I sit down on a fallen tree, my fists clenched. I really felt I was making a friend, somebody I could talk to. Tommy's diamond watch flares on my wrist; I feel like taking it off and throwing it as far as I can.

I make my way slowly back to the hotel, dragging my sandals through the dust. I'll stop in a cafe for a drink, then go and tell Tommy that I can't stand it any more. I want more for my life than money from ruined buildings.

I can't stay here, because that will mean taking money from Tommy. No; I'll go back to Glasgow alone and get a job, so that I can get money for college. I really want to better myself. There are things Mr Mackintosh says about art. If I don't understand them at the time, how can I write them later in my chronicle?

But Tommy isn't in the hotel. He'll be away at the post office, sending another of his telegrams to his foreman. We're booked in here for another week; I want to go this afternoon. I can stay with Mummy for a while.

142 LORN MACINTYRE

Who do I see from the balcony walking along the street? I don't care; I rush out to meet Mr Mackintosh. I could hug him.
Me: 'I went to the Rock but you weren't there. I've been so worried that you'd been taken ill somewhere because of the cherries.'
Mr M: 'That's very considerate of you' (he means it). 'But I went to draw the Fort instead. I have to keep several works going at the one time if I'm to have forty paintings for my Leicester Gallery exhibition.'
He's put his drawing folder down on the reception desk. CRM is painted in stylish black letters. This is my chance, at last. I take a deep breath.
Me: (touching the folder) 'What does CRM stand for?'
Mr M: 'It was a lovely morning.'
I have to risk it, because I know that this is the last opportunity I'll have, so I repeat myself.
Mr M: (with great reluctance): 'Charles Rennie Mackitosh.'
I try not to show in my face that I'm no wiser. But I can't offend him by dropping it, so I have to think quickly because he's now got his drawing folder under his arm, his foot on the bottom step.
Me: 'I think I've seen some of your paintings in Glasgow.'
Mr M: 'Really? You couldn't have seen them in a gallery; it must have been in a private house. A few of my friends have one or two. We must have mutual friends.'
I want to change the subject, but he's watching me closely.
Me: 'I just don't know; but your name means something to me. It's going to niggle at me all day.'
He hesitates, his hand on the banister.
Mr M: I wasn't a full-time painter in Glasgow. I was an architect.'
This is getting out of hand; he must be able to feel the heat from my face.
Me: 'That's what it is; I've seen your name on a building.'
Mr M: 'But my name isn't on anything I built in Glasgow; not that I built very much.'
Me: 'Name some of them, then I'll know.'
Mr M: (reluctantly) 'Well, there's the Art School, and Miss Cranston's tearooms — '
I know it now! I'm a wee girl again. Daddy doesn't work on Saturday afternoon. I fetch the horn so that he can put on his brightest boots. He's getting his watchchain looped across his waistcoat. Half-way up Sauchiehall Street I begin

to girn, and he has to carry me.

It's always the same ritual. Up the strange stairs in his arms; through the glass doors that look like broken bits of mirror stuck together. He sits me down on the high-backed silver chair.

Here's the game. I have to peep round the chair, staring at the big panel on the wall. Daddy says that as soon as I see the fairy queen stepping from the panel, I've to wish for something nice.

When I turn round, there's a big creamy cake on my plate, and a funny looking spoon to eat it with. I always get cream on my chin, but Daddy wipes it with the handkerchief from his breast pocket.

That's the panel that's between Mr and Mrs Mackintosh in her bedroom upstairs. I would like to tell him that his Room de luxe in the Willow Tearoom, Miss Cranston's, was a magic grotto to a wee girl; but Daddy didn't come back from France, and I've never set foot since in the Willow. (Is it still there?)

Me: 'I think I'll go and lie down; the sun's given me a headache.'

I slept through dinner. When Tommy came up, drunk, I pretended to be still sleeping. He soon gave up.

Sunday 29th May

I am down early to breakfast, but Mr Mackintosh is already there. Is he going queer? He sweeps his hand slowly over his wife's chair, as if trying to summon up her spirit. Then he holds his hand up against the glare of the window-pane. There is a membrane of a cobweb between his spread fingers.

When he passes my table he asks: 'Are you feeling better this morning?'

I'm confused.

Mr M: 'Your headache?'

Me: 'Oh, that's gone; I had a sound sleep. And you: will the Rock be finished today?'

He shakes his head. 'I never work on a Sunday.'

He obviously sees my disappointment because he says: 'I'm going for a walk; would you like to come?'

We are walking in a cool shaded place of trees and flowers, perfume in the air.

Mr M: 'We call this Happy Valley; my wife and I often come here.'

Me: 'Will she be coming back soon?'

Mr M: 'A few more weeks; I'll take the train to Perpignan to meet her.'

Me: 'You'll have done more paintings by then?'

Mr M: (laughing) 'If I don't she'll think I've been lying in my letters. I write every day, but may not post it for several days. I have to watch the weight, for the cost.' I stumble where stone is exposed. He has my arm.

Me: 'Why did you give up being an architect in Glasgow?' (I could add: there must be plenty of opportunity, the number of buildings my husband's knocking down).

Mr M: 'It didn't work out, for various reasons; I don't like talking about it. When the past goes wrong, you have to try and put it behind you.' Just like me, with Tommy.

Mr M: 'Anyway, I'm a painter now, or trying to be. Paper's easier to work with than stone. You don't need to get planning approval, and you can tear it up if you aren't satisfied.'

Me: 'Does your wife paint?'

Mr M: 'No, but she believes in me; that's the great thing.'

Me: 'Does your wife — '

Mr M: 'I think we'd better turn now, before we get sunstroke. Look at that.'

He pulls out the pocket of his green corduroy trousers, to show me the hole.

Mr M: 'I've probably lost money through that.'

Me: 'I'll sew it after dinner'; I've got a little kit in my room, and a husband who's always tearing things.

Mr M: 'Thank you; but I'll ask the *patronne*.'

Me: 'She thinks the world of you — and Mrs Mackintosh.'

Mr M: 'We've been there a long time, summer and winter. I suppose it's our home now. In fact' (he stops) 'I would like my ashes scattered here.'

There are a lot of smart motor-cars parked outside the hotel, and the dining-room is quite full. Two little children have been put at Mr Mackintosh's table. (The parents are at the next one, with even more children).

They look angelic, sitting either side of him, the little girl in Mrs Mackintosh's chair. But then they start kicking at each other under the table, and poor Mr Mackintosh's shins get in the way. Still, he smiles through it all.

I am on the balcony with my cigarette after lunch.

Mr M: 'There's a sailing ship in the harbour, crammed full of wine.'

Me: 'Perhaps we should stow away on it.'
Mr M: 'No; I think I've done enough moving about. Anyway I only like wine in moderation.'
Tommy comes in behind us, searching for Sunday papers. He drank a bottle with his lunch.
Me: 'Tommy, Mr Mackintosh is an architect. He built the Glasgow Art School.'
Tommy: 'That's the place above Sauchiehall Street?'
Mr Mackintosh nods, pleased.
Tommy is sucking his Craven A alight. Then: 'It would be a difficult demolition job because of all that glass.'
Mr Mackintosh is no longer there. I slap Tommy; then I run upstairs. But the *patronne* is standing outside his door, waving her arms.
'Non, non, il écrit (she scribbles on her palm) à la Comtesse.'

Monday 30th May
I have had a dream; my father with bloody face, his uniform in tatters, staggering out of the Mackintosh mural in the Room de luxe.
    I listen for Mr Mackintosh going. He's probably slipped out early, quietly, after Tommy's insult. I've decided; as soon as the shops open I'm going to sell the diamond watch, and go and find Mr Mackintosh. I want the strength of the Rock on my wall in whatever future I have.
    But it's a grey morning, with mist swirling in. There will be no work done on the Rock today, by the looks of it; but I'm still determined to buy it in advance.
    Mr Mackintosh is at breakfast. He nods to me. He doesn't look angry about Tommy's insult. (I shall explain to him later what I'm married to).
    The *patronne* comes in and puts a telegram on Tommy's napkin. I look at it upside down and see the Glasgow postmark. We've still got another week here, and I want longer. I'll make him buy me a paintbox today.
    I would tear up that envelope on his plate, except that the *patronne* (obviously a gossip) will tell him about it. Mr Mackintosh is now breaking bread in his fists.
    Tommy opens the envelope with a filthy finger. Then he rises again.
    'Got to get moving,' he says.
    I turn the telegram round.

SERIOUS TROUBLE OVER FINNIESTON
CONTRACT stop Macleod foreman
Me: (vehemently) 'I'm not having my holiday interrupted
by that. You can go.'
Tommy stands over me, his big gut pressing against my
arm.
'This is about money; you can't stay.'
I look for Mr Mackintosh but he's left the hotel. As I
pack, crying, the fog lifts like a curtain. There are three huge
grey battleships outside the harbour. I must put this book
into my luggage.

Postscript
Charles Rennie Mackintosh died in London in 1928, from a
cancer that had started in his tongue.
The Rocks is now the property of a private collector in
England.

Valerie Thornton

ONLY THIS

Jim has brought some dumpling, he said, there's a piece for you too.
Dumpling. The stuff you get in the butcher, shiny brown slices with liberal quantities of little black currants, hard and burnt tasting, sometimes with nasty little crunchy bits of stem or pip left in. Dumpling which the butcher gathers with hands bloody from mince and livers. He slaps the slices on the weighing machine's spattered surface and wraps them up with the raw sausages. Sometimes there's little red bits clinging to the cooked dumpling which you have to pick off. Dumpling with plastic round the outside, which you grill with the sausages and black pudding and which always burns hard and dry. The only dumpling now.
His mum made it for his father's birthday or something, he adds.
A vague memory stirs, but you let it rest.
Until you feel peckish and wander through to the kitchen. The dumpling's in the cupboard, wrapped in an opaque polythene bag, hidden from the cats. As soon as you open the bag, the smell seduces you, melts the years, dissolves the present. A smell unknown for what — you stop to count — ten, maybe twenty, years?
The mixed spices rise warm and friendly. The sultanas gleam quietly in the soft brown mixture of dried fruits and orange peel, flattened moon slices encircled by that wonderful thing — the skin of a clootie dumpling.
You loved them then. This one, Jim's Mum's one, is good. But it is only the key to the memory of heavenly ones.
When it was drawing near your birthday, you would ask Mrs MacDougall please to make you a dumpling. And she would give your mother a list of the things she needed because your mother never kept them in the house. Mixed spices — cinnamon, ginger and nutmeg, lots of sultanas, a bag of flour, a red, blue and yellow box of suet, and maybe other things. Little silver secrets, wrapped in greaseproof paper and hidden in the mixture — a thimble for an old maid, a

horseshoe for luck, a ring for a wedding, a coin for wealth.
Mrs MacDougall would swing out the kitchen table with
the red formica top into the middle of the room and put up
the leaf so that she had room to work, with her sleeves rolled
up, beating and mixing, raising a spicy cloud around her.
A clean linen dishcloth would be waiting nearby, the fine
white kind with the blue or red borders. If you weren't already
there, Mrs MacDougall would call you down when the bowl
was ready to lick, when the mixture was tied up in the towel
and simmering in a pan on the cooker. It would cook for
hours, for all the morning, while Mrs MacDougall cleaned and
ironed and washed and tidied and told you things. She knows
everybody and tells you about them, about what a terrible
time Mrs Thomson's husband gives her and nothing wrong
with him but bad temper. She knows about Mrs Cairn's shed
which blew down and about who's died and who's had babies.
She had six babies, six sons, six men, and she tells you about
them and their wives and their children, her grandchildren.
When she was a little girl she used to have long dark plaits,
long enough for her to sit on. You laugh, because you can't
imagine her as a little girl or with dark hair, this round, jolly
person who has been this way since you came here. You were
four and four days when you moved here and when you were
four and five days Mrs MacDougall came to the door and
offered to help your mother with the new baby, your little
brother.

You would leave your room in a terrible mess. Your
mother would rant at you to tidy it up so that Mrs Macdougall could clean it, but you knew that she would also tidy
it for you if you didn't. Sometimes she'd tidy things away
and you couldn't find them and you'd have to wait till the
next day to ask her where she'd put them. But she was wonderful when you'd lost something. Have you seen this — my
green scarf or my necklace with the elephant with the shiny
pink stone or the hanky with my name embroidered on it?
She always knows exactly where it is, and if she doesn't she
will hunt until she finds it.

Some nights she comes and babysits, when your parents
go off to a party or to a dance. Your mum will shimmer in
before she leaves, beautiful as a princess in her down-to-the-
ground shiny dresses. Midnight blue with diamanté, or ivory
satin with pearls on the bodice, or your favourite with the
pink and grey layers of net and the marcasite beading round
the low neckline. You sometimes go and open the door of

the downstairs wardrobe in the spare bedroom and stand and gaze at the dresses hanging there. They seem unreal, magical, and the satin feels cold when you stroke it. They need your pretty mother's slim figure to bring them to life, her face perfect with powder and eyeshadow and bright lipstick, her long golden hair piled softly on top of her head that morning by the hairdresser, her sapphire and diamond ring flashing on her finger, a cloud of soft perfume floating behind her. Sometimes the next morning there is a bouquet of flowers in the sink, exotic behind cellophane and satin bows, their raw stems, bruised and dark green, resting in an inch of water, waiting for Mrs MacDougall to arrange them in vases all over the house.

You have fun when Mrs MacDougall comes in the evening. She too has make-up on and jewellery. Pretty red beads and little gold earrings. She brings a handbag with her instead of her shopping bag and doesn't wear her overall. You know her and yet you don't know her like this. But soon you are laughing — telling riddles and jokes and tongue twisters. She teaches you one about eenty teenty fickery fell, ell ell dominell, about Jack in the hazel tower. A hazel tower sounds wonderful. A tower is a magical thing and hazel is a creamy brown and hazelnuts are nice to eat and you know a girl called Hazel and she is pretty, not like you with your short straight hair and glasses.

Then she starts singing. She loves singing, and knows wonderful songs. They make you kind of sad inside too and you ask her to sing them and sing them until you can sing them too. You learn The Northern Lights of Old Aberdeen, which makes you sad, and when you ask her if that's where she comes from, if that's really where she longs to be, she laughs and tells you it's just the words of the song. You sing about the high road and the low road, and the bonnie bonnie banks of Loch Lomond. You sing about westering home with a light in the eye, back to my ain folk in Isla. But she doesn't come from Isla either, no more than you do. It's just the words of the song. You learn the descant for The Skye Boat Song at school and she loves it when you can sing together in harmony.

Then, long after your parents said you should be in bed, she begins to get you upstairs. She says get ready for bed and I'll come up and see you. You giggle and laugh a lot and plot tricks on her. One night, when she comes up the creaking stairs, you curl giggling under the covers. You have left a

potty at the top of the stairs for her to trip over. But all she
does is empty it for you and say nothing.
    Then the bedroom games start. Wonderful games. You
play The Minister's Cat, then I Spy, then you want to bounce
on the bed. Then you play Throw the Sock Down the Back
of the Bed. You have to get out of bed and sit at the bottom
of it, with Mrs MacDougall in a wicker chair nearby. Any old
sock will do, and all you have to do is hurl it at the dark head
board until it falls down the back. You are all in stitches, because a sock is not very easy to throw. Sometimes it sticks
and hangs over the back without falling down. When it does
go down your little brother is always the one who has to go
and get it. Mrs MacDougall takes a long time to bend down
and reach in there, and you are scared of oose lurking in
fluffy grey clouds on the brown linoleum. Your skinny little
brother doesn't like going under the bed either, so he wriggles
in and out as fast as he can.
    Once, there is a sudden panic because you hear their car
in the drive. Quick, into bed, she says, and puts the light out
fast. She is downstairs and sitting by the fire on her own
when the key turns in the door. You creep out of bed to hear
what they say. No matter what you've got up to, she always
says you've been as good as gold, and no bother at all. Her
loyalty to you makes you all warm inside.
    Sometimes you go to her house for tea. It's a real treat
because she makes chips. Your mother won't let her do it in
your house because she's afraid the kitchen will go on fire.
You never have real chips at home. Chips and macaroni and
cheese, and slices of buttered bread. And as a special treat
you can eat in front of the television. Peyton Place is on, and
you fall in love with Mia Farrow, you want to be her, pretty
and elfin and with such lovely long hair. Sometimes you stay
late enough for Coronation Street, with the lovely sad music.
You like the lady with the sharp face and the hair net; even
her name is sharp, Ena Sharples. She's so deliciously fierce,
but it's safe because she's behind the screen and can't get at
you.
    When Mrs MacDougall goes on holiday to Blackpool she
always brings you back a present, although your mother
always tells her not to. You have a little wooden box, with
varnished shells on the lid. You swing the lid sideways from
one corner to open it. And a big lump of real crystal which is
very heavy and clear and sits on the dressing table on a mat
your gran crocheted. A green one with tiny roses worked into

it. But your favourite is the little heart-shaped silver box with the red velvet lining. You keep your teeth in it. The ones the fairies didn't take away. One of them still has a speck of dried blood on it. It feels so strange when you put it into your mouth, not like it was yours at all.

Mrs MacDougall lives down by the river, but she doesn't like frogs. She's terrified of them and shudders uncontrollably when she tells you about the time she found a huge green one on the stone landing. She had to get a shovel and when it hopped on, she carried it all the way down to the back, so afraid it would jump off and land on her foot. You laugh and laugh at her, because you love frogs. You get tadpoles every spring but they mostly don't make it into frogs. One time you did have some little frogs but they hopped down the back of the washing machine which was bolted to the floor. You didn't tell anybody, especially not your mother, because you would have got a row and she would have got a man to take the machine out and look for frogs.

One summer you and a friend brought a lot of little baby frogs back from a pond. You had a sink in the garden and they could live there. But instead they crawled all over the rockery and were baked dry against the hot stones. Little flat frog shapes, grey and thin like burnt paper.

Another time, when you were at school, someone visited with a child, who went to play in the garden. The child knocked over your basin of tadpoles and Mrs MacDougall who hates them so much, was down on her hands and knees picking up the slippery little black things because she knew how you loved them.

She used to take your old bread for the hens. The hens were up on the wasteground beside her mother's house. Then when they built houses there, and the hens went away, she still took the bread. But she would bring potted hough which she had made herself for you. And always she would make a big pot of soup for the weekend, and wash and peel all the vegetables and leave them on top of the washing machine in a big bowl of water. She was so fast at peeling potatoes. You would stand by her elbow and watch her hand whizzing round a potato so fast you could hardly follow it. Then she would fish in the basin of cold water, thick with skin and earth, and bring out another dark potato to peel. You would talk about lucky potatoes, which she too remembered buying when she was little. Sweet cinnamon-dusted slices of delicious crumbly white stuff, with a gift concealed in it. She used to get silver threepennies when she was little, but now you get plastic soldiers or aeroplanes. You have to lick and suck and poke the sweet potato out of the tiny spaces on the gift. She never eats sweets herself now; she used to ice cakes in a baker's shop and that put her off for life. But she likes pepper. She loves to see your face when she tells you she gets through a carton of pepper a week. And just to prove it, she always puts pepper on her cheese sandwich for elevenses.

One day when she was cleaning the stairs, there was a loud ripping noise — her whole knee had come through her stocking. You both laughed, shocked at the sight. Sometimes when she cleaned the stairs and you were at the bottom, you could see she wore peach coloured bloomers, but you didn't tell her because that was a private thing. She told you that she cleaned her knees with brillo pads and you laughed at the idea, but your mother was quite shocked.

When you went on holiday, she took the cats and the goldfish. She loved to have the cats because they liked playing games with bits of bootlace and little balls of foil. She always had lot of people around who could play with them. One time, one of the cats ate the fish and she was distraught when you got back. It didn't really matter, though, because fish are not the same as cats. You didn't even cry.

You left school and went away to study. She was still there, but you weren't. When you came back and saw her it was a little bit like strangers. She treated you not like you were a little girl, but like someone she had once known. You couldn't ask her for sweeties any more. She was a lot thinner and you saw her as someone between your mother and your grandmother's ages. Then, your mother persuaded her to stop. To retire. You and your brother were both away from home and there was so little work now.

Once, you and your brother visited her. You stood on her doorstep, and you were all embarrassed. She was humble and respectful in a way you hated. She said you were a young lady now. You didn't want to be that kind of young lady. You wanted Peyton Place and macaroni and chips.

Then one year, the day after Christmas, your mother sees one of her sons pass the window. He comes to the door and tells you his mother has died. Suddenly. A heart attack. You are stunned. You don't cry. Not then.

It is snowing on the day of her funeral. You walk up the white road with your brother, slipping and giggling. Behind are your parents. Then you stop laughing when you get to the church and there are lots of cars, and a hearse, with its back door open, up in the air. There is no coffin. At the church door there are two wreaths of flowers on the wet tiles and inside the church there are lots and lots of people and a coffin on the floor in front of the pulpit. Suddenly it's all real and sad. You squash into the back row and wait for the last to arrive, her six sons and her husband, looking small, and bowed and old. As the service begins the snow starts to fall, thickly, past the gold and green and rose panes of glass. Mr MacDougall has asked for one of her favourite songs to be sung, and Cathie Jordan sings The Old Rugged Cross, and brings tears to your eyes and a huge lump to your throat. The minister says lovely things about her, and about how you should be glad to have known her and how there is a place for her in heaven, and you have to wipe your eyes and your nose. You try to think of something else, in this church decorated for Christmas with a tall green fir tree hung with shiny gifts and shimmering mists of angel hair and bright little strings of fairy light. The snow is swirling outside, beyond the pretty windows but you are inside and there are so many people mourning that crying seems to be the right thing to do, so you cry. Men are crying too. Your brother has forgotten to bring a hanky, so you give him a grotty one of yours but he doesn't seem to mind. You try to sing The Lord's My Shepherd, but you cannot sing. Your throat has closed up tight. You are trying hard not to sob.

You all stand as her six sons carry out her coffin. You are surprised at how small it is. They all look like her. You don't know whether this is happy or sad, but you cry anyway. Someone begins to sob loudly. The minister helps Mr Mac-Dougall out of the church and everyone files out slowly, shaking hands with her sons, her sons in tears. The coffin is in the hearse, with flowers around it, with thick snow falling, covering the tracks and the footprints. You leave feeling desolate. It's the first time you've been together as a family for a long time. Your father takes you under his umbrella and offers you his arm. You have high-heeled boots and the snow is slippery, but you can't giggle about it any more. You hold his arm all the way home, feeling the warmth of your father by your side. It is the first time you have done this and it is comforting.

Although it was over already, it is really over now. You want only her to comfort you for this loss. But there is nothing.

Only this slice of dumpling, here, now, bringing her back to you. But it hurts too much right now. You can always eat it later. It looks lovely, but not as perfect as her birthday dumplings for you. Nothing can ever match the perfection of the memory, the reality of then, in the sudden emptiness of now.

Ewan R. McVicar

ADEN INCIDENTS

DEVILMENT
The searchlight on the Crater rim rakes our shroudless windows. Again. Gritting teeth, we plot to pay them back. Lift a mirror from the chummery wall, perch it on our balcony. When the beam flicks by again a flash rebounds. Dropping beneath the parapet, dissolved in terrified giggling, suddenly realising a flash means a hand grenade, awaiting the rattling tracer machinegun bullets the squad at the door the room kicked in the blood on the tiles the tear gas smoke bomb mortar rocket. Or worst of all a formal complaint to our manager. Stalag National Bank is quiet. Again.

REVERENT
Guitar strapped to back I motor-cycle the bunkered curfewed stuckdown Maalla Road night. A Duck In A Shooting Gallery. The shuttered shop I have just passed on the left is where George my next-but-one-door neighbour took me to buy this machine. And subsequently chid me for failing to purchase a safety helmet.
The next corner on the right is where George my next-but-one-door neighbour stood beside his bike removing his gauntlets and safety helmet while a freedom fighter shot him in the neck. On the grounds that he might have been a soldier.
Three corners away is the balcony where the two lads who share a house with me sat drinking beer when one hand grenade gate crashed their Ku Klux Konclave of the Aden Police/Army Intelligence mafia. Fortunately the grenade was twenty years old and only pierced their legs.
Fortunately George received the finest medical care and is only paralysed from the neck down.
Fortunately

SAPIENT
The farmer at the counter is shouting. So am I.
The interpreter edits out the mutual insults.
Insisting that he paid off last year's overdraft, the farmer

156   EWAN R. McVICAR

considers the local sheikh's letter of support all the authority needed to unlock our vaults.
I have not yet discovered that the maze of variant clerk spellings of names — six common ways to spell Mohammed/five for sheikh/a minimum of three for any family name — and the local habit of juggling name order — mother's clan name replacing father's if the latter is being politically or socially unsupportive/a visit to Mecca adding Al Haji/social climbing tagging on a title — means he probably did pay us off and has one thousand shillings credited in a now forgotten nomenclature.
He unslings and points his rifle, states 'If you were a Muslim I would kill you'. His friends, concerned for their own seed loans, hustle him away.
Soon the Chief of Police appears. 'Where is he? I will put him in jail for twenty years.'
The Chief of Police has a very large overdraft.

TUMESCENT
Mohammed extols the beauty of a perhaps-young female form behind a lattice above Zingibar office. Two unveiled women are of a sudden standing near us. Light blue head squares/dresses narrow banded in silver and dark like a Scots song about heather/barefooted/the younger hides her plump mouth with a hundred shilling note/the older impassive. Women get shot for going barefaced here. I ponder local community mental health policies.
'Who are these?'
'They are protestutes. From Palestinian. They want an introduction for they think we have too much money.'

DIFFERENT
Astride motorbike, considering ordering another pair of bespoke trousers.
Round the corner, arms-in-arms, a well suited arab/a leggy taller-by-half-a-hairdo blonde/a well suited arab.
Oh hell, I'm racially prejudiced.

AFFERENT
In Lahej sub-branch we are currently blessed with electricity and the fan has blown for over an hour.
Outside our local guards — baggy khaki shorts on spindle shanks, washed out bundled turbans, scuffed sandals, prayers five times a day — kid and tease and tickle each other. I have previously established that these slim defenders of a heavy

prince earn a plebeian thirty shillings per month.
'How can they joke and enjoy life like that?'
'If you have nothing, you might as well be happy.'

EFFERENT
No Lahej electricity this week. And termites have eaten the
cash drawer. I tell the clerks about the Kenya customers who
buried their coffee crop wealth in wooden chests. Then
brought the confetti the termites had blessed, in hopes we
could annul the rape.
My favourite local guard comes in. Wirelashed eyes brimmed
with tears. He must go. Word has come. His four year old
daughter has just died.

TRANSIGENT
A colleague stops off from a steamer. A former boss whom I
saw age twenty years in six weeks. The whalebone of his
shoulders dried sharper with each coded cable confirming 'No
thousand bags of coffee at this railway halt.'
Fleshbags dragged his jawline down with the weight of missing
millions of shillings. His work demands became favours be-
seeched while he tried in vain to penetrate the hedge of
lawyer/doctor/nursing home around the chief debtor.
He wandered the office seeking the spectacles perched atop
his head or dangling from his mouth-corner. He rubbed raw
his temple, seeking three wishes.
Only one was granted. He goes home.

FRAUDULENT
Parked near the Ja'ar Sultan's office, eating. A small hardshell
loaf, beheaded, soft innards replaced by goat and lady's finger
stew. Drinking sweet-well water from coke bottles — costing
more than The Real Thing. Farmers lounge, awaiting word of
rain in the mountains thirty shimmering miles north. Each
straps a serviceable rifle and a silver-bound dagger. As the
only infidel for forty miles, I am keenly interested in how
many of them are fundamentalist Muslims who believe that
to kill an infidel will passport them direct to Paradise.
A man of influence arrives, crossed bullet belts laced with
grenades, an honest-to-badness tommy gun. Not a prince, he
waves his bunduk, shouts he will drive the devil British into
the —— . Someone points out my presence. He comes over to
chat re increasing his overdraft.
The young Sultan, on hols from English prep, emerges/takes

matter-of-fairness petitions / extravagant compliments / hand touched-to-old-woman's mouth-touched-to his-foot.
A few minutes later she gives her symbolised kiss to my foot. Just for luck.

SEDIMENT
The second-biggest banking cheese, Deputy Lord High Some-one-or-other, quite enjoys the industrial strife.
Every hour, upon the hour, in answer to a shop steward's whistle, all the clerks rise from their desks, shout DEATH TO IMPERIALISM, subside again to wait us out.
We officers bustle, signing ledgers, paynotes, bills of lading, cables, tables, expense fables, balance vouchers.

SALIENT
Lord What's-his-face takes photographs on the beach ten miles from anywhere while I pull a stroke on the union.
The cash and ledgers, soldiers, me, Lord Toby Jug, and the contract driver dash off to open office in far Zingibar main drag.
The union driver union clerks and union guard are left to tag along at go-slow union speed. A prime target for bandits.

FLOCCULENT
Standing in the street half watching the landrovers being loaded up.
In the gutter lies an oldfashioned fat brown fountain pen.
Half thinking of an old Jack Hawkins wartime film in which the Germans dropped booby-trapped torches, I make a half joke to the bank guard that the thing is a bomb.
Returning four hours later we find the street cordoned off and must twiddle thumbs till the disposal types say 'All clear and false alarm.' I half murmur 'Serves me right.'

AFFLUENT
At the door of his dark green high rise castle the prince displays the puny injury the bazooka shell inflicted on his curtain wall, then bids us come and have our hands washed.

ALIMENT
I appeal to my assigned aide, who hacks a leg from the boiled sheep before me. I bid him down, armed with a chrome-peeling teaspoon tackle three pound weight of mutton. Relaxed, since my line manager is with me, so I am spared the eyes.

PURULENT
In the grubby loose sand of the compound, small depressions like the tops of ants' nests. Each is an inch from its neighbours. It must have rained last night.
Perhaps it will rain again next year.

ACCIDENT
As the landrover rolls down the slope my hands break through the windscreen. I fall towards Hassan who falls towards the driver who is suddenly not there. My legs saw against the jagged glass. Now Hassan falls towards me. I am suddenly not there, but flying through blackness, ending in a thump, thinking 'That was fairly easy. Could have been a worse end by far.'
Light breaking through, I realise with dismay that there is afterlife after all, and fear my fracturing lack of belief will result in lack of courtesy to a kindly angel.
Sight clearing, down on the level ground, the landrover, is back on all four wheels, shivering, like an undrowned dog.
I wrench air into my lungs, and expel 'Oh God, Oh God, Oh God.'

OCCIDENT
Hassan asserts we are born again.
I begin a lifetime of fearing other drivers.

G.F. Dutton

flat

like much of Scotland
this is a flat land,
stretched between

mountains and shore,
grey cloud grey haar
most of the year

and no doubt
has often been
as flat

though shrugged about
various seas,
dipped and raised

time again,
kindled, braised
iced to the bone;

yet nevertheless,
smoothed with pale green
under a weak sun

and offered to
shall we say man,
it had its attractions.

whether or no
any remain
or any new

have come in
is less certain.
these constructions

dot it sadly, though
big at the feet,
for this is not

climate for concrete
and mud
too rapidly succeeds

ideas of grass.
people and weeds
have to thrive here

roots and seeds
have to explore
momentary silt

have to cherish
leaf or even flower
of the one result.

a pointed spade

you need a pointed spade
for ground like this;
to be of use

in this last rock and turf.
a square-edged blade
so good to double-trench

that first allotment
would be bent,
never penetrate

this kind of earth.
you need to wrench
then drive it straight,

lever to and fro
spoon up the stones
deep as you can go,

maybe an inch or two
to start but once
you're in, no further doubt

than time, and how
to find the soil to fill
the hole you've lifted out.

after brashing pines

brashing is
lopping off dead branches, old
entanglement, outgrown

gesture; so your trees
rise calm and clean into their own
September. when

you leave them, go home
they resume
high business, needle on needle

repeating, gathering
the night wind; and
you do not mind,

you do not look behind
at what's beginning again, what storm,
what growing collision of darkness;

you have no concern,
the job being done
and they putting up another season,

the tall leaders
quarrelling together
against their stars.

on passing

no it is not repeat
repeat, it is once
only and enough;

these juniper berries bunched,
sun-bosomed through the frost-
needles in the bright

snow-light, meet their first
chance to last next
spring, and no more;

rounded-off tough
sky-blue bloomed, their green
one-year-behind

successors crowding about them.
it is enough
to have seen a stiff

laden juniper branch,
pausing as you are
passing, just now once

out of the snow and never,
coming back how often,
to see it this way again.

the prize the primacy of it
the instantaneous thousand
cold needles ever

afire and berries
thrusting their one spring
aware out of the cluster.

Alan Bold

HARVEST

By the frontiers of a farmer's field,
In shadow cast by the hawthorn hedgerow,
A body lies bleeding. Come close:
See the features growing old

While the barley brightens in the sun.
A body lies bleeding. The ground
Is stained with blood, red on brown
Supporting yellow stalks. The wound

Is fresh, still oozing as the sun
Shifts from pale yellow to blood-red
In a cloudless sapphire sky.
The body darkens in the shade.

Another body, running for its life,
Holds the horizon as the sunset dies:
A silhouette sharp as the scythe
That comes to the barley, bringing death.

Tom Nairn

THE MARK

Fresh in a sharp steel cast
And hard as a wire this neck,
And like the swan,
This dry, patterned limb,
The moulding of a pummelled head
Designed and coiled in beaten lead.

The tongue is silver —
Only the sun moves
On eyes cut
In cold, slick glass.

In a quiet hunger,
In the shadow and stone,

Waiting for the mark
And flash of warm meat
To conjure animation.

THE SKELETONS

I
Looking to pictures by Bruegel
Of lepers and markets,
His bucket-brown canvasses
Of wide-faced
Maimed and mediaeval men,
And picturing poems
I might wrap
In pictures like these,
Mediaeval machinations maybe
To Dunbar via Villon.

II
You're lying sick and hot
In tired and twisted sheets,
Pale, weak and wiry as a plant
I forgot to water:
In the night I bring
Cold jugs to your lips.

III
Then seeing
The puffing and ploughing
Of flesh
Below my mother's jaw.
I can't see her mother's face
In her face, but still
It's not the face I filed.

What have my eyes
Been doing with me
Recently anyway?

IV
I walked in the night
From my window,
The early smells
Of cut damp grass,
And on the hill
At the city's heart
A car turning in the high dark
Spun its headlights around like a beacon
Over the streets: I look behind me.

V
Until turning wondering,
What to do with all
Of the skeletons
I never found cupboards for?
They follow me around,
Jangling their bones
Like maracas
For attention.
My own unending statuary
Propped behind me, now
Brittle stringless puppetry
Still not unmoving,
They stand behind me
As I write in half-darkness,
Still try to guide my hand.

SHE LOOKS AHEAD

Wide and brown as a plum
She carries her child,
A packet or parcel
Skin-tight and round,
Tiny, smiling, toothless
Without sound.

Her eyes are black-rimmed,
Deep and dark,
She looks ahead and walks slowly.

Beginning already to know,
Intricate, accurate,
Spinal spiral severe as a leaf
Gnarled in first frosts.

Wide and brown as a plum
She carries her child.
High-eyed and deep-skulled,
Feeding in that darkness
Uncaring.

Carrying with her
Her life
As if a precious toy,

They are strange
And tenacious,
Will not let go.

David Cram

TRIOLET: DINNER AT THE LAST DAYS OF THE RAJ

A cast awaits us to produce
The meal that we are there to order.

The lights are dimmed. Demure and spruce,
The cast is ready to produce.

We enter. Ushers introduce
Us from the wings. On set a broader
Cast awaits us to produce
The meal. We extras come to order.

William Gilfedder

THE GOOD OLD DAYS

O fur the good old days
When the worst thing that could happen tae yi of an evening
Wis if a draught of wind came doon yur chimney
And blew yur fire oot
When the favourite subject of conversation among the
    educated classes
Was to blame the French Revolution
On those daft tumbril drivers
Fur drivin oan the wrang side o the road.

LAST OF THE 7 SAMURAI

I who once trailed the magic corridors of the east
Who in all things jade rule like an emperor
Am reduced to this.
I who in the heyday of my youth bestrode the silver screen
Like a colossus
Am shrunk to this size.
I who from dawn to dusk, championed at no extra cost
Freedom, justice, eternal optimism
And anything else you care to mention
Am catapulted into obscurity.
I who was once, almost nearly, made sub-editor of wishful
    thinking
At the emperor's palace
Am doing this.
Demonstrating the most noble and ancient art
Of pear-splitting
In of all places Glasgow.
May the ancestors of my genes forgive me.
God what next, lecture tours at sunrise?
Banzai!
Banzai!

David Scott

KITE

That's me up there
caught in the wind's claws
held slant to the land
at the end of my string. I'm
a scrap of orange
in a blue bowl
a fingernail scraping thumbed
against the sky and I laugh
for the wind can't tear me,
though I toss from side to side.
People stop by lochs
or come out of their houses
on the flat brown moor
laughing and pointing.

'This is me up here!'
— as the big wind buffets
and gusts —
'Just doing my job.'

And I want to chase after the sky
to swoop down behind those islands
to the blue sea.
But they tug me in.
They play me like a fish.

Then they put me in the garage
with my string wound up beside me.
And I wait.

WHITE

We drifted (these old words
will have to do) chartless,
rudderless, captain gone, no land
in sight, etc. — who knows how long
we drifted? No song was on our lips;
no, not a word.

We saw no boats, at night heard
flapping sails and
muffled cries; at dawn
strange messages we did not understand
were scrawled across our decks.
Our days were spent in
                    putting notes in bottles
                    (which we kept), sleeping,
                    breathing, cleaning the
                    decks, getting a nice tan,
                    cleaning the decks, starving,
                    making decisions, dying of
                    thirst,
and looking for the captain —
drowned
or just hiding? We searched
but didn't find —
the ship was large.
The bosun took six men
into the sails;
saw nothing, billowing,
and would not return.

                    We couldn't weep

but had a party for him! Cleaned the decks
until they shone! The sails were bright,
our uniforms, hands, faces, bright with salt.

The sun was white,
the sea was white as snow
and white the glad shout
when the bosun called out from the rigging —

'Is it land?'
      (we cried)

'No flames! And white fire in the sails!'

Raymond Friel

THE BUTTERFLY

Farewell, farewell, lost soul!
you have melted in the crystalline distance,
it is enough! I saw you vanish into air.

D.H. Lawrence, 'The Butterfly'

I
I tap, tap, tapped the earpiece,
remembering: the poised Veterano bull,
testes and all; the bully-stare of police;

the hills that sleep in long-past lands,
ochre, crusted, dotted vine-green,
hills that would crumble in your hands;

monstrous palm-trees fingering the night,
the Magno bottle, quarter full,
the bar across switching out its last light;

the bluebottle noise of a moped, louder,
loud, the sudden look of the girl,
Drew's dead, she spoke, I'm really sorry, it's

II
A girl on a starved Atlantic beach,
cross-armed, swaying wrapped, staring
at sand-pictures, still out of reach.

So sad, so sudden, the details are
I move across the losing sand . . .
she starts, pipes, 'Vete! Vete!'

What sin? Why sin-talk
when roots pressed in thin soil
finger rock, and rock, and rock?

Yet every night I am torn, unpinned
by violet dreams, mutterings rain
like shied stones on a woman sinned.

III
I came to the girl in need of a clue.
I did not weep, only repeat his name
with a little O, rocking like a Jew.

All there in today's paper. Is . . .
Two days ago, in Cumbernauld, she said.
Wednesday: Salamanca, breathless heat,

I read the column grandmothers read
stoically, youngly awakened to death's
character in life, doubt's in faith,

mobility's in doubt, I couldn't sit,
I reached high and patted around
for a lost thing, panicky, where *is* it?

IV
Stood at Unamuno's nicho, the seer,
unaware of his 'Agony' 's receipt,
took a photograph and went for a beer.

He went religious before the calamity,
God over a pint, eucharist in the pub.
I thought it *was* religion, not insanity.

What's push sent him reeling
at twenty-two, lawyer, thinker, friend?
What sucks, sucks, life's meaning?

What's push impels some to wreck it?
Stuff, stuff, the easy, easy:
no job, smack, The Smiths, Beckett.

V
... the reason, a tip? We waited, smoking.
Reunioners chipped out eulogies of course.
Clergy, family, kept inside, coping.

Atheists, theists, maybeists, somedayists,
by death, good shepherd of -ists,
were gathered in the pen of Catholic faith.

The priest-poet called him a butterfly,
imagine, a wingèd psyche, in 1984!
But is he, is he dancing over fields and

Or kept down, appalled by Rachel's cry,
the life of grief which tugs, tugs,
to break its roots. Or did he simply die?

VI
Every morning I am born, unpinned
by unseen hands, noises thrash
like corn in wild-gone wind.

I reach high and pat an arc
for a lost thing, panicky,
reach, reachings irradiate the dark!

Every morning I am born, unpinned
by unseen hands, noises crash
like seas on seas, life undimmed.

Fields of longing sunflowers, lifted
by sound as deep roots yield,
lifted by dust rising, lifted?

Gavin Sprott

DIANA

'I suppose I'll hae tae get ein o' thae.' Meg pointed to the row of crash helmets that sat on display on top of their boxes. 'Ay lass. It's the law. And besides, ye dinna want tae bash in that bonnie heid o' yours. There's brains in't as weil as beauty, eigh?'
'If ye say sae' she half laughed. She had not thought of all the extras and what they would cost. But she was committed now.
'Whit about that reid ein?' The colour matched her shoes. He handed it down. 'Try it for size onywye. It should fit snod or it's nae yiss.' At first she couldn't figure out the way it went on. But it fitted perfectly. She looked in the mirror provided. The helmet framed her elfin face. She twisted and shaped the odd curl of her fair hair that peeped out. 'That's fine.' She rather liked it.
She signed the papers and he wheeled the scooter out between the ranks of shining new bikes. Meg followed him with a growing panic of misgiving. When she had risen that morning, she had not even thought of it. To spend so much on herself. She could hear her father's perplexed comments to her mother when she was maybe just within earshot — about young folk and the value of money. Even worse, it wasn't her money — she was getting the thing on tick. Jeez — mak shair he duisna get tae ken about that!
'Nou lass, hae a shot here first.' He showed her the controls. 'The main thing, learn hou tae stop. The front brakes's the maist pouerfae, but the back's safest. If yer front wheel skytes, ye'll cowp. Aye mind that.' Gingerly she seated herself on the machine while he held it. 'Get yer balance nou. It's like ridin a bike. Ye've ridden a bike?' He started the engine.
'Ay.' She put out one leg to keep her balance and he let go. The jeans were right enough, but he glanced at the impractical slim high-heeled shoe with resignation. He feared that her foot would slip on the brake pedal.
'Lat the clutch out gentle nou.' He lumbered alongside as

the machine began to move. 'Stop nou. Haal in the clutch and brake.' They did this several times until he was satisfied. Then unbidden she did a U-turn in the little street, then a neat figure of eight. She came to a halt at his feet with an excited giggle. 'Hei lass, ye're a natural' he said, patting the back of her hand. 'Caa cannie nou, and ye'll be fine. Lat's ken if there's ony problems.'

'Thanks Mr Lamb.' Without hesitation she drove off and turned into the main street.

She headed out towards Glamis, going south across the Howe, and then west along the old side road to Kettins. It was magic. The energetic hum of the little engine, the roadside trees wheeking by, waltzing through the bends and over the rises. Fancy ye was on a fleet wee horse out o' thae fairy tales. Oh, ye'd ging fleein through the wuids, alang the burnsides and up the smaa dens whaur the spinkies grow, chase the hares across the parks and fleg the pairtriks out o' the stibbles. Suddenly she found herself braking hard. The back wheel skidded. Her heart leapt into her mouth as she steadied the machine out of the bend, the verge rushing close under the left side. She stopped to regain her composure. She hauled the scooter back on its stand and sat on the seat sideways, her legs crossed below the knee, swinging childlike.

What would she say to her dad? — or her mum? Oh, ye'll yaise it tae get til work and that. Ye'll can gang hither and thon. Then mentally shrugging her shoulders she smiled. It's mine and I'll pye for't.

A car came round the bend where she had nearly come off. On sighting her the driver slowed and stopped alongside. Leaning over the passenger seat, he wound down the window and spoke to her, but she couldn't hear distinctly because of her helmet. She took it off and shook her hair loose. The man got out and came round.

'Canaan' he said, 'anywhere near it?'

'Ay. Juist doun the road. Onybodie ye're seikin?'

'You know the place?'

' 'Course. I bide juist out o't.'

'Franklin House?'

'Ay. In the Main Street. Ye've bocht it?'

'No. Just renting it. But yes, I'm moving in.'

'Weil, I can get ye doun the road. If ye dinna ken the turnins, ye can miss it aesy. Fallae me.'

'Hey, thanks. That's great.'

To her relief, the machine started first time, and she sped off down the hill, looking back at the two junctions to make sure he followed. She stopped in the middle of the road outside the house. As his car drew up, she started moving off, but he halted her with a raised hand.

'Where did you say you lived?'

'Up thonder. Rashiehauchs.'

'Rashie . . . ?'

' -Hauchs. Ma faither's tractorman there.'

'You really zapp along on that thing. See you around. Thanks.'

'Cheerio.'

She had to slow to a crawl on the farm road, negotiating the holes and skirting the lumpy ridge that formed the centre of the track. She halted in front of the cottarhouse door, determined to tackle the matter head on, and so she went in. Her mother was sitting with a cup of tea.

'Ay Mum. Whaur's Dad?'

'In the gairden. Hou? Somethin wrang?'

'Na, na. I've a surprise.' She smiled brightly, and went through to the back. 'Dad. Come through and see.'

'See? Fat, lass?'

'Juist come.'

They both looked at the scooter solemnly. 'Michty. A wee motor, kind' said her mother. Her father walked round it, as he would eye a beast at the Kirrie Show. Meg half expected him to put his fingers on the black plastic hide of the seat, to see how much flesh it had on its backbone. Slowly, hands in his dungaree pockets and leaning back for balance, he stretched the toe of his boot and gently touched the back tyre.

'Ay ay. A richt smert-luikin wee thing. Ay. Juist . . . ay. Fat d'ye get it for?'

'The wark . . . and that. Gittin about, like.'

'Ye ken I'd gie ye a hurl in the car ony place ye fancy.'

'Ay . . . but . . . .'

'Come on lass. I ken hou ye got it.' There was unexpected kindness in his voice. 'I ken ye've cast out wi'm. — Dave was't ye cried 'im? Nivver likit 'im. Sleikit wee bugger, eigh Ma?'

'Weil, that duisna mak it ony aesier for me. Had ye thocht on that?'

'Come on lass, I ken that was a daft thing tae say. But

that's juist life, eigh.' He put his arm round her shoulder and gave her a squeeze. 'Luik at ye — 's bonnie 's they come. Ye'll nae want for company. Come on lass.'
    'Oh, it's mebbe nae company I'm wantin ee nou.' The tears were rolling down her cheeks.
    'Weil I dinna ken . . . ' Dod Hendry shook his head. 'But stervation cauld yon thing in the winter shairly' he said, changing the subject. 'I mind fan we got the Fordson. Nae haetit cabs then, by Christ. Eince I was that frozen harryin, I fixed a line til the steerin wheel and walkit ahent it like I was back drivin a pair o' horse.' He gave her shoulder another squeeze and left her as gently as he could.

    The air was blue with smoke, and numerous conversations competed against the mellifluous drone of the piped music. A futher layer of sound was added by the muted thump of bass drums filtering through from the new function suite at the back, where a wedding dance was in progress. It was the lounge bar of the Pitfergus House Hotel.
    Meg was with a crowd from the office in Kirriemuir in which she worked. They were taking out one of the other girls who was getting married the next week. The details of the wedding plans were anticipated yet again, the presents discussed, the little flat in Kirrie described, and the bridegroom's prospects guessed at. ' 'Course Jim's a sales executive. He gets an Escort. Nae as airy as yer scooter, eigh no, Meg!' Meg smiled. She was usually quiet in company. 'Can ye get somebody on the back?' they asked. 'Could be cuddly, eigh!'
    She laughed and shook her head. 'I made shair it was a single seat, juist.' They knew this was a direct reference to the recently dismissed Dave.
    'Weil, there's ither people'll wish they stuck tae a single seat. Ye ken about Helen Findlay?'
    'Oh ay, I just heard!'
    'Whit's wrang wi her?'
    'A bun in the oven.'
    'A bun in . . . yer jokin! Daft bisom. But ye wad nae 'ae expectit it, eigh? I mean, ye ken her mum was aye on at her nae tae dae onythin daft.'
    'Wha's the man?'
    'Naebodie kens. I dinna think she does. She was fou, she admittit it. She's in an affae state.'
    'But whit's she gaein tae dae?'
    'She's nae notion. I suppose she'll pit a stop til't some

wye.' Nobody wanted to use the word abortion.
'God, ye feel sorry for her, eigh, I dinna ken whit I'd dae.'
'Same again fowks?' Meg was on her feet. It was her turn.
She was glad of any excuse to break away from the conversation, for she'd had a near enough miss herself, so she sus-
pected. The days she had spent waiting for her period to
come was something she never wanted to repeat ever. But
that's the thing, she thought. Ye think that's the kind o'
thing ye'll nivver dae yersel, sae ye dinna tak ony precautions.
Ye think ye'd be makin a hoor o' yersel aeven if ye nivver got
that length. But Meg knew there was more to it than a bit of
drunken folly, something concealed by her incapacity to recall the details, and her mind shied away from it.
    She elbowed into the bar. 'A Pernod, a couple o' Bacardis
an' Coke, a half o' lager and lime, an orange juice. And can I
get a tray plaese.' Her mind drifted onto other things while
she waited. She would give her dad a hand with the calves
when everyone else was having their long lie. Still, she liked
the calves, their affectionate suckling of her fingers if she
held them out. She would be just as happy to change her
shiny new boots for her shairny wellies.
    She was aware of somebody tapping her on the shoulder,
and turned.
    'Hello there.' It was the man from the car. 'What would
you like? You scarcely gave me time to thank you.'
    'Oa, that was naethin. I've got somethin, thanks.' She
pointed to the orange juice.
    'Come on, it's my pleasure.' But she shook her head.
    'Twist your arm. Put a shot of vodka in it, there you go.'
    'Aw weil.' She smiled ruefully. 'Leastwyes, yer findin yer
wye about.'
    'No doubt about it. Although I could think of better
places than this, — but they don't exist here.'
    'Whaur 've ye come fae onywye?'
    'Edinburgh. I'm setting up a studio at the house there.
Bags of room you see, the old shed at the back's perfect. My
cousin's renting it to me.'
    'Come tae think on't, there was an artist boy there eince
afore. He was a teacher in Dundee. But he was a bit funny
though.'
    'Funny perculier? Maybe I will qualify too. Yes, but
that's why it's right. He put big windows in, and there's a perfect north light in that old gig shed.'
    'Whit d'ye want that kind o' licht for?'

'You see the colours properly that way. In direct sun-
light you see them out of balance. I can't explain it better.
Come and see for yourself.'

'Weil ... I dinna ken if I could mak onythin o't.'

He paused before replying, smiling gently as he recon-
structed her country tongue into his own language. Then his
expression changed to unexpected earnestness. 'Please come.
D'you know why? I'd like to paint you.'

'Pent me!' She laughed out loud, so that the heads next
to them turned slightly, and she felt the blood rising to her
cheeks. She put her hand to her mouth and gave a little
giggle.

'Yes, paint you. Just as you were, sitting on your scooter,
where I found you. Exactly the same!'

She shook her head. 'Na na, nae me!' The notion was so
absurd, she rejected it casually. Then she realised the others
would be waiting for the drinks by now. 'Thanks. But if ye're
wantin ony eggs, ye'll get them fae ma mum. Richt walkin-
about hens' eggs.'

'Thanks. What's your name?'

'Meg Hendry.'

'Well, mine's Stephen. See you.'

'Who's that?' Meg was flattered by the chorus that greeted
her return with the laden tray. She sat with her back to the
bar, so that she would not have to see his reaction to all her
friends stealing a glance at him with none too much discretion.

'I come across him last Setterday. He'd got hissel a bittie
lost. Tryin tae find his wye til the village. He's some kind o' a
painter.'

'Has he got his ain business? Canaan's a funny place tae
set up as a painter, eigh? Ye think he'd dae better in Kirrie or
Farfar.'

'Nae a house painter, silly! ... a pictur painter.'

The exotic dimensions of this revelation caused a stir. An
artist ... ken whit like they are! Hou auld was he, about
twenty seiven mebbe. That was a fantastic gansey, wi its
green and reid stripes, hand knitted it must be, cost a bomb
must 'ae. But luik at thon breiks! — they luik like a tramp's,
aa that paint on them. But he luiks nice, eigh Meg! It was on
the tip of Meg's tongue to mention his offer to paint her, but
caution stopped her. It 'ad seem settin yersel up, kind, and a
bittie daft, seein as ye refused.

That shot of vodka in the orange cost Meg a slight hang-

over — not by itself, but because in the face of her resolution
she had got the taste for the rest of the evening. Nothing
much, just a slight dryness in her mouth and fuzziness in her
head, but she didn't like it. Rising early on a Sunday morning
was one of her pleasures. Even on the February mornings,
when the ground was white with rime but the days were beginning to lengthen, she liked it. Then there was renewed
strength in the sun as it shone horizontal between the opened
doors of the lambing shed, flooding directly onto the ewes
and their young settled in the nests of straw her father had
made for them. But now, in the spring, the sun had been up
for hours when she woke. Too late to help her father with
the calves.

Her mother was getting ready to go to the kirk, hurrying
before the toneless clink of the bell carrying across the parks
would tell her that she was late. 'I'll get ye doun the road,
Mum . . . for the daunder, like.'

'But ye'll nae come wi's, eigh no?'

'Ye ken whit I think. It's borin. And whit about Dad? Tell
him, eigh? C'm on Mum. I'll nae faa out wi ye ower it. I'll
get ye the length o' the village, and turn back alang the burn-
side and nae embarrass ye.'

'Aa richt lass.' Janet Hendry smiled in wan resignation.
'Ainly this. Mind, if ye want tae get merriet in yon kirk ae
day, ye'll hae tae ging til't. Yon young minister's got strick
notions on that kind o' thing. It's yer ain business, but dinna
say I nivver tell't ye.'

'Ok Mum. I ken whit ye're sayin. I'll cross yon brig whan
I come til't — if I come til't.'

They were walking arm in arm along the farm road, the
older woman short and strong with her tweed coat, simple
hat and lace-up shoes and stocky stride, the younger one
longer in the leg and with her father's slighter build, but the
squareness of her shoulders developed by physical work, emphasised by the old jersey that she wore. Meg went through
the puddles in her wellies, allowing her mother to remain
dryshod.

'Cross yon brig if ye come til't' mused her mother. 'Weil,
I s'pose ye're auld eneuch tae ken yer ain mind. But that's
nae fat ye mean, is't? Ye're nae thinkin ye'll nivver get in tow
wi anither man. Na, ye'll juist ging and bide wi'm, eigh?'

'Na Mum, ye're up the wrang dreil. I'll nae be nae man's
bidie-in.'

'Weil, that's a relief! I canna pictur it onywye' she chuckled.

'Ye've owre muckle sense in yer heid.'

Meg blushed to herself. Her mother would have been speaking differently if chance had dictated the other way, and she had been, as her grannie would put it, on the fang. The drink clouding her memory made it worse, not better. There was something so hurtful that she detested him for but blamed herself, but her mind refused to place it.

'Aw weil lass, a'bodie has tae find their ain road' her mother added, and to Meg's relief, let the matter drop.

The kirk was at the far end of the road that formed the main street of the village. On one side were a dozen cottages strung along in groups of three, the other was open to the fields, looking back across the Howe to the hills of Prosen and Clova rising beyond. The shop and post office took up half of one house, and the *Tav* or Tavern, the pub, took up another house. They were all single storey except the one at the near end. It was Franklin House, grandly named by its builder after the great American. It contained two rooms on each floor, and an assemblage of sheds in the yard at the back. It was also the point at the beginning of the village where Meg would have to part from her mother.

'Watch the denner duisna burn, it's in the oven, mind.'

'Ok Mum, I'll pit the tatties on. See ye later.' She stood for a moment, watching her mother go. She was about to take a quick glance at the house and turn down the path when she heard the front door scrape open.

'Hi there. Like a cup of coffee?' He stood leaning on the door jamb, hands in the pockets of the same trousers as the night before, the same brilliant striped jersey. The only difference was he had not shaved. Meg glanced down the road. The only folk on it had their backs turned to her, headed for the kirk. He gave a little toss of the head, summoning her with good natured impatience. She hesitated, pursing her lips, then with another glance up the road, smiled cautiously and crossed to the house. He led her through to the kitchen at the back.

'Take a pew.' He motioned her to the one timeworn arm chair by the fireplace. 'Is that your mother — of the walking-about hens?'

'Ay.'

'You don't go to church with her?'

'Oa, I yissed tae. But I havena been for some while. I've plenty else tae be gettin on wi.'

'I'm sure. You look the energetic sort. I like that.'

'Ye've nae muckle option on a fairm' she said, accepting it as a matter of fact. He handed her a cup of coffee. 'Thanks. And hou d'ye like it here?'

'Great. At least I think so. Have to get myself organised though.' He waved round, indicating the disorder in the kitchen. He still stood, leaning with his back to the sink, then impulsively reached out to the table for a packet of cigarettes and offered her one. She shook her head.

'No? You were smoking last night.'

'That's juist in company.'

'The way we all start I suppose. Makes you less nervous. I've been trying to stop for ages, but it's no use. Must have lungs like the inside of a street-cleaner's barrow by now.'

She laughed and relaxed a little. 'And hou's yer paintin comin on?' She told him how her friends thought he was a tradesman painter. It was his turn to laugh. 'But you know' he added, 'some of your old tradesmen could teach artists a thing or two. They had to mix their own colours from the pigments — you know, the thing that gives paint its particular colour. And they had skills that artists should envy. The way they could do graining — imitation natural wood — in paint. Some of them used to let their thumb nail grow extra long and cut it like a toothed edge, and that way they rattled over the woodwork with a few strokes of their hands. And there's the way they could do imitation marble. You'll see some up at the Pitfergus, but rather battered now — next time you go up for a smoke.'

'D'ye paint aa the time, like?'

'I'd like to think so, but I don't. I take fits at it — paint like a fanatic until I drop. Then I get pissed off with what I'm doing. Manic depressive — that's my wavelength. What's your neurosis?'

She shook her head. 'Nane o' that things. I think I'm a happy person. Sounds daft, eigh? A'though whiles ye want for somethin different.'

'The big wide world?'

'Mebbe. But I'm nae shair. Na, things could be the same some place else and different here. Depends on the wye ye luik at it.' She drank her coffee, and he lit another cigarette, eyeing her enquiringly.

'Come and have a look at the studio' he said after a long pause. 'What was it you said about the guy that was here once?'

'Mr Danet? Oh, he was clean aff his heid. I think he was

cairted aff til the mental hame, puir man.'
'Crikey! You have a blunt way with words around here. I found some of his work left in that cupboard.'
'Ony yiss?'
'Pretty landscapes. Not my kind of thing. But I'll use the canvasses.'

As he had said, one whole side of the old gig shed had been replaced with glass from the eaves to near the floor, the glazing bars left in the natural timber, giving the place an open airy feel. The studio framed the side of a little court-yard, looking across an overgrown flowerbed to the back of the house. It was secluded and private.

'I'm going to make a little Japanese garden there.'
'Whit's that? Flouers or tatties?'
'Neither' he laughed. 'Mostly stones and gravel, and per-haps some small trees or shrubs.'
'Oh ay.' She felt slightly nettled at her show of ignorance, as she recalled reading something about such gardens in a woman's magazine.

'Whit d'ye want tae paint me for' she said, turning to him unexpectedly.

'Well, let's start by saying how I wouldn't paint you. Not like the top of a chocolate box. I wouldn't make you look like Miss World, or like Page Three. Indeed, I wouldn't dream of asking you to take your shirt off, nice though your figure may be. On the other hand I wouldn't move your eyes onto your shoulder, or put your ear into your pocket. I wouldn't ride my bike around the canvas with paint on the wheels. Does that put your mind at rest?'

'It was nivver onywye else' she replied, with enough tart-ness to bring him to the point.

'Look Meg, I don't want to tell you' he said simply. 'Just let me paint you — exactly as I saw you the other day — in your jeans and jersey, red high heels and helmet, sitting side-ways on your scooter. You will find your answer in the picture.'

She looked out at the ragged flower bed again and con-sidered. 'Ok' she said, 'I s'pose that's whit picturs is for.'

At first they went to the exact spot, and she sat as she had been. He moved her a little up the road nearer the bend, then back again. He turned her slightly on the seat, crossed her legs one way and then the other. She tried to be serious, but found it funny. He didn't seem to mind. It was a large canvas, and he worked hard to sketch in the outlines he wanted. It was when they started down in the studio that she found it tiring. He wheeled her scooter in and set her on it, manoeuvring her by the shoulders with a firm touch that was neither rough nor sensual. He would not allow her to read or talk, because he said it would change her expression. Her thighs developed pins and needles after a while, and her back ached. When she felt she could sit no longer, he sensed it, and made her a cup of coffee and offered her a cigarette. She took it and looked at the canvas. It was still mostly outlines, with broad areas painted in simple bland colours.

'It's like yon fillin-in books I mind whan I was a bairn' she remarked. 'But ye ken whit ye're daein, eigh?'

Whan iver did ye sit still like this? In the skail, watchin the telly, in the kirk? — nivver. Teachers, ministers, aa yon actor fowk and politicians and that, yappin their heids aff at ye. Ye'd be kirnin about on yer erse, scartin and fitterin, waitin 'or they feinish.

She tried to sit relaxed, but her back soon ached again. 'Sit up' he said with mock authority. To her surprise, she found that it made it possible to hold her position of quiet immobility. She became aware of the muscles and sinews in her back and hips. She listened to the patter and scratch of his brush on the canvas. Paintin ye! But it's like he is paintin ye, his brush flein ower yer face, kind. Without moving or touching it, she could feel her skin.

'Meg, how do you do it? — I'm knackered!' He rose to stretch himself. 'You've been like that for over two hours. But I couldn't miss it, just great. But quite exhausting really. Hope you're not exhausted.'

'Hou should I be?' She shook her head with a smile. 'It's ye 'at's daein the wark.' Without asking she went to make him a cup of coffee. Only when she returned did she glance at the canvas. The bland image was crumbling under a hailstorm of ruby reds and emerald greens. Even the developing flesh tones had a translucent jewel-like quality.

'Will ye be famous?'

'I kid you not' he replied. Then a serious face peered out from behind the mask of habitual jokery. 'You will make me famous.'

On another day he took the canvas back up the road, and

she went with him, not to sit, but to watch. She brought a
thermos and pieces filled with ham.

'That's delicious. Never tasted anything like it.'

'It's the pig.'

'A walking-about pig?'

She liked that. When he poked fun at her, it was always
at her meaning, never the way she spoke. Even with her
friends in the office, she was aware of her country tongue,
but with Stephen, never.

She watched him quietly as he painted. Has onybodie
paintit him? Oh, ye could say he is nice. Nice! — whit is nice?
It seemed a blind alley, and her attention wandered. She
thought of her scooter. It had been a good buy, giving her a
freedom she had not even known she wanted.

Her eye came back to the canvas. Strange, he's moved
trees, ye can scarce mak out the dykes, a lot o't's juist wild
colour. Whit season 'ad ye pit thon in if ye didna ken? Nae
winter, there's nae frost in't, nae bare trees. Na, ye couldna
say it's the hills and wuids ahent Canaan, nae if ye didna ken.
It's somethin in his ain heid, a kind o' fairyland.

'Fancy a pint?'

'Nae a pint. But ye can hae yer pint.' He packed up, and
they went down to the Tav in the village. She made no
attempt now to conceal their acquaintance. But when people
hinted at what was going on, she shook her head. 'There's nae
romance' she would say, 'we're juist freinds.' Folk found it
hard to imagine, a good looking young man and woman going
about just friends, but there it was.

He completed the painting on his own. Familiar though it
had been in the making, this fresh sight of it astonished Meg
and even frightened her slightly. The fairy land was not the
one in his head, but hers, — a remote beauty of colour that
stretched into the horizon beyond what she could imagine.
Her own figure was familiar, but altered. Her legs were longer,
and the shoes, encompassed by the background of the scooter
wheel, had a winged energy of their own. Her breasts were
not so full and more pointed. Her head was slightly turned,
the muscles across her neck tense with alert energy. Were
those her features, the escaping curls of her hair, her eyes?
They were only a few brush strokes, but the high cheekbones,
the straight but narrow nose, the neat set of her mouth and
jawbone, it was all there. She could not distinguish the colour
of her eyes, it was the way the light caught them. The light!

The vivid red glossy surface of her helmet, of the scooter body and her shoes caught white light from one direction, in the landscape it came from another. ' "Diana the Huntress" ' he said, standing at her shoulder. 'An ancient goddess of the woods and wilds. Or Artemis to the Greeks. The virgin huntress of the secret places, worshipped by women and slaves. The classical education I never had. Don't worry, it's in the reference library. But you have a look at it.' To her relief, he then left her to absorb it by herself.

It's in a strange tongue, she mused, struggling to translate the artistic conventions that were so foreign to her. Yet it touched her heart, left her exhilarated because it was her. But the same thing which was locked in her mind was locked in the picture, and she found the effort to grasp it brought her to tears.

The exhibition in the village hall was a great event. The pictures dramatised what everyone took for granted — the towering grain silos at Myreside against the wild sky of a rainy dawn, Jim Boag welding in the muddy scrap yard behind the old smiddy, Dod Hendry rolling silage in the makeshift pit bound by railway sleepers that everyone knew had been commandeered free of charge when the line had shut: the ranks of empty cars parked outside the floodlit Pitfergus House Hotel, their shapes and colours surreal in the blackness and the glaring light. The paintings and sketches were the cause of more than a few arguments — those who thought they were junk, and others who liked them, and some who said they appreciated them but didn't like them. All were agreed that there wasn't a pretty picture among them.

There was one picture not shown in the Canaan Hall, the second one of Meg Hendry. She did not want him to show it, it seemed so personal.

'But the others are just as personal' he had said. 'Your dad, your cousin. That's why I did them.'

'Ye ken whit ye're paintin. Ye should ken whit I mean.'

So he agreed. 'But you'll let me take it to Edinburgh?'

She shrugged her shoulders. 'Nivver been near the place.'

But that did not stop her going to have a look at it where it lay in the studio. In the height of summer they had gone down to the banks of the Isla, to a pool where the older children sometimes swam, Stephen with his sketch pad, Meg with a magazine. While appearing to read, she had watched him as he worked, maintaining a fiction by turning the pages

of her magazine. She had followed his muscular hand as it
kneaded and floated the pencil over the sheet. She had been
taken by the simple beauty of the movements, and for the
first time for months, had felt the stirring of desire. Not understanding what it was, she had concealed it in an irritable restlessness. 'I'm juist gaein for a bit daunder.' She had walked
up the bank a little, vacantly watched a man fishing on the
far bank, and returned to a spot not far from where he was
sketching. Taking off her shoes, she had rolled up her jeans,
and stepping on the round stones green with soft fine weed,
had waded to the rock off which people dived into the water.
She had lain full length on the rock, her chin resting on her
folded arms, studying her reflection in the passing water. So
as she had watched him, he had sketched her, unawares. In
the painting, her toes just trailed in the water, and her body
curled over the stone, the stretched limbs tense, powerful,
and quietly but unmistakably sensual. The mood had passed,
and she had returned to her tranquil self, but the canvas was
a reminder that both pleased her and left a ripple of unex-
plained disturbance.

   Stephen could not persuade her to come to Edinburgh
for the exhibition. What was stopping her?
   'Naethin, I s'pose. Nae ma scene, juist.'
   'Your scene will be plastered round the walls, with you
and your scooter zooming through the middle of it. What
d'you mean? — that you won't fit in somehow? You don't
have to. It's the other way round.' It was the nearest they
had come to a quarrel. With something near sullenness she
helped him pack up the pictures and load them, and saw him
go.
   And when he was gone, she missed him. She felt a childish peevishness that he had taken the picture of herself, the
Leopardess, and then scolded herself for being daft. She had a
disturbing dream of a painting of her looking at the picture
of her looking at her reflection in the water, the thing that
she sought drowned in an infinite regression of images. Now
that he was absent she was surprised by the obvious questions
about their friendship she had never asked — he's aye that
cheerfae, daft tae get on wi his paintins, he duisna ask onythin o' ye. Na, that's nae true. He picks it, like an aipple fae
a tree, ye ken it, but its painless. And ye wonder, is he queer,
— duis he fancy ye or duis he juist like ye? — is that whit
fowk thinks mebbe? Weil, damn the hail tribe o' them.

And so the conversation in the Tav went knowingly, — it must be love, — aa this speak o' juist freinds and nae romance, it's juist havers, stuck up rubbish. She thinks that gies it a touch o' class, him bein a bit o' a toff like. Oa, she got shot o' thon Dave mannie, nae guid enough for her. And God, was she nae doun there the first Sunday he come. And man, d'ye nae think he got stuck in there, eigh!

On the Saturday he was due to return she took a turn up the road on foot. It was the nearest she had come to admitting to herself that she was seeking him. She knew now that those brown eyes and short muscular fingers darting over the paper or canvas held the key to the shadow inside her.

She walked a long way, right across the carseland to where the Sidlaw hills rolled up on the south side of the Howe. It had been a fairly dry summer, and she was not surprised to see the first combine out. Yet for somebody brought up in the countryside all of her twenty three years, never had she been so aware of it as this summer. She noticed the things she remembered her grannie pointing out when she had been fit enough to walk, — wild plants growing at the dykesides that had their uses, the little patches of uncultivated meadow grass where you could still find mushrooms, the things to be sought in the woods and the little dens where the burns ran down off the hills into the Howe. She had even peeled the bark from a birch tree and Stephen had watched as she gathered the thick juice that lay over the naked sapwood.

'Juist a notion,' she had said. 'Seeminly ye can yaise this for shampoo. Gie's yer hair a richt shine.'

And so she walked on, now for miles. She had long ago given up expecting to see the yellow and rusted car appear round the bend or over that ridge. She reckoned to drop down to the main road by Eassie and get a bus back. Then on a long straight she picked it out in the middle of the road, framed by the verges and the dykes. She stopped walking, waiting for him to draw up in front of her.

'Ay ay. Hou d'ye get on.' She smiled brightly as she climbed into the car.

'Absolutely great. Went down like a bomb.'

'Eigh! Sae ye made it?'

'So did you. The Huntress and the Leopardess. You're a celebrity.' The old jokery, but the tone was flat. 'And how are you?'

She ignored the question, turning herself in the seat to

look at him. 'Fat's wrang wi ye?'

'Dunno. I'm just done. Fed up. It's all too much.'

'A'richt. Dinna chow ma heid aff.'

'I'm sorry. It's just the way the mood takes me some-times.'

And so they reached Canaan, in dour silence. He insisted on leaving her at the farm road end, and went on to Franklin House alone. 'It's better that way' he said. 'I don't think you will like me like this.'

Sae that's it! He said he had yon turns whiles, but God, naebodie's gaein tae thole that. It's nae juist the notion o' pittin up wi't. There's nae wye ye'll can get through til 'im. And so she returned home, footsore, hungry and quiet.

And that night she lay, thinking that he would be gone with his paints and his easel and all his stuff crammed roof-high on the back seat of the rusty car. A shopper who has forgotten to pay for a small item of his purchases, he would be gone with the images that lay behind those brown eyes.

She rose early, but there was nothing to do. The calves were away, and the harvest had not yet started at Rashie-hauchs. She could not drive the bogie to the combine, or get going with the baler. It was an age before her mother got ready for the kirk, adjusted her new hat in the mirror, fiddled with the dinner Meg already had in the oven, and finally started down the road. Nervous but determined, Meg went with her.

He was not busy packing up as she had expected, but still in bed. The bottle of Glenmorangie on the kitchen table was empty and the precooked frozen meal only half eaten. She cleared the mess aside, and took him a cup of coffee.

'C'm on m'n, sit up.'

He lay with his eyes open to the ceiling, motionless.

'Whit is't ye're seein?'

'Black light.'

There's nae yiss for speakin til'm. 'There's yer cup aside ye. Dinna skail it.' She went back to the kitchen and set to, tidying up. Then she sat and smoked one of his cigarettes. She knew she should be getting back for her dinner, but stayed where she was, thinking. She lit another cigarette, but before it was half smoked, threw it into the fireplace and went through to where he lay, the coffee untouched.

'Stephen, up ye get. I want ye tae dae somethin.' She gripped his forearm and shook it.

'What?'

'I want ye tae draw me.'
'I've done that.'
'But this is different.'
'What's different?'
'I've nivver askit ye afore. Juist dae't, eigh?'
The tone in her voice just penetrated that small window in his mind still open to the world. Not a muscle in his body moved, only his eyes, which shifted their unfocussed stare from the ceiling to herself. She watched as ever so slowly he brought his image of her into sharpness.
'Is this what I owe you?'
'Ye owe me nae a thing.' She shook her head vehemently. 'But ye can gie it.'
His body began to stir, little uncoordinated movements that took time to take on any semblance of purpose. 'Ok' he sighed, heaving himself upright. He had slept in his clothes, and as he threw the covers back, it released a tang of stale sweat. Sitting on the edge of the bed he ran a hand through his hair and gulped down the cold coffee. 'Give me a minute.'
He came down to the studio to find her on the platform he had devised at one end. She lay on her side, her head propped on her hand. They did not look at each other. He raked around for suitable paper, throwing debris aside as he went. She looked vacantly at the flowerbed that was to have been a Japanese garden, but sported instead a ripening crop of weeds. Eventually he settled, and stared at her.
She thought he would never start. Aware of his eyes on her, she felt conscious of her body, and a growing anger of shame that she had laid herself out thus: aware of her breasts filling out the shape of her blouse, light catching the sun-bleached down on her forearm, the twist of her midriff and swell of her hips. She had kicked off her wellies, and now even the nakedness of her slender ankles and bare feet shamed her, that the sight of them alone would reveal every secret of her body to his pencil.
He did start, then stopped again, and her heart sank. 'It's nae yiss, is't.' She sat up and looked away.
'Stay where you are. As you were. Exactly.'
She resumed her position, resentment blazing that she should turn to this man, any man, for knowledge that they would never understand. But now his pencil was going, his fist swerving and curving over the creamy paper, and she did not hear it. Her elbow became sore and her wrist ached under the weight of her head and shoulder. Her spine sagged painfully

under the pull of her torso, tearing at the muscles in her back, but still she lay, with the dumb patience of the wounded animal.

'That's it.' He unclipped the paper from his board, came over and put it on the floor in front of her. She straightened herself only with difficulty, her body was now set so stiff. She stared down, concentrating hard. For all the way she had lain, the image of her body was closed in, her expression withdrawn. Even the hand on which her head had rested was clenched. With a wail she pitched her body forward, and with her head between her knees and protected by her folded arms, she wept until she was on the point of retching. Then her sobbing died and she sat silent, still hunched, trembling. She remained so for a long time, and he sat on a chair near her, quiet, grim, hands in his pockets, trying to understand what he had drawn.

'Do you know what it was now?'

She nodded her head silently.

'It is still your secret — whatever it was happened.'

This time she shook her head. 'Oa, nae juist mine, Stephen, nae juist mine. And mebbe nae juist his. Mebbe he blaws aff about it til his freinds. Or nivver gies't a second thocht — wha kens? But there's it.' She reached forward with both arms open, and grasping opposite ends of the paper, crushed it into a crumpled mass in a single furious movement.

Stephen picked it up, awed at the strength of her anger. 'The things people do' he said softly, rocking it on the palm of his hand. He struck a match and lit a corner. The ball of heavy cartridge paper expanded in its own heat, the scraps of convoluted image grotesque as they twisted in the flames. He held it until his fingers were scorched.

She rose and turned to him, stalling on the verge of further tears. He kicked the ashes on the floor. They rose and settled in the same place. 'Oh Meg, it's not as simple as that, is it? But it's a start' he said, touching her hand.

David Neilson

AL-QAHIRA
(from *Robert the Vole*)

The lizard, clinging upside down, breathed very distinctly and
flexed its long head to the left. Then it darted into a crack,
flicking its tail once. The sun turned up something to glint against on the high
inner walls of the city. The prayers of sunset were being
called, echoed in successive voices from the eastern quarters
to the west. Mehmet cracked a pistachio, sighed, and slid the
kernel into his mouth while it was still open.
'*Za'alaani*,' he mumbled, chewing. 'I am pure sick, by the
way.'
They were sitting in the courtyard of a tea-garden under
the shade of a weeping fig where the top leaves only now
caught the sun. As Mehmet spoke, Omar became aware for
the first time that the crickets had stopped sounding.
Mehmet's posture was dejected, his legs thrust out before
him and his heels dug into the stony ground; but the frowning between his eyebrows and the narrowing of his eyes
spoke more of irritation than despair.
'*Ma'ak, ya Habibi*?' asked Omar, looking at Mehmet while
he turned over an unsplit nut, feeling for the cleft. 'How,
whit's the problem, son?'
'Ah'v this message to go,' said Mehmet, turning his neck
and trying to peer through the star-patterned *meshrebiyya*
set in the courtyard wall.
'Where is it?' said Omar.
'El Fustat.'
Mehmet stretched out his arm, holding it up. The sweep
of his white surcoat showed that he had an entire city to
cross.
'Well, how no jiss go it?' said Omar. 'It's olny Tuesday.
Ye've git the rest a the week.'
Mehmet shrugged.
'Ah could go,' he said, 'but there's the brother's soap con-
cession.'
'Your brother git a soap concession?' said Omar.

'That's whit ahm sayin,' said Mehmet, 'he's goat a soap concession.'

'Could he no jist concede it himsel?' said Omar.

'Yiv no idea,' said Mehmet. 'There's hunners a crates, an tubs a oil, an millions a labels in this two gigantic bags.'

'How's there two bags?' said Omar, pulling down a branch of the fig and nipping off a leaf.

'Different labels,' said Mehmet. 'Wan says "Pure Soap" an the other yin says "By The Way".'

'Is that no a bit ae a caper?' said Omar.

'No really,' said Mehmet. 'There's two other brothers.' He flicked the mound of pistachio shells from the table. 'Anyhow, ahv tae be back at nine wi three big boattles ae Attar a Roses.'

'Is that no dead dear, that stuff?'

Mehmet looked at Omar.

'No oota Ahmed's, naw.'

'Send wan a the other brothers, then.'

'Canny,' said Mehmet. 'Yussuf's feart tae go oot kiz a big guy that sells birdseed doon at Amr Ibn El As says he wid jump him, and Idris has tae stey in kiz the polis ur still lookin fur the guy wi the crossbow.'

'Send yer maw,' said Omar.

Mehmet brightened for a second, then slumped.

'Naw,' he said, 'she's in the huff.'

'Bit ye did her livin room last week fur her.'

'It wiz that wallpaper wi the rectangles,' said Mehmet. 'She says it jumps in an oot an gies her a sore heid. She wanted a farmyard scene wi ducks.'

Omar tucked his legs under the garden seat, bent forward and looked at Mehmet.

'Dye want me tae go?' he said.

'Naw,' said Mehmet. 'Naw, naw.' His eyes flashed urgently and he waved a finger for Omar's attention.

'Ye canny get a farmyard scene here,' said Omar. 'They wullnae allow it. It's olny squerrs and wee circles an that.'

'Ah know,' said Mehmet, with a sudden laugh. 'Ye get tired a talkin.' He jerked his head anxiously at the *meshrebiyya* behind them. Omar could see only the walls of the street outside through the lattice of stars.

'Send a wee guy fae here,' said Omar. 'Jiss stick im a tube a Smarties an tell him the score.'

'Too chancy,' said Mehmet, grimacing. 'Need sumdi ye can trust.'

'Ahl go,' said Omar, rolling a leaf into a thin cylinder. He turned. 'Another two coffees!'

'Naw, naw,' said Mehmet. 'Ah don't mean that, ah jiss mean it isny ferr.'

Mehmet took the rolled leaf, pinched the end and inscribed a name in the dust. *Daoud ibn 'Aruus Issaghreer*, Omar read, grinning. Mehmet jerked back his head again, and Omar nodded.

'Lissen, did you hear that there's aw these guys oot in the desert?' said Omar.

Mehmet's eyebrows raised suddenly, frowningly.

'Whit like,' he said. 'Bedouins?'

'Naw,' said Omar derisively. 'Franks.'

'Is that a fact?' said Mehmet, nodding.

'A hale big troupe a them, an somethin lit a castle oan wheels.'

'That's amazin. An whit ur they daein aboot it?'

'Jist the usual, run oot an shout evribidi in. Toon's choc-a-bloc, ye should see it.'

'Who dye reckon it is?' said Mehmet. 'Ur they comin here?'

'Oh, they'll get a knockback here. Big Sahn-al-Hummus canny go that patter.'

'Whit patter's that?'

Memhet started. The tiny *fanajeen* of coffee, black with a touch of thick brown froth, were set down beside them.

'Nearly hid a heart attack therr, Ali,' he said to the patron. 'Naw, this billetin Frankish armies caper. Ye canny be bothered wi it.'

'Dono,' said Ali. 'It brings in a few bob.'

'Good for the caterin trade, right enough,' said Mehmet.

'Aye, an when they've been oot in the desert fur two months they like a good wash as well,' said Ali, picking up his tray and wandering off. Mehmet glowered.

'So who's likely to be operatin roon here?' said Omar.

'God knows,' said Mehmet. 'Although there isny exactly a big selection. Either it's a gang a headers fae Strathclyde or it's Robert the Vole.'

Omar's mouth opened.

'Robert the Vole?' he said. 'Bit ye never git Robert the Vole gaun aboot wi a big army.'

Mehmet lifted his cup and sipped carefully.

'Ah know,' he said. 'Robert the Vole's likelier to come in somewhere himsel, hiv a look aboot, make the occasional contact. Fur aw ye know, he could be here the noo, in the

other side a the city, co-ordinatin messages, waitin fur word
. . . ,
  'D'ye reckon?' said Omar.
  'Widny be surprised,' said Omar.
  'Whiddye think they aw say tae wan another?'
  'They probbli, lit, pass oan objects, an that. Like ye send
a hauf-eaten Monster Bar an that means ahl meet ye at the
Post Office on Tuesday.'
  A package had appeared in Mehmet's lap. Omar did not
see it get there. It was oval in shape, the size of a hand, bulkily
wrapped in linen.
  Mehmet was mouthing something at Omar.
  'Sorry?' said Omar.
  Mehmet continued, adding pantomime.
  'Sorry,' said Omar, 'gauney speak up? This is jist not
comin across at all.'
  'Ah wis sayin,' said Mehmet. But he broke off immediately, smiling generously and stretching out his arm in a gesture
of welcome.
  'How're ye doin?' he said.
  Omar looked up. Beside them, with a jaunty air of recognition, stood a man in a white robe and headdress. At his
temples, Omar noted, were strands of blond hair, and his eyes
were light blue, set in a long and rather red face.
  'Peace be upon yiz, by the way,' he said, lifting his hand
in benediction.
  'No problem,' said Mehmet. Omar noticed the swift tran-
sit of confusion across the stranger's face, and, though it took
him a moment longer, the fact that the parcel had disappeared
from Mehmet's hands. 'Take a pew.'
  The stranger nodded at Omar.
  'Daoud ibn 'Aruus Issagheer,' said Mehmet, winking.
'Omar 'Abd ur Rahman Qirdati.'
  'You honour us,' said Daoud.
  'Don't mention it,' said Omar. 'Whit ur ye fur?'
  'Are you on the bell?' said Mehmet.
  'Ah think so,' said Omar. 'Whit is it, then?'
  Daoud sat.
  'Well, wan a thae wee coffees,' he said.
  'Right,' said Omar, turning and raising a hand. 'Three wee
coffees.' He turned to Daoud again. 'Don't fancy a pickled
egg or anithin, dae ye?'
  'Naw, it's OK,' said Daoud.
  'Three coffees, Ali,' shouted Omar.

'Wherr yiz off tae the night?' said Daoud. 'Roon tae the Casbah, ur whit?'

'Nothin planned,' said Mehmet. 'See how the land lies. Mebbe take a wee walk roon the walls ur that.'

'Ah says ah wid meet Haamid 'Abd ul Karim at the Three Falconers later oan, if ye fancied a jaunt roon,' said Omar.

'Is that wee Hamid that went tae Wali Hassan?' said Daoud. 'His maw used tae clean oot the *madrasa*?'

'Naw, ah know who you mean,' said Omar. 'They flitted tae Nishapur. His sister wis a big daft lassie?'

'Ah canny mind,' said Daoud. 'Mebbe sumdi else.'

'An whit ur ye up tae yirsel?' said Mehmet. 'Oot fur a few wee corianders an honey?'

'Ah do no,' said Daoud. 'Ah fancy a quiet night.'

Ali was at his shoulder, setting down the coffees. He bent over to light a candle at the table.

'Did ye hear aw that clatterin oot therr?' he said.

'Whit wis that?' said Mehmet.

'Must jist be at the back,' said Ali. 'A hale platoon runnin past at the double. Ye must a heard them. *Waahid, ithnayn! Waahid, ithnayn!* Dye reckon they're gauney fight this?'

'Better no botherin,' said Mehmet. 'Jiss let it wash ower ye.'

'Yiv to know who yir friends are,' said Daoud. 'Know whit ah mean? Whit's the point in arguin if ye kin dae a wee deal?'

'Very good if yir sellin hatchets,' said Ali. 'Thir a couple a things ah better go an plank.' He went off.

'We wir jist sayin,' said Omar, 'that this is either Strathclyde or Robert the Vole.'

'Dye reckon?' said Daoud.

'Well, it isny Prester John, is it? Ah widny mind if it wis Robert the Vole, though. Ah canny go thae other nutters.'

'How dye mean?' said Daoud.

'Apart fae evrithin else, thiv ate evrithin fae Isfahan tae Damascus. An thur nothin bit a lot a heathens.'

'So's Robert the Vole,' said Daoud.

'Aye, but he isny a nutter. Whit aboot that other wan?' Omar looked at Mehmet.

'Ah heard they were climbin through the Caucasus wan time,' said Mehmet, 'an this monster came along. So they aw crapped it aff the monster and ran intae a cave. Big Eat-the-Breid ur whatever his name is looks oot an sees this mental thing jumpin up an doon an roarin. So he says, OK boays, been in this situation hunners a times. Another wee minute an there'll be another wan a thae things up here an the two a them'll lock in combat an roll ower that ledge an plummet tae thir dooms.'

Daoud, Omar saw, was becoming uneasy.

'Here, right enough, does another thing wae a big scaly heid no turn up an start pawin the ground an thrashin its tail. The other wan squerrs up tae it.

'Right, men, he says, javelins at the ready, we'll jist slip by here, an they aw creep oot.'

Mehmet lifted his cup and took a sip.

'Whit happened?' said Omar.

'The two monsters took wan look an charged them. They were in the cave fur another six weeks.'

'That isny true,' said Daoud. 'That's lit the kebab grilled rat an the folk that wir hivvin the party an thir flerr collapsed.'

'Whit aboot it?' said Mehmet.

'They complained to the factor and he says look at the small print. Doon at the bottom it says they're only allowed a hunner an seventy dancin in the wan room.'

'Where wis that?'

'Tangiers.'

'Ye must admit though,' said Mehmet, 'that guy is totally aff his heid.'

'Yir better no gaun intae politics,' said Daoud. 'People's got different political opinions.'

'How does politics come intae it?' said Mehmet. 'The guy's jist a bampot.' He swept up from his seat, rattling the gravel and grasping the folds of his surcoat.

'Look at Omar,' he said. Mehmet stood behind him, placing both hands on his shoulders. 'He's a Jehovah. Urnt ye?'

'Sure,' said Omar, nodding. He was conscious of something awkward and foreign working into the folds of his robe, catching at the right shoulder. He resisted the temptation to squirm. 'Ahv been witnessin since ah wis three.'

'See how you're a Jehovah,' said Mehmet. 'Whidde Jehovas think aboot evribdi else?'

'Yiz ur aw damned,' said Omar, still nodding.

'An ye go roon sellin that Watchtower, don't ye?'

'Aye, roon the doors,' said Omar.

'Don't sell a lot, though?' said Mehmet.

'Naw, no here,' said Omar, shaking his head. 'We'd shift merr if we hid some pubs.'

'Bit we kin still get oan,' said Mehmet, 'although ma

opinions ur quite different. Whidde ah think aboot folk that urny Muslims?'

'Wir aw damned,' said Omar, nodding.

'These are massive differences, yit he's still quite high in ma estimation,' said Mehmet, patting Omar on the shoulder. 'Sorry. So it disny matter whit yir opinion is. It isny politics. He's jist daft.'

'How dyou manage wi the polis here?' said Daoud.

'It's amazin,' said Omar. 'Ye'd think wi aw these monumental differences that ye wid encounter prejudice at every turn. Bit here ye don't.'

'People kin be really tolerant, kint they?' said Daoud.

'Ah know,' said Mehmet. 'Really tolerant.'

'No the Spanish, right enough,' said Omar.

'Naw,' said Daoud, 'no the Spanish, bit jist the same. An there's no anti-Jehovah feelin at all?'

'Mebbe up Al Azhar on a Saturday night,' said Omar, 'but no really.' He made to stretch, but stopped halfway through.

'Anyway,' said Mehmet, 'who dyou reckon it is?'

'Ahv goat this feelin,' said Daoud, 'lit ah dono whit it is, bit ahv an intuition ur somethin, that it's probbli Strathclyde.'

'Is that a fact?' said Mehmet.

'Naw, it's an intuition,' said Daoud. 'A presentiment. Caw it whit ye will.'

That's funny,' said Mehmet, as Daoud lifted his *finjaan.* 'Sumdi wis sayin they saw Robert the Vole oot in the street yesterday.'

Daoud spluttered out coffee.

'Imagine,' said Mehmet.

'Credit that,' said Omar.

'How did they know it wis Robert the Vole?' said Daoud.

'Well, whit they actually seen wis a wee herry guy, lit a kinna walkin beard. They said he wis done up lit an Arab. He looked right stupit.'

'Aye,' said Daoud. 'He wid. Naebdi wae im?'

'Naw,' said Mehmet. 'Who wir ye thinkin?'

'Naebdi really,' said Daoud. 'No even a big tall guy haudin his erm funny?'

'Never mentioned that,' said Mehmet. He hunched down over the table and gestured them together.

'Keep a secret?'

'Aye,' said Daoud. 'Nae bother.'

'Can you?'
'Aye,' said Omar. 'Is it yir brother?'
'Naw,' said Mehmet. 'That's another wan.'
'Is it Robert the Vole?'
Mehmet looked round. Daoud was holding the edge of
the table.
'Lissn,' he said. 'Ah better no let oan. It's a secret.'
'Naw, tell us,' said Omar. 'That's rotten.'
'Ah shouldnyive said,' said Mehmet.
'Go,' said Omar. 'Jiss tell us. Will you let oan?'
'Naw,' said Daoud. 'Go.'
Mehmet looked around again. He paused. Ali appeared
from the side door of the teahouse and began collecting used
cups and saucers. Daoud looked round with a grimace.
'You boays OK the noo?' said Ali.
'Aye, fine,' said Mehmet.
'Aye, we're awright,' said Daoud, waving. 'We're fine.'
Suddenly Ali was shouting over them. A small boy was
standing at Omar's side, holding out a brown paper packet.
'Here,' Ali cried, 'on yir way!'
'Haud oan,' said Mehmet, turning to Daoud as Ali bustled
over. 'Dye fancy a nut?'
'You encourage them,' Ali snapped as he ran, grabbing,
past them. The boy, barefoot and quick, dodged under a
table. More quickly than Ali could bend he was disappearing
round the gate.
Ali stood for a moment, breathing heavily. Then he
gathered their tiny cups, slapping them together on his tray.
'This is a teahoose,' he said, 'no a nuthoose.'
He stomped off.
As Daoud watched him go, Mehmet said, 'This is it. Ahv
tae go up an see him.'
'Who?' said Omar.
'Him wir talkin aboot,' said Mehmet. 'Robert the Vole.'
'How?' said Daoud, his voice low and astonished. 'How?
Wherr is he?'
'Here,' said Mehmet. 'In this very city.'
'How're ye daein that?' said Omar.
'Jist a wee joab,' said Mehmet. 'Here, ah better get up the
road.'
'Dye no fancy another wee coffee?' said Daoud. 'Actually
it's ma shout.'
'Naw, ye kin drink too much a that stuff,' said Mehmet.
'It makes yir tongue go funny.'

'Aw kinna black?' said Omar.
'Aye.'
'So's mine. Gie it a swish roon wi orange juice. Here, whit
is it yiv tae say tae Robert the Vole?'
Mehmet bent suddenly over Omar.
'The big man grabs me,' he said. 'Get a haud ae him. Tell
him tae get oot a here this minit. Gie him this back. We hivny
goat any, tell him. We dono how they make them. Skedaddle,
ur yiv had it.'
'Ye never know whit he's oan aboot,' said Omar.
'Bit wherr is he?' said Daoud.
'Up by the Five Pillars,' said Mehmet.
'The Five Pillars?'
'Of Islam,' said Omar. 'Ah canny go up therr.'
'How no?' said Daoud.
'Cause ahm a Jehovah,' said Omar.
'Ah better hit the trail,' said Mehmet, sitting back.
'Haud oan,' said Daoud, 'Ahl get ye up.'
'Ah better make a move an aw,' said Omar. 'The old sun-
dial says it's time tae go.'
'How's that?' said Daoud, peering through the candle-
light.
'Cause it's too dark tae see it,' said Omar, standing.
Mehmet rubbed his hands.
'Fancy a wee smoke?' he said.
'An excellent plan,' said Daoud.
'No me,' said Omar. He slung one trail of his burnous
around his neck. 'Right,' he said. 'Ma name is Gough an ahm
off. Ahl grab Ali on the road oot.'
'See ye when ye're better dressed,' said Mehmet.
'Cheers the noo,' said Daoud.
Omar bent slightly and walked off. Daoud stared after
him.
'Ah never noticed your pal's got a hump,' he said, nod-
ding in the direction which Omar had taken. 'Ahm no bein
cheeky ur nothin, it's jist ah never noticed.'
Mehmet nodded.
'The thing is,' he said, 'he isny bitter or anythin. A lot o
guys wid hiv a chip on thir shooder.'
'That's a hale fish supper,' said Daoud.
'Naw, he's dead cheerful. He disny let it bother him.'

Omar faced into the darkness of the street. Only the light
of Ali's behind him let him unwrap the parcel bound in cloth,

which he had dug out, with a struggle, from the back of his neck.

Lying in his own hand, with the cloth around it, was another, stranger hand.

Its palm and inside fingers were cold and leathery, the top joints curled in and the nails were short and broad. The back of the hand was covered in coarse hair, thick as the hide on a coconut, but black. From the wrist protruded two jointed metal tubes and something that looked like a spring.

Omar wrapped it again.

'See ye, Ali,' he said. 'That's a watter pipe, wan wee coffee, an a pint a export fur that daft spy that thinks he can talk Arabic.'

Maurice Lindsay

ON TRIAL

1
The Prisoner

She stumbled from the cells into the dock,
constables corseting her, and roundly glared
at the swivel faces, each, she imagined, paired,
few of them having found their flesh's lock
picked and sprung by a friend; the sudden shock
of warmth withdrawn, the emptied things once shared
spat at by tender words flung back to mock.

But the evidence closed her in; how, high on fury,
she'd threatened the tender throats of the little boys
he'd gotten on her; as the picture built, she
recalled the discovering neighbours, folk like the jury,
the resistant knife, the gashed unnatural noise,
and, then as now, the eyes that chorused *Guilty*.

2
Business Man

Firmed by the strictures of self-rectitude
that years of work and marriage couldn't bend,
and having checked his standards that it could
in no way pious principles offend,
clearing his throat, why yes, he said, he'd lend
his long consideration to becoming
the Jury Foreman. He would comprehend
disordered facts the others might find numbing.
Authority then set his fingers drumming
impatiently with those who faltered doubt,
despite his easy clarity of summing
up statements rung with truth and those without:
pity was weakness that he couldn't own
while compromise was failure, weakly shown.

3
Sociologist

He flopped the inequalities of the world
on a hard seat, let attentiveness unfold
and, though he felt as if his spine had curled,
heard the snap of a tether lose the hold
it briefly strained on the flawed reality
of a system proffering only its crust to the poor,
keeping the softer postures of society
for those advantage rendered worth the lure.

Guilt and conviction simply didn't arise
when the weakness of manipulated shame
let a sociologist widely visualise
what shaped the contours that are miscalled blame.
Did she or not?, the impatient foreman rasped;
drowning in straws, *she did*, the false one gasped.

4
Pop Singer

He must have been down on the uppers of his luck
to touch that broad, the pop musician mused
on the small screen of his mind as it reviewed
the groping hand, the skirt pushed into a ruck,
the struggle with pants, then the quick loveless fuck.
How otherwise could a guy be so little cued
as to marry the bitch and beget a battering feud
that left her big with a second and him stuck?

You'd think from then on he'd have had no truck
with women, yet he'd got his pecker glued
to the next available ass that needed screwed,
or offered herself in the street for an easy buck:
Guilty or not?, he heard the foreman say,
rousing the answer. *Eh? -- Oh, yeah, yeah.*

5
Schoolteacher

A funny thing, thought the vagueing classical scholar
after the hours of evidence and the weight
of having to measure out the disposable fate
of a woman smudged away by grinding squalor
Medea, Jeannie Goldsmith, whatever you call her
didn't matter — centuries couldn't abate
the risks the legs rode when the animal state
let naked lust bestride its reeking holler.

Without a wasted second, thankfully back
in the paper streets that argued Ancient Rome,
he surveyed his pupils, oddly never at home
in the past, and sighed at their present lack
of respect for certificates and the clean-limbed rule
that bested all the days of his life at school.

6
Novelist

Truth, grey prophets beard, is stranger than fiction!
As a novelist, I'm sure I'd never have got
away with such an unoriginal plot;
two people rubbing into open friction,
whatever they said implying contradiction,
the straight thing twisted into counterplot,
exasperation tindering the knot
that joyed them once in fleshing benediction.

Starved of his sex and lacking love's conviction,
with jewellery and drink he easily bought
the only element he'd ever sought,
leaving her oiling jealousy's affliction.
How odd our thoughtful glands secrete a mess
that oozes murder. Then she did it? Yes.

7
Charlady

I wuz luikin fur a leak in the washin machine,
the door wuz aff the sneck fur the watter tae rin
oot, whan all o a sudden I heard the quean
screich. An awfu commotion. It was kin
o eerie like, sae ah sez tae masel, I'll see gin
onythins wrang wi Jeannie. Whit wi her man
cairryan oan wi lassies he'll nivver see
again, her heidaches, an she sae deidpan
wi it all, ah thocht, ah'll gie her a cup o tea.
But when ah opened her front door, losh me!
she was cooriean, cover't wi bluid on the hall stair,
a carvin knife in her haun, an baith the wee
laddies mangl't deid on the livin-room flair
Ah've kill't the bairns, she sabbed; *life maks nae sense* . . .
Nothing to ask, snapped Counsel for the Defence.

8
The Undecided

A face that burrowed a moustache to hide in
sat amongst those who never held strong views;
good people, always eager to confide in
others just how hard it was to choose,
preferring always movement with a crowd;
readers of tabloids tarting up the news
to titillating entertainment, loud
with scandals, murders, rapes and sexual stews.
All of which shook their heads to virtuous *tuts*,
yet proved essential reading for relaxing;
this was for real, a maze of *ifs* and *buts*,
the arguments, bewilderingly taxing;
a flock of fundamentalist *Don't Knows*,
Guilty, if you all say so, I suppose.

9
The Q.C.s

There are pressures in life that cannot be withstood
Defending Counsel proclaimed in defiant mood
to the dusty Gothic rafters; *however good
us humans are; the pressures that obtrude
on reason can betray the normal heart
from such affections as it holds most dear.*
Said Counsel for the Prosecution: *The part
the defendant played on the fatal night is clear
beyond all possible doubt — She cut the throats
of her sons with full responsibility
for her actions. That's the matter's nub.*
After the jury had cast its clumsy votes,
Pretty well cut and dried, said the old Q.C.
to the younger, over sherry in the Club.

10
The Judge

The voice which penetrated from the wig
that justice evened centuries with, pronounced
its final measured peroration, big
with public gravitas, before it pounced
upon the prisoner's forfeit liberty:
Crime passionel, peculiar to the French
and not the outcome of conspiracy,
in Scottish law affords no just defence.

Weeping, the broken woman disappeared;
reporters raced to hype her story up
to catch a morning's glance; the courtroom cleared;
the judge disrobed and wandered home to sup,
then take down Homer for the umpteenth time,
lost in the ancient lineage of crime.

Aonghas Macneacail

fitheach is calman

1
robh stiùir an fhir dhuibh
cho gleusda

2
robh biathadh nan dìle
na shàsachadh

3
cha b'e sìol
a dhiathad
riamh

4
robh saorsa
san ablach

5
mìlseachd do chlosaich
ma bha thusa cho gòrach

6
cha b'ann gun eisimeil
fasgadh sabhail

déirceadh tarruingeach
sa chomain

7
thill am fear bàn
gu tràilleachd an t-sìl

raven and dove

1
was the black one's compass
as finely tuned

2
was there food on the flood
to satisfy

3
seed
was never
its diet

4
was there freedom
in the carrion

5
sweetness of your corpse
if you were so stupid

6
it's not without dependence
barn shelter

there's enticing beggary
in obligation

7
the white one returned
to the slavery of seed

Alan Riach

THE BLUES

The lights are on all over Hamilton.
The sky is dark, blue
as a stained glass window in an unfrequented church
say, by Chagall, with grand and glorious chinks
of pinks and purples,
glittering jewels on those glass fronted buildings
where the lifts are all descending
and the doors are
being closed.
    You're out there somewhere,
going to a concert in wide company or maybe
sitting somewhere weaving a carpet
like a giant tapestry, coloured grey,
pale brown, weaving the wool
back in at the edges of the frame, your
fingers deft as they turn the wool in tight and
gentle curves.
       Or somewhere else.
       What do I do
       except imagine you?
       The river I keep crossing
       keeps going north. The trains
       in the night cross it too.
       Their silver carriages are blue.

AT SPIRITS' BAY, THE EMPTY SEA

'You cannot miss the ships that miss each other
ships that the wide earth parts'
    the sliding waters meet
them all, and all the ships come in.
The Tasman nudges off the Cape
the shallow stern of long Pacific slants.
The Cape runs ragged down the land
and susurrates into the oceans:
auratic, yet the sand is scald, is
beaten gold, the rocks as black,
the grasstopped hill
bright emerald, the lighthouse
lighthouse-white.
'Have I come these 20,000 miles
to be beaten by an empty wind?'
(The ruin or the blank in our own eye.
The axis of vision is not coincident
with the axis of things. Therefore the words
(world) lacks unity. Said Emerson. He sang:
Don't fence me in.) The palisades
surround the lighthouse.
                    Even out there
where the 2 seas say hello
to each other they're shaking hands
with rippling knuckles, as
white as waves are
on cobalt.

Christopher Salvesen

PSYCHOSCOTIA — A COMPLAINT

The sunset — she made me watch,
A blackbird, listen,
Lady my mother Macbeth.
Another day's boredom
Burnt out at the end:
In the branches rain-song, cold,
The beginnings of spring.
I have sucked ever since
Those rainy clouds
Those runs of song.

Sometimes I seem to be nothing
My Lady mother Macbeth
Or an idea, nothing but,
Turned up in a touring actor
A moorland shifting mist
On the way from there to here.
Or else my mother, bored with me,
Willed me into life
And almost, wailing, back again
To my reedy native shore.

Who wouldn't have a soldier father?
Guns he had fired — such batteries —
The river-hole he swam in
That summer afternoon,
They deafened him, confused his head.
Lady Macbeth my mother
He deserved his wound
The fields of Africa and France,
And Hannibal, a master, his marches
And — in the end — defeat.

To manage an estate —
A farmer king.
Who will carry it on?
When floods flowed in across our fields
Mother my Lady Macbeth
And the new grass failed
I waited by the thorn hedge
Till he went. A wintry wind,
The wire pulled taut,
A fence repaired.

Valerie Gillies

THE ROCK OF HAWTHORNDEN

At the rock of Hawthornden,
steep outcrop well-loved by men
since the day they first fortified its crag,
put a hand to the rockface,
it is magnetized in place
by the fiery core of the old magma.

Marked with clefts and caves,
ferns and trees within its waves,
sewn with deadwood petrified in seams,
crystals and glittering stones embed
shining eyes upon this head
while through its ivy wreath there darts a wren.

In India such rocks
worshipped like beasts or gods
are visited by pilgrims walking on the plain;
only here in Scotland
it takes a solitary stand
among discords of chainsaw and firing range.

River Esk so far below
turns sunwise in its flow
round the rock and the house on its rampart,
where wooded shades sun never clears
keep dark four hundred years
since the man of Hawthornden lived at its heart.

His was a white melancholy
suspended on this promontory
washed by weathers high above the wooded valley,
a house rich in angled shapes,
turrets and crow-step gables:
for the art of thinking he rebuilt his sanctuary.

Now Drummond of Hawthornden
once wrote to a true friend,
'Where I love, there I love for years'
and from this place he loved
his spirit cannot now remove;
he is at last his own rockform here.

Gael Turnbull

A POEM CONTAINING THE WORD: LAUNDERETTE

containing the word: launderette
the words: finest equipment
the words: oily overalls, horse tack and muddy sports
    gear you must not, repeat underlined must not
    attempt to wash, in these machines
the words: load drum, amount detergent, add appropriate,
    desired wash, select cycle, coin in slot, proper
    amount, push slide, fabric softener, add before
    'rinse light' ON, again after 'rinse light' OFF,
    not complete until 'lid light' OUT, will not open
    until 'lid locked light' is also
then by pressing the words (it distinctly says
    'pressing the words') 'High' 'Low' 'Permanent Press'
    as required, ensure you follow in sequence the words
    to pre-set the dryer, then by pressing the word
    'Start' and re-pressing if need be
compressing, expressing, rinsing and cleaning,
    refreshing and drying, restarting, resetting
in a word, with words: a launderette, containing a
    poem

Norman MacCaig

TWO NIGHTS

The real night, the one
that keeps coming back on time,
never begins
with a gash of black.

As though, politely,
it makes a noise on the gravel
and coughs and knocks at the door
before coming in.

Not like the other one, that
on the most summer of days
gashes the light and pours through
a black dark with no moon, no stars.

NOTES ON CONTRIBUTORS

TOM BERRY Born Barrhead, Renfrewshire, 1927. Educated Barrhead and Paisley. Degree in architecture, Strathclyde. Lived and worked in Glasgow area except for 2 years in India and 8 in West Africa. Poems in various magazines, *Noise and Smoky Breath* anthology and broadcast on BBC Scotland.

ALAN BOLD Born Edinburgh 1943. English poems in *In This Corner* and Scots verse in *Summoned by Knox*. His poems have been performed by Glenda Jackson and Tom Fleming; set to music by Ronald Stevenson and Edward McGuire; interpreted visually by John Bellany and the poet himself in exhibition of his Illuminated Poems.

RON BUTLIN Born Edinburgh 1949. Brought up in village of Hightae, near Dumfries. Has published three books of poetry, a collection of short stories and a novel, *The Sound of my Voice*. At present completing another novel. Awarded a Scottish Arts Council writer's bursary earlier this year.

ALISON CAMPBELL Born Aberdeen 1950. Educated Aberdeen High School, Jordanhill College, Glasgow, and Stirling University. Has lived in Australia and New Zealand. Now divides her time between parenting, social work and writing. Belongs to a very supportive writing group in N. London. 'Ti Amo' is her first published story.

DAVID CRAM Born Lincolnshire 1945. Early childhood spent in China where his parents were missionaries. Studied at universities of Oxford and Cornell. Resident in Scotland since 1973. Currently head of Linguistics Department, Aberdeen University. Verse translations and poems in various British and American journals.

ROBERT CRAWFORD Born Glasgow 1959. Recent English poems in *Cencrastus, London Magazine, London Review of Books* and Scots in *Sterts & Stobies* and *Severe Burns*. Is an editor of *Verse*. His *The Savage and the City in the Work of T.S. Eliot* is forthcoming from OUP.

G.F. DUTTON   Born 1924 of Anglo-Scottish parentage. Travelled much of globe, most of life in Scotland. Publications from enzymology to mountaineering. First collection of poems, *Camp One* (Macdonald 1978) won SAC New Writing Award. Latest collection is *Squaring the Waves* (Bloodaxe 1986).

A. FENTON   Born Shotts, Lanarkshire, 1929. Returned to North-East almost immediately. Schools: Drumblade, Auchterless, Turriff. Universities: Aberdeen, Cambridge, Edinburgh. Dr Fenton is currently Research Director, National Museums of Scotland. Numerous publications on Scottish country life; translations from Danish and Hungarian.

ANDREW FOX   Born Bristol 1953. Resident in Scotland since 1958. Educated Dundee High School, Edinburgh and Aberdeen Universities. Has worked as a bank clerk, civil servant, teacher, editor; is currently working on the Frigate Unicorn in Dundee. 'Bathsheba (After Rembrandt)' was a prizewinner in the Scottish National Open Poetry Competition.

RAYMOND FRIEL   Born Greenock 1963. Educated St Mary's, Blairs, Aberdeen; St Patrick's College, Thurles, Eire, and Glasgow University (English Literature and Language). 'The Butterfly' is his first published work.

ROBIN FULTON   Born Scotland 1937. Edited *Lines Review* 1967-76. *Selected Poems 1963-1978* (Macdonald) gathers work from several volumes. Latest collection of poems is *Fields of Focus* (Anvil 1982). Also edited Robert Garioch's *Complete Poetical Works*. Noted as translator of Scandinavian poetry.

WILLIAM GILFEDDER   Born Glasgow 1945. Educated Our Holy Redeemer's, Clydebank. Left at 15 with no qualifications. Has had various jobs: van boy, apprentice motor mechanic, driver and at present works as a gardener/handyman. Only two poems published previously, in *Scottish Review* and *The Glasgow Magazine*.

VALERIE GILLIES   Born Edmonton, Canada, 1948. Grew up on the upland moors of Lanarkshire. Universities of Edinburgh and Mysore, India. Poet, writer in schools, harper's roadie, collaborator with artists and musicians. Wife of William Gillies, Professor of Celtic, and mother of three children. Latest collection *Bed of Stone* (Canongate 1984).

ANDREW GREIG   Born Bannockburn 1951. Graduated Edinburgh University 1975 (philosophy). Now a full-time writer, he has climbed with three major Himalayan expeditions. His most recent books are *Kingdoms of Experience* (Hutchinson 1986) and *A Flame in Your Heart*, with Kathleen Jamie (Bloodaxe 1986).

W.N. HERBERT   Born Dundee 1960. Currently at Oxford, writing a thesis on Hugh MacDiarmid. Has worked as a part-time apiary assistant. Editor of *Gairfish* and co-author of *Sterts & Stobies* (Obog Books 1985). Work published in *Akros* and *Verse*.

DAVID KINLOCH   Born Lennoxtown 1959. Has spent most of his life in Scotland. Graduated Glasgow University 1982. Since then has studied in Oxford and Paris. Currently a Fellow of the University of Wales. Is co-editor of *Verse*. Contributed to *NWS* 1, 2 and 3. Work forthcoming in *Lines Review*.

MAURICE LINDSAY   Born Glasgow 1918. Trained as musician — an injury ended performing career. Became music critic and broadcaster. Former Controller, Border TV and Director, Scottish Civic Trust. Retired 1983. Has written and edited over 60 books. Latest collection of poems is *The French Mosquitoes' Woman* (Hale 1985).

NORMAN MacCAIG   Born Edinburgh 1910. Educated at Edinburgh University (classics). Has been teacher of various sorts — primary schools to Stirling University. Has published over 15 books of poems including, in 1985, his *Collected Poems* (Chatto & Windus).

KENNETH MacDONALD   Born Paisley 1959. Married and works in an office in Glasgow. When not writing collects John Fahey records and supports Motherwell F.C. 'The Silver Tin Can Will Visit You Tomorrow' is his first published work.

LORN MACINTYRE   Born Argyll 1942. Educated Stirling and Glasgow universities. Free-lance writer resident near St Andrews. Three novels published so far in Chronicles of

Invernevis series. Also short stories in anthologies and magazines, and, after a long silence, poetry.

ALASTAIR MACKIE   Born Aberdeen 1925. Educated Robert Gordon's and Aberdeen University. Taught English at Stromness Academy and Waid Academy. Retired 1983. SAC bursary 1976. Publications in Scots: *Clytach* and *Backgreen Odyssey*. Latest collection, *Ingaitherins* published this year (Aberdeen University Press). Now returned to English after 30 years given over to Scots.

AONGHAS MACNEACAIL   Born Skye. Native Gael. Poet, journalist and broadcaster. Experienced reader of his own poems. Has toured Ireland, West Germany, U.S.A. and Canada reading Gaelic poems. His collection *An Seachnadh/ The Avoiding* was published in 1986 (Macdonald).

EWAN R. McVICAR   Born Inverness 1941. Second chance Aden 1964. Mostly a social worker but other activities include peace busking, writing songs and allotment-holding. Work published in *Folk Roots*, *The Scotsman*, *Edinburgh Review* and *NWS 4*, among others.

GORDON MEADE   Born Perth 1957. Educated at Dundee University. Lives as freelance writer in East Neuk of Fife. Poems in many magazines including *Blind Serpent, Cencrastus, Chapman, The Glasgow Magazine* and *Lines Review*. Forthcoming first collection from Littlewood Press, Yorkshire.

NAOMI MITCHISON   Born Edinburgh 1897, mother Kathleen Trotter, father J.S. Haldane. Early education Dragon School, Oxford. V.A.D. nurse in World War I. Married Dick Mitchison, later Labour M.P. Five children, lots of grandchildren and great grand-children. Written about 80 books, mostly historical novels and stories, also SF and straight history. Still writing.

WILLIAM MONTGOMERIE   Born and educated in Glasgow. M.A., Glasgow University; Ph.D., Edinburgh University. Taught and lectured in Dundee, retired to Edinburgh. First collection of poems published in 1933. Selected poems, *From Time to Time*, in 1985 (Canongate). With his wife Norah published collections of Scottish rhymes and folk stories.

TOM NAIRN   Born Perthshire 1955. Moved to Edinburgh 1973. Has MA from Edinburgh University where he is currently working on a Ph.D. Poetry and criticism in various magazines including *Cencrastus* and *Scottish Literary Journal.* Reviews editor of the latter.

WILLIAM NEILL   Born Ayrshire 1922. Educated Ayr Academy, Edinburgh University. Ex-airman, ex-teacher. Six collections of verse in Gaelic, Scots and English; essays and broadcasts. SAC Bursary 1984; SAC Book Award 1985 (*Wild Places*). Lives in Galloway.

DAVID NEILSON   Born Glasgow 1953. Author of *XII from Catullus* (Mariscat 1982) and illustrator of Michael Munro's *The Patter* (GDL 1985). Works in further education, is married and lives in the Crosshill district of Glasgow.

TIM NEIL   Born 1962. Currently working on a thesis in history at Edinburgh University. 'A Christening' is his first publication.

TOM POW   Born Edinburgh 1950. First poetry collection *Rough Seas* from Canongate earlier this year. Poster poem *In Old Galloway* one of four commissioned by Book Trust to celebrate *Poetry Live*. Lives and works in Dumfries.

ALAN RIACH   Born Lanarkshire 1957. Degree in English from Cambridge, doctorate from Glasgow on later work of Hugh MacDiarmid. Currently on a Fellowship at University of Waikato, Hamilton, New Zealand. Has produced and given a number of readings and his work has appeared in *Cencrastus, Chapman, Edinburgh Review, Radical Scotland, Verse,* etc.

CHRISTOPHER SALVESEN   Born Edinburgh 1935. Brought up in Dumfriesshire. Educated at Oxford. Teaches English at Reading University. Has published two volumes of poetry: *Floodsheaf: from a Parish History* (Whiteknights 1974) and *Among the Goths* (Mariscat 1986).

DAVID SCOTT   From Gourock. His poems have been printed in *Cencrastus* and the *Edinburgh Review.*

IAIN CRICHTON SMITH   Born Isle of Lewis 1928. Full-time writer. Writes in English and Gaelic, novels, shorts stories, poems, plays. Most recent books: *Towards the Human* (Macdonald), a book of criticism, and a novel, *In the Middle of the Wood* (Gollancz).

GAVIN SPROTT   Born Dundee 1943. Father a parson, mother an artist. Hopeless at school. Various jobs. Eventually studied Scottish history at Edinburgh University. Married with 3 children. Head of Working Life Section, National Museums of Scotland. Story published in *NWS* 4.

VALERIE THORNTON   Born Glasgow 1954. Educated in Stirling and Glasgow. Has enjoyed periods of employment on feature films and with film festivals. Stories and poems have appeared recently in *Scottish Short Stories*, *Cencrastus* and she has had work in *NWS* 1, 2 and 3.

GAEL TURNBULL   Born Edinburgh 1928. Now lives in Cumbria. Recent publications: *A Gathering of Poems 1950-1980* (Anvil Press); *From the Language of the Heart* (Mariscat and Gnomon); *A Year and a Day* (Mariscat); *Spaces* (Satis); *A Winter Journey* (Pig Press). Has the curious distinction, through his father's family, of being a Hereditary Freeman of Berwick-upon-Tweed.

FRED URQUHART   Born Edinburgh 1912. Has published four novels and twelve collections of short stories. The BBC has broadcast most of his stories including the series about 'Alice Buchan, Babysitter' on Radio 4. Received Arts Council bursaries in 1966, 1975 and 1978. Now working on a sequel to his last novel *Palace of Green Days*.

ISABELLA WALKER   Born Dowies Mill, near Cramond, 1934. Father's people from the Orkneys. BA (literature) Open University (1980); MA (Hons) in History of Art, Edinburgh University (1984). Is currently researching the life and work of the artist Joan Eardley. 'Eardley Painting' is her first appearance in print.

ASSOCIATION FOR SCOTTISH LITERARY STUDIES

The Association for Scottish Literary Studies exists to promote the study, teaching and writing of Scottish literature, and to further the study of the languages of Scotland. It was founded in 1970 by members of the Scottish universities, and is now an international organisation, with members in 22 countries.

The ASLS fulfils its aims of promoting the study, teaching and writing of Scottish literature and of furthering the study and the use of the languages of Scotland, by publishing annually an edited text of Scottish literature, scholarly journals, and *New Writing Scotland*. It also produces material for use in schools, texts for students and other publications.

Membership of the ASLS is open to all who support the aims of the Association and who pay an annual subscription. Please address enquiries to:

Association for Scottish Literary Studies
c/o Department of English
University of Aberdeen
Aberdeen AB9 2UB

Honorary Members

Norman MacCaig, Sorley MacLean, Naomi Mitchison
Edwin Morgan, David Murison, Iain Crichton Smith

Officers

President: Thomas Crawford, University of Aberdeen
Past President: David Daiches, University of Edinburgh
Secretary: David Robb, University of Dundee
Treasurer: David Hewitt, University of Aberdeen
General Editor: Douglas Mack, University of Stirling
Convener Language Committee: Derrick McClure,
    University of Aberdeen
Convener Schools Committee: Ronald Renton,
    St Aloysius' College, Glasgow
Convener Publications Committee: Felicity Riddy,
    University of Stirling